LOGGING FRAMEWORKS IN JAVA

LOGGING FRAMEWORKS IN JAVA

Neha Kaul

www.arclerpress.com

Logging Frameworks in Java

Neha Kaul

Arcler Press

2010 Winston Park Drive,
2nd Floor
Oakville, ON L6H 5R7
Canada
www.arclerpress.com
Tel: 001-289-291-7705
     001-905-616-2116
Fax: 001-289-291-7601
Email: orders@arclereducation.com

© 2019 Arcler Press

ISBN: 978-1-77361-288-1 (Hardcover)

Arcler Press publishes wide variety of books and eBooks. For more information about Arcler Press and its products, visit our website at www.arclerpress.com

ABOUT THE AUTHOR

Neha Kaul is an experienced Java consultant currently residing in Paris, France and working for one of the leading financial companies in France. She received her double Master's Degree in Computer and Communication Networks and Information Technology from Telecom SudParis and University Paris-Saclay in 2016. She is a recipient of the prestigious Telecom Scholarship for Excellence provided by Fondation Telecom, France. She received the Bachelor of Engineering degree in Computer Engineering from the University of Pune, India in 2011. From 2011 to 2014, she was employed as a Software Engineer with Geometric Ltd, Pune, India. Her major interests include Advanced Java frameworks, Logging Frameworks, Network Security and Data Mining.

Dedication

To my mother Anita, Thank you for bringing the joy of writing into my life. This would not have been possible without you.

TABLE OF CONTENTS

PREFACE

Logging plays a vital role in the maintenance of any software application. Logging is simply an action of maintaining a log of the events that take place in the lifetime of an application. Log statements are nothing but simple messages that note down the transactions/communications-taking place between different elements within the application. These messages are written to a file called as the Log file. In other words, logging is documentation of all the events that occur in a system.

Logging, when used wisely is an extremely powerful tool to debug, administer and maintain your applications. It provides you with information about what your underlying code is doing. This helps rapidly debug the code, analyze the code, monitor the application and manage complex applications. Additionally, logging can serve as a means to measure application performance.

Logging is an intrinsic part of many object-oriented languages such as Java, C++ Python, etc. To make the process of logging effortless, many powerful logging frameworks have been provided to facilitate the process for the concerned end users. With the use of frameworks for the purpose of logging, a developer can better maintain his application in an easy, developer-friendly way. For example, in the case of complex client-server applications, logging helps to understand the activities of the server/servers being used thereby aiding in deciphering the incidents that take place in such a context. Java logging frameworks not only ease the process of logging, but also help standardize the process.

In this book, various logging frameworks have been presented in the context of Java, a language that is very well suited to object-oriented programming and design. This book covers the basics of logging, its implementation in Java and describes in detail some logging frameworks that are used in a Java context. Several samples of java code implementing logging functionality and tested against Java versions 7.0 and 8.0 have been provided.

CHAPTER
1

INTRODUCTION TO LOGGING

CONTENTS

1.1. WHAT IS LOGGING?

Logging is nothing but the act of recording an activity. It is an action of maintaining a record of the events of an application.

It is the process of writing log messages during the period of execution of a software application to a common central place. The activity of logging allows us to maintain and report all types of statuses of the application such as error messages, warnings as well as a general status of the application. These messages are stored centrally and can be retrieved for analysis at a later point.

The logs serve a wide variety of uses; they can be used to debug the system to figure out the cause of problems in the system, perform system analysis in terms of performance or to run a statistical analysis of the system.

1.2. WHY DO WE NEED LOGGING?

Logging is a simple low-tech method of debugging (log4Delphi.sourceforge. net, 2017). Logging is essential because in certain situations it may be the only way to debug the application. In a multithreaded Java application or a large distributed client-server application, this serves as the only way to know the status of the application. Particularly in case, an application is at the production stage where a debugger cannot be used, logging is the best and sometimes the only way to get information about the program this is running. Additionally, logging can help in determining and analyzing timing related issues as well; with the help of time-stamped log statements.

Over the years, logging has proved to be instrumental in the SDLC lifecycle as it has several benefits. Logging has the capability to provide specific context related to the current execution of an application. Logging is devised and built to let a simple Java program or advanced Java components such as servlets, applets, EJBs etc. generate useful messages that are of interest to the developers, administrators, engineers and the end users. Once log statements are added to the code, the log output is generated automatically. Furthermore, the logs can be persisted thereby allowing developers to analyze them at a later stage. Apart from the use of logging in the software development life cycle, a logging framework that is API rich can be used as an auditing tool.

1.3. WHAT IS A JAVA LOGGING FRAMEWORK?

A **Java logging framework** is a computer data logging package for the Java platform (Java Logging Framework, 2016).

Logging is generally a standard for software development teams. In order to ease the process of logging, there are several frameworks that simplify and standardize this process of logging for the Java platform (Java Logging Framework, 2016).

A logging framework is designed in such a way that it is easy to incorporate in an existing application with minimum overhead and configuration requirements.

A logging framework is typically made up of the following components:

1. Logger

The most important component of any logging framework is the Logger. This is the object which performs the logging operation in applications and is typically just called 'Logger' (Lars Vogel, 2016). A log entry can have different levels of criticality based on the nature of the application. Typically, a log message can be of type DEBUG, INFO, ERROR, WARNING etc. This is called as a logging level. The logging levels vary based on the logging framework. The logger provides the ability to define different levels of importance of the logged messages and the ability to use different destinations for the output such as the console, a file, etc. Additionally, a logger is configurable and hence we have the choice of disabling certain types of log messages from the log output. For instance, in a production scenario, we may not want to see all the log messages that are of a particular type such as debug. The logger essentially captures the log messages.

2. Appender

Once the log messages have been captured by the logger, this logging information needs to be sent to an appropriate destination. This destination is the appender, which writes the log messages to the specified destination. The appender is attached to the logger and it listens for messages of particular logging levels (Error, debug, etc). Its main goal is to take the logging information and post it to the correct destination such as a console or file. The appender is capable of writing messages to the following destinations:

- File;
- Console;

- Send via email;
- Append/add to a table in a database;
- Network Socket; and
- Distribute it via Java Messaging Services (JMS).

3. Formatter

A formatter is the component that is used to configure the format of the log messages. A formatter usually displays the log in a string format. It is used as a means to enhance the quality of the log and provide additional information about the logs such as time zones in addition to the log level, date and time and log message. Formatters help represent the data in a better way that is suited to needs of the application.

In order to ensure that log messages can be added in a java program/ application, the framework is built with powerful API that renders logging to be as inexpensive as possible. With the use of a logging framework, the stakeholders of the application can ensure that the log visibility can change dynamically; the code can produce detailed logs when required (in case of critical errors) and limit the logs produced under normal use. The API within a framework provides mechanisms to change and control the display of logs dynamically, which makes logging an inexpensive yet extremely helpful activity. The API differs from framework to framework, but most frameworks provide interfaces and classes that serve as hooks for developers to extend the existing API provided by the framework.

1.4. LOGGING FRAMEWORKS IN JAVA

There are several logging frameworks that have been developed over the past few years for the Java language. Some of the commonly used Java logging frameworks are as follows:

1. Java logging;
2. Log4j;
3. SL4J;
4. Logback; and
5. TinyLog.

Each of the above frameworks is discussed in detail in the upcoming chapters. It is assumed that all the readers are familiar with Java and have a good understanding of programming with Java.

CHAPTER
2

JAVA LOGGING FRAMEWORK

CONTENTS

2.1. INTRODUCTION

This is the default logging framework provided as part of the Java Language Packages. The Java API provides a sub-package in the java. util package called the logging that consists of the logging API. The java.util.logging package was introduced in the Java SE 4 (1.4) release in 2001.

This package provides several classes and interfaces that support and implement the core logging functionalities. This package was introduced in order to provide a means to maintain, troubleshoot and repair the software at the client side in a simple way.

Logging was put into place in order to handle the following different scenarios:

1. Resolve issues found during software development

Logging may be used to aid the developers during the course of development of the software. The API could be used to obtain additional information about the application that is currently under development. A developer can generate logging information for the target application to determine at which point his application's behavior has changed. This could help him locate the root cause of the bug/issue. Although a developer has access to debugging and profiling tools in his current development environment that help him resolve issues found during the development cycle, logging can be used as an additional hassle-free method to obtain information about the application under development.

Additionally, in a distributed environment with several clients and servers or in an environment without a development environment such as servers, a developer can easily test his application with the help of logging.

2. Resolving issues detected by System Administrators and End Users

Logging can be used to analyze, track and fix issues that are found by the users of the system and the system administrators. The logging functionality can be used to obtain logs of the target application to fix these issues. The development team can focus on generating logs for the specific part of the application that seems to pose a problem and then analyze the logs to determine the cause of the issue and resolve it.

This includes regular day-to-day bugs/issues that can be analyzed, tracked and fixed in a local environment such as basic configuration issues, security issues, memory issues, etc.

3. Issues detected at the client end

Logging is an excellent method to fix issues that are detected at the client end. These issues are the ones that are found in a production context when the software has already been deployed at the client location. Issues detected in a client environment are considered to be of the highest priority and they need to be resolved with minimum delays. Moreover, in such a scenario, the development team may not have access to the production environment. This usually happens in large distributed teams where each aspect of the software development is handled by different teams. Hence, in such scenarios logs prove to be beneficial. The logs that have been generated at the client end can be provided to the development team which can further analyze the logs and resolve the issue. In such cases, the logs are fairly detailed containing a lot of information about the activities of the system. Moreover, in such a situation the tracing level of all the components may be as detailed as possible. Another possibility is that the logging information for a specific sub-component/sub-components might be traced in a deeper way as compared to the others such more information on their execution internally within the sub-component.

All these configurations can be done with the properties file that serves as the configuration file. This will be discussed in detail in further sections.

4. Issues detected by Service Engineers

These issues are the ones that are found by the service and maintenance team that is located at the client location. Issues found in this context are similar to production issues. Logging can be used by the Service Engineers to diagnose and resolve issues that were detected. Similar to the production environment, the logging information needs to be extremely detailed and complex as compared to that provided in a development environment. In this situation, all or some of the components/sub-components will require a deeper tracing level as compared to other components.

A detailed logging/tracing level can be pre-configured at the time of development of the software. This will be discussed in detail in upcoming sections.

2.2. COMPONENTS OF A LOGGING FRAMEWORK

The logging framework in Java is composed of the following components. (Figure 2.1).

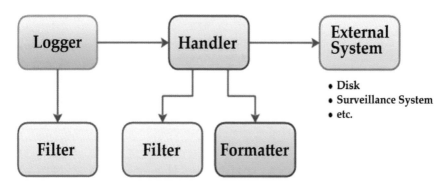

Figure 2.1: Components of the java logging framework (Jenkov, 2017).

2.2.1. Logger

As explained in Chapter 1, the logger is the main component of the logging framework. In the java logging package, a Logger class has been provided that does the work of a logger. Typically, the application calls a logger object to perform a logging operation.

Loggers are entities that are named similar to dot-separated java packages (com.oracle). The logger namespace is entirely hierarchical and it is managed by the class Log Manager.

The naming convention for a logger is the same as that for java packages.

Loggers constantly observe their parent loggers in the logger namespace tree for logging. The parent of a logger is its closest ancestor in the tree. The root logger (also named """) is the Logger that is highest up in the namespace and hence has no parent. In case the logger is declared to be anonymous, its parent is root.

All the loggers may inherit some attributes from their parents which may be any of the following attributes:

• Log level

If a logger has a log level of null or it has not been set at all, then the Logger will traverse up the family tree to find a Logger with a Level that is not null and use this level.

- Handler

The default behavior of loggers in the Java logging framework is that a logger will send its output to the handlers of its parents in a recursive manner up the family tree.

- Resource bundle names

If a resource bundle has not been defined for a logger or it is null, it inherits the resource bundle from its parents. If its parents do not have a resource bundle defined, then the logger scans the parent tree recursively until a valid bundle name is found.

The concepts of Handlers, Bundles and Log levels have been discussed in the next section.

To create a logger an instance of the class Logger is typically created. The instances of the Logger class are organized hierarchically. This means that if a Logger is at the lowest level in the hierarchy, it will forward its log messages/data to its parents/ancestors. A child Logger may inherit certain properties related to logging configuration from their respective parent/ parents in the tree/namespace.

This enables filtering of entire branches of Loggers in a particular sub-tree.

Log requests are maintained in the form of a Log Record object, which passes the requests between the Logger and the Handler. A Log Record object is an instance of the Log Record class which holds the contents of the log message and its level.

2.2.2. Handler

This component receives objects from the Logger object and publishes the object. Each and every logger object can have access to one or more handlers.

The handler receives the log message from the application logger as in input and then further exports/sends it to a certain destination/target. Standard targets for a handler include consoles, output files, System log files, remote files, etc. Each logger must have at least one handler.

The java.util.logging package provides the following standard handlers:

Stream Handler

This is the simplest type of handlers that is used for writing formatted logs to an object of type Output Stream. It is basically a stream-based handler. A log record is output to a particular stream []. The main aim of this handler class is to serve as a base class that can be further used in the implementation of other handlers for logging.

Console Handler

This is another straightforward handler class that is used to write log records to the System. Err stream. It is a system-based handler that publishes the log output to the console. In a development environment that consists of an IDE such as Eclipse, the log output is displayed in the console tab as shown below.

File Handler

The File Handler is a handler that writes log messages to a single file or a set of rotating log files (File Handler, 2017). Rotation of files is done to ensure smooth memory management. As each log file reaches a particular size, it is closed for writing, rotated out and a new file is opened. Typically, the order of naming is numerical and successive; the numbering starting from 0 is appended to the filename.

Additionally, we have the possibility of rotating the files on the basis of days, weeks or months.

Socket Handler

The Socket Handler is a handler this is used to send log records over a network. It writes the logs to remotely located ports (TCP). The records are published to a network stream by the Handler.

Memory Handler

The memory handler is a handler that stores log records in its buffer. The buffer is circular and hence the earlier records are discarded from its memory. This handler stores the incoming Log Record object received from the Logger into its buffer and simply drops the previous records/inputs. This handler serves as a cheap method of buffering and further helps reduce costs related to the formatting of the log messages.

This handler can be thought of as a temporary memory handler that saves the log records until a certain condition is met. Once this condition is met, the Memory Handler will publish the log records to another Handler which will then publish it to desired target location.

This condition is handled by the **push Level** parameter which will be discussed in Section 2.5.

Developers also have the possibility to write their own customized handlers. This can be done by either writing a completely new handler from scratch or by subclassing one of the existing handlers.

A handler can be set on and off using the set Level() method provided by the handler API.

A Log Manager is generally used to set the default properties of a Handler. This shall be discussed in the upcoming sections.

2.2.3. Filter

The filter, as its name suggests is used to filter the log messages. The filter has the power to decide whether a log message gets published or not. This is extremely useful in case of production environments where only specific types of messages are printed and published in order to avoid large quantities of logs. In the java logging framework, the Filter class provides this functionality.

Each logger has a filter associated with it. Whenever a log message is given to a logger, it first has to go through its filter. By default, the logger does not have a filter set. But, if a Filter has been configured for the logger, the message can be either accepted or rejected by the filter. A filter basically decides if a Log record is of any interest to it or not.

If no filter has been configured, each message is accepted by default.

2.2.4. Formatter

Before the log records are published to a destination, the handler has the possibility of formatting the log messages before they are sent to an output stream. Additionally, the messages can be localized as per a particular geographical region.

Each handler has a Formatter associated to it. But the use of a formatter is optional.

In order to format a message before publishing it, the Handler classes use a class called Formatter to format an object of type Log Record.

By default, the Java logging framework provides two in-built formatter classes. These two formatters inherit from the parent class: Formatter.

They are:

a.   Simple Formatter

This is a fairly simple type of data formatter that writes the log messages in a format that is easily readable by users. Summaries of logs are generated using this formatter.

b.   XML Formatter

This formatter is a slightly advanced and structured formatter. It writes the log data in detailed fashion in XML-based format.

The handler classes in the logging API make use of either of the above two formatters. But, a developer can also develop his own custom formatter.

Similar to a Handler, this can be done by subclassing the Formatter class.

2.2.5. The Log Manager

In the Java, logging framework there exists a special component called as the Log Manager.

It is a global component that tracks and manages all the logging information. It contains a namespace of all the loggers in a hierarchical manner. It also contains logging control properties that are read from a configuration file. The configuration related to the logging shall be discussed in section 2.7.

2.2.6. Log Levels

Each log message that is logged using a logger has a log level associated to it. The level is nothing but the level of importance of the message. In the java.util.logging package, the Level class holds the different levels that can be attributed to log statements. A log level is simply an integer that determines how critical the log message is. The level is an integer which determines how important the message is (Level, 2017). It is a rough guide that denotes the urgency and importance of a particular log message. The higher this value, the more critical the message is. A higher value indicates higher priority.

The following 7 levels (descending order of importance) have been provided by default in the java.util.logging package in the class **Level**: (Table 2.1).

Table 2.1: Log levels (Level (Java Platform SE 7), 2017)

Log Levels
SEVERE
WARNING
INFO
CONFIG
FINE
FINER
FINEST

Each log level corresponds to a constant that is declared in the class **Level**.

Log levels can be used for filtering purposes as well. All the log messages that are valued below a particular level can be rejected or suppressed. The logger class can make use of the setLevel() method to configure the logger to accept log messages only above a certain level. For example, if we set the log level to INFO, all the messages of type CONFIG, FINE, FINER and FINEST are ignored.

This has been illustrated with the help of examples in Section 2.5.

2.2.7. Control Flow

As shown in Figure 2.1, the flow of control for logging is simple. The java application creates a Logger. This object is called by the application. A logger is generally organized hierarchically (using namespaces). Each logger surveys the log level that it is focused on and rejects other log requests that are do not satisfy its requested level demands or are below this defined log level.

When the Logger instance is called, the logger object creates an object of type Log Record. Once a Log Record is created, this is passed to the Handler which handles publication of log messages. Moreover, a Logger and a handler both can use Filters or log levels to focus on a particular Log Record. Furthermore, the handler has the possibility to format the message before it is sent to the output stream (external environment). Localization of a log message specific to a particular geographical, cultural or political region can be done with the help of a Formatter. The external environment can constitute the console, a file, a remote file, etc.

All the output Handlers of a logger are tracked by it. A logger can be configured to ignore certain handlers which have been configured below a certain log level.

As discussed in the previous sections, Handlers can also send output to another Handler. The Memory Handler is one such example. It maintains a buffer of records and wits for a trigger so that it can publish the records to an external source. In this case, the Formatting of the log record is done by the last handler in the control flow.

The logging API is developed and structured in such a way so as to minimize the cost of logging. Events such as Formatting and Localization are delayed until they are requested by the Handler. Also, with the use of a Memory Handler, formatting does not need to be done, thereby saving costs of formatting.

2.3. LOGGING API

This section covers useful API provided by the java.util.logging package.

2.3.1. The Level Class

- Fields

Table 2.2: Fields in the Level Class (Level (Java Platform SE 7), 2017)

Field Name	Description
Static level ALL	This field denotes that all types of messages should be logged by the logger.

Static level FINE	This field denotes the messages that give tracing information and that these messages should be logged by the logger.
Static level FINER	This field denotes slightly more detailed FINE messages.
Static level FINEST	This field indicates a very detailed tracing message.
Static level INFO	This level denotes informational messages.
Static level CONFIG	This field denotes simple and static configuration messages.
Static level WARNING	This field denotes a level that means there is an issue.
Static level SEVERE	This field denotes a level that means there is failure in the application.
Static level OFF	This is a particular level that is used to switch off logging functionalities.

- Constructors

Table 2.3: Constructors in the Level Class (Level (Java Platform SE 7), 2017)

Constructor	Description
Level (String name, int value)	Create a level with the given name and integer value
Level (String name, int value, String resourceBundleName)	Create a level with the given name, integer value, and localized resource name

- Methods

Table 2.4: Constructors in the Level Class (Level (Java Platform SE 7), 2017)

Method Name	Description
int Value ()	This method returns the integer value for the current Level.
String get Localized Name ()	This method returns the localized name of the current Level for the default locale.
String get Name()	This method returns the non-localized name of the current level as a String.
String get Resource Bundle Name ()	This method returns the localized resource bundle name for the current level or it returns null if no bundle has been defined for the current level.

Table: Constructors in the level class (Level (Java Platform SE 7), 2017)

2.3.2. The Handler Class

- Constructor

Table 2.5: Constructor in the Handler Class (Handler (Java Platform SE 7), 2017)

Constructor	Description
Handler()	This is the default constructor of the Handler.

Table: Constructor in the handler class (Handler (Java Platform SE 7), 2017)

- Methods

Table 2.6: Methods in the Handler Class (Handler (Java Platform SE 7), 2017)

Method	Description
Filter get Filter()	This method returns the current filter for the handler invoking this method.
void set Filter (Filter filter)	This method sets the specified filter which controls the output that is written to the Handler.
Level get Level ()	This method returns the Level specified for the Handler that invokes this method.
void set Level (Level level)	This method sets the log level of the Handler to the level specified as an input.
Boolean is Loggable (Log Record log Record)	This method checks if the given input level will be logged by the Handler.
Formatter get Formatter()	This method returns the Formatter for the current handler.
Void setFormatter(Formatter formatter)	This method sets the formatter for the Handler.
Abstract void publish(LogRecord record)	This method publishes a log record to the output stream.
String getEncoding()	This method returns the encoding for the Handler in the form of a String.
String setEncoding(String encoding)	This method sets the character encoding that has been provided as an argument for the current Handler.

2.3.3. The Logger Class

- Constructors

Table 2.7: Constructors in the Logger Class (Logger (Java Platform SE 7), 2017)

Constructor	Description
Logger(String name, String resourceBundle-Name)	This constructor creates a new logger object.

- Methods

Table 2.8: Logger Class Methods (Logger (Java Platform SE 7), 2017)

Method	Description
Static Logger get Logger(String name)	This method returns a logger object for the given resource.
Static Logger get Logger(String name, resourceBundleName)	This method returns a logger object for the given name and resource bundle specified.
void fine(String msg)	This method logs a message of level FINE.
void finer(String msg)	This method logs a message of level FINER.
void finest(String msg)	This method logs a message of level FINEST.
void config(String msg)	This method logs a message of level CONFIG.
void info(String msg)	This method logs a message of level INFO.
void warning(String msg)	This method logs a message of level WARNING.
void severe(String msg)	This method logs a message of level SEVERE.
String get Name()	This methods returns the name of the logger.
String get Parent()	This method returns the name of the parent of the logger.
Boolean is Loggable(Level level)	This method checks if the given input level will be logged by the logger object.
void log(Level, String msg)	This method logs a message with the given level and message input.
void log(Level, String msg, Object params)	This method logs a message with the given level message input and input parameters.
void log(Level, String msg, Throwable ex)	This method logs a message with the given level message input and an object of type Throwable.
void log(Log Record log)	This method logs a LogRecord.
void add Handler (Handler handler)	This method adds a Handler to receive log records.
void remove Handler(Handler handler)	This method removes the specified Handler.

Handler [] get Handlers()	This method returns all the Handlers for the logger object invoking this method.
Filter get Filter ()	This method returns the current filter for the logger invoking this method.
void set Filter (Filter filter)	This method sets the specified filter which controls the output that is written to the logger.
Level get Level ()	This method returns the Level specified for the logger that invokes this method.
void setLevel(Level level)	This method sets the log level of the logger to the level specified as an input.

2.3.4. The Log Manager Class

• Constructor

Table 2.9: Constructor of the Log Manager Class (java.util.logging (Java Platform SE 7) 2017)

Constructor	Description
protected Log Manager()	This is the default constructor of the Log Manager

• Methods

Table 2.10: Log Manager Methods (java.util.logging (Java Platform SE 7), 2017)

Method	Description
Boolean add Logger (Logger logger)	This method adds a named logger and returns false if a logger with same name exists.
static Log Manager get Log Manager ()	This method returns the global Log Manager object
String get Property (String name)	This method retrieves the value of a logging configuration property
void read Configuration ()	This method re-reads the configuration file and reinitializes the logging properties.
void read Configuration (Input Stream in)	This method re-reads the configuration file and reinitializes the logging properties but reads it from a given input stream.
void reset ()	This method resets the logging configuration.
void add Property Change Listener (Property Change Listener l)	This method adds a listener to listen for changes in the configuration properties when the logging properties are being re-read and reinitialized.

| void remove Property Change Listener (Property Change Listener l) | This method removes the listener that listens for changes in the logging properties. |
| Enumeration<String> get Logger Names () | This method returns a String enumeration of all the known logger names. |

In the Log Manager, as we can see from table 1, the read Configuration () methods allows the configuration file to be re-read. When the configuration is loaded once more, all the values that have been updated programmatically will be overridden by those from the configuration file.

It is crucial to note that all methods provided by the Log Manager class are thread-safe. Hence, logging can be used in a multithreaded environment without having to worry about concurrency among threads.

2.3.5. The Filter Interface

Each logger and appender has a filter tagged to it. The filter interface consists of the following method:

Table 2.11: Filter Interface methods (java.util.logging (Java Platform SE 7), 2017)

Method	Description
boolean is Loggable(LogRecord logRecord)	This method returns true if given record can be published, else it returns false.

2.3.6. The Formatter Class

The formatter class is an abstract class that serves as the parent class to the Simple Formatter and XML Formatter class which are used to format log records. It takes a Log Record object as input and processes it to convert it into a string.

This class has the following methods:

Table 2.12: Formatter Class Methods (java.util.logging (Java Platform SE 7), 2017)

Method	Description
String formatMessage(LogRecord logRecord)	This method returns the localized and formatted LogRecord as a String.
String getHead(Handler handler)	This method returns the main header string for a set of formatted log records.

String getTail(Handler handler)	This method returns the tail end string for a set of formatted log records.
abstract String format(LogRecord logRecord)	This method is an abstract method that is used to format the given record and returns the formatted record in the form of a string. This method is implemented by the SimpleFormatter and XMLFormatter class.

2.4. ENVIRONMENT AND CONFIGURATION

As the java logging framework consists of the logging API, no specific installation with respect to the logging component needs to be done. Once the JDK has been installed, we have access to the java util logging API.

But, in order to enable logging, we need to configure it first. The configuration for enabling logging in any Java application is done with the help of a configuration file that is read when the application is started. This configuration file is a standard file of type 'java.util.properties'. The Properties class in java represents nothing but a persistent set of properties (java.util.logging (Java Platform SE 7), 2017). It is a file that stores key-value pairs and is thread-safe which means that it can used in a multithreaded environment.

The configuration process for logging in Java can be done in two ways; by use of a properties file or by writing a class that handles the initialization of the configuration. We describe the above methods with examples as shown below.

2.4.1. Using a Properties File

As the java logging package is a part of the JDK API, a configuration file has been provided by default by java. This file is named as logging.properties.

This file is located at the following location:

Local path to jdk\jre\lib\ logging.properties

By default, the logger is set to output the log messages to the console and the default log level is set to INFO. A Simple Formatter is used to format the log messages that are sent to the console as output. Also, the File Handler has been configured that formats the log output using the XML formatter.

The contents of this file are as follows:

📄 logging.properties ⊠

```
###########################################################
#    Default Logging Configuration File
#
# You can use a different file by specifying a filename
# with the java.util.logging.config.file system property.
# For example java -Djava.util.logging.config.file=myfile
###########################################################

###########################################################
#    Global properties
###########################################################

# "handlers" specifies a comma separated list of log Handler
# classes.  These handlers will be installed during VM startup.
# Note that these classes must be on the system classpath.
# By default we only configure a ConsoleHandler, which will only
# show messages at the INFO and above levels.
handlers= java.util.logging.ConsoleHandler

# To also add the FileHandler, use the following line instead.
#handlers= java.util.logging.FileHandler, java.util.logging.ConsoleHandler

# Default global logging level.
# This specifies which kinds of events are logged across
# all loggers.  For any given facility this global level
# can be overriden by a facility specific level
# Note that the ConsoleHandler also has a separate level
# setting to limit messages printed to the console.
.level= INFO

###########################################################
# Handler specific properties.
# Describes specific configuration info for Handlers.
###########################################################

# default file output is in user's home directory.
java.util.logging.FileHandler.pattern = %h/java%u.log
java.util.logging.FileHandler.limit = 50000
java.util.logging.FileHandler.count = 1
java.util.logging.FileHandler.formatter = java.util.logging.XMLFormatter

# Limit the message that are printed on the console to INFO and above.
java.util.logging.ConsoleHandler.level = INFO
java.util.logging.ConsoleHandler.formatter = java.util.logging.SimpleFormatter

# Example to customize the SimpleFormatter output format
# to print one-line log message like this:
#     <level>: <log message> [<date/time>]
#
# java.util.logging.SimpleFormatter.format=%4$s: %5$s [%1$tc]%n

###########################################################
# Facility specific properties.
# Provides extra control for each logger.
###########################################################

# For example, set the com.xyz.foo logger to only log SEVERE
# messages:
com.xyz.foo.level = SEVERE
```

As we can see the default handler is the Console Handler and it is set to the INFO log level.

Additionally, an example for specifying additional customized configuration has been provided for the users.

If we want to use the default configuration provided by java, we can simply instantiate the logger object in our class.

Consider the following class:

```
FirstJavaProgram.java

    public class FirstJavaProgram {

        public static void main(String[] args) {

            System.out.println("Hi! This is my first Java Program!");

        }
    }
```

If we want to enable logging in this program, we instantiate a logger object as follows:

```
FirstJavaProgram.java
    import java.util.logging.Logger;

    public class FirstJavaProgram {

        public static void main(String[] args) {

            final Logger logger = Logger.getLogger(FirstJavaProgram.class.getName());

            System.out.println("Hi! This is my first Java Program!");

            logger.info("My first Log statement!");

        }
    }
```

We declare an object of type Logger and use the getLogger() method of the Logger class to load the default logger provided by the Java logging API.

This method returns an instance of the default logger provided by java.

Once, we have the default logger, we simply use it as shown in the class above.

The output generated by the above class is as follows:

The default configuration doesn't take up a lot of space. It doesn't bombard the user with a lot of information but ensures that critical logs are provided to the end user.

This configuration defines and maintains a single handler on the root/parent logger which sends the output to the console.

Although the use of the default configuration is easy, it is limited in terms of functionality. In case a developer needs additional logging capabilities in an application, the default logging configuration falls short. In this case, it is advised to provide your own configuration. This is done by creating a separate properties file for your application.

The steps are as follows:

a. In your java application in eclipse, create a 'resources' folder. In this folder, add a logging.properties file as shown below:

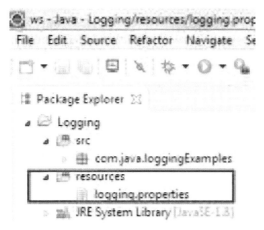

b. Edit this file and provide the custom logging configuration that you wish to implement in your application.

```
📄 logging.properties ⊠
  # This is the properties file used for configuring the java logging facility

  handlers=java.util.logging.ConsoleHandler

  #Default Logging Level: This level may be overridden by Loggers and Handlers

  .level= INFO

  #Loggers
  #-------------------------------------------------------------
  com.java.loggingExamples.level=ALL


  # Handlers
  #-------------------------------------------------------------

  #------Console Handler--------------
  #Override the global logging level
  java.util.logging.ConsoleHandler.level = SEVERE
  java.util.logging.ConsoleHandler.formatter = java.util.logging.SimpleFormatter
```

In the above logging.properties file, we have configured a single handler: console handler.

The console handler is configured to print only the messages with the level SEVERE.

It should be noted that the default logging level has been set to INFO but it has been overridden by the Handlers.

c.   Instantiate the logger and add log statements to your Java class

This is shown by the class Logging Example as shown below:

```
📄 LoggingExample.java ⊠
  package com.java.loggingExamples;

  import java.util.logging.Logger;

  public class LoggingExample {

      // Instantiate the logger object
      private static final Logger logger = Logger.getLogger(LoggingExample.class.getName());

      public static void main(String args[]) {

          // add log messages of different log levels
          logger.info("Info message");
          logger.severe("Severe message");
          logger.warning("Warning Message");
          logger.severe("Another Severe message");

      }
  }
```

As we can from the above class, three different types of log messages have been added in the class.

d.   In order to load the custom logging configuration on to the classpath, the runtime system will look for the following property: **java.util.logging.config.file**

By default, the Java runtime will load the logging.properties that is located within the JDK.

e.   If we want to load the custom properties file we need to provide the path of the new properties file as the value for the **java.util. logging.config.file** property at runtime. In order to do this, we need to specify the path of the new configuration file when we run the java program. This can be done in the following two ways

-    **Loading the configuration file at runtime**

-    **Programmatically (explained in the next section)**

In case of the first way of loading the file, if you are executing your java application via the command prompt, use the following command:

java   -Djava.util.logging.config.file=my   Logging   ConfigFilePath <classToExecute>

The above command is used directly when run from the command prompt.

But, in Eclipse, we need to specify this argument in the Run Configurations as follows:

The following screen is displayed. Go to the Arguments tab.

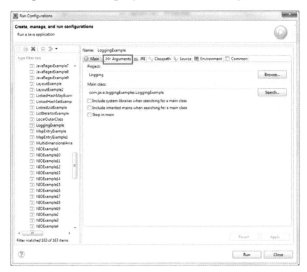

In the arguments tab, edit the VM arguments component and add the following parameter:

- Djava.util.logging.config.file=<Path to custom logging file>

In our case it is the following:

- Djava.util.logging.config.file=C:/Users/books/ws/Logging/ resources/logging.properties

Edit the field as shown below and click on run.

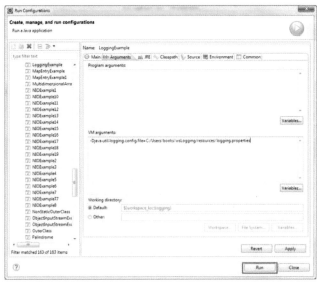

The output is as follows:

```
Console ⊠  Problems  Javadoc  Declaration  Annotations  Call Hi
<terminated> LoggingExample [Java Application] C:\Program Files\java\jdk1.8.0_92\bin\java
Oct 03, 2017 6:07:57 PM com.java.loggingExamples.LoggingExample main
SEVERE: Severe message
Oct 03, 2017 6:07:57 PM com.java.loggingExamples.LoggingExample main
SEVERE: Another Severe message
```

As we can see, only the log messages that have a priority SEVERE have been displayed on the console as we have configured this in the configuration file logging.properties.

If we want to display all the log levels on the console as well, the configuration file needs to be changed as follows:

```
logging.properties ⊠
# This is the properties file used for configuring the java logging facility

handlers=java.util.logging.ConsoleHandler

#Default Logging Level: This level may be overridden by Loggers and Handlers

.level= INFO

#Loggers
#---------------------------------------------------------------
com.java.loggingExamples.level=ALL


# Handlers
#---------------------------------------------------------------

#------Console Handler-------------
#Override the global logging level
java.util.logging.ConsoleHandler.level = ALL
java.util.logging.ConsoleHandler.formatter = java.util.logging.SimpleFormatter
```

We need to change the level of the console handler to ALL so that it accepts and prints log messages having different types of log levels.

The output generated after this small change is shown below:

```
Console ⊠  Problems  Javadoc  Declaration  Annotations  Call Hie
<terminated> LoggingExample [Java Application] C:\Program Files\java\jdk1.8.0_92\bin\javav
Oct 04, 2017 9:25:35 AM com.java.loggingExamples.LoggingExample main
INFO: Info message
Oct 04, 2017 9:25:35 AM com.java.loggingExamples.LoggingExample main
SEVERE: Severe message
Oct 04, 2017 9:25:35 AM com.java.loggingExamples.LoggingExample main
WARNING: Warning Message
Oct 04, 2017 9:25:35 AM com.java.loggingExamples.LoggingExample main
SEVERE: Another Severe message
```

The output clearly displays all the log messages (INFO, WARNING, and SEVERE) that we have logged in the class LoggingExample.

It is important to note that the loggers and handlers override the default log level that has been set in the configuration file.

2.4.2. Loading the Configuration Programmatically

Alternative to providing the path at runtime, the logging configuration can also be initialized by providing a Java class that would be used for reading the initialization properties. This is done by loading the file with the use of the read Configuration () method that loads the file. This is shown below:

```
// LoggingExample.java

import java.io.FileInputStream;
import java.io.IOException;
import java.util.logging.Level;
import java.util.logging.LogManager;
import java.util.logging.Logger;

public class LoggingExample {

    // Instantiate the logger object
    private static final Logger logger = Logger.getLogger(LoggingExample.class.getName());

    private static final LogManager logManager = LogManager.getLogManager();
    private static final Logger LOGGER = Logger.getLogger("com.java.loggingExamples");
    static{
        try {
            logManager.readConfiguration(new FileInputStream("./resources/logging.properties"));
        } catch (IOException exception) {
            LOGGER.log(Level.SEVERE, "Error in loading configuration",exception);
        }
    }

    public static void main(String args[]) {

        // add log messages of different log levels
        logger.info("Info message");
        logger.severe("Severe message");
        logger.warning("Warning Message");
        logger.severe("Another Severe message");

    }
}
```

As shown in the class Logging Example, first an instance of the Log Manager is obtained. Then, the read Configuration () method is invoked on this object. This method takes an Input Stream object as its input parameter. Hence, the path of the configuration file has been provided to it.

This way of configuration is more flexible and permits the configuration information to be read from various sources such JDBC, LDAP and so on. As we have seen, the configuration files specify levels for the loggers.

It is interesting to know that this level that has been set via the configuration file is set for the logger and its children in the tree. The levels are defined and applied in the exact order as mentioned in the configuration file.

The default structure of the java logging APIs are such that the initial logging properties of an application are read from a file. This default configuration may be later changed programmatically using the methods provided by the Logger class API.

But, if we reload the configuration file, any changes that have been performed programmatically will be overridden by the configuration that has been specified in the configuration file.

The logging API permits the user to dynamically configure the properties at runtime as well. New Handlers having different attributes can be created. Handlers can be added, updated or removed. The same goes for loggers.

They too can be created, modified and configured to use specific handlers. The log levels for the handlers can be set dynamically at runtime via the code.

These configurations have been explained with the use of examples in section 2.6.

2.5. EXAMPLES

Example 1: Simple Default Logger example

In this example, we make use of the default logging configuration that has been provided by Java to log messages. We demonstrate the use of log messages in case of Exception Handling. This example is an extension to the Logger Example class that we have previously used to demonstrate the logger configuration.

```java
LoggingExample1.java

package com.java.loggingExamples;

import java.util.logging.Level;
import java.util.logging.Logger;

public class LoggingExample1 {

    // Instantiate the logger object
    private static final Logger logger = Logger.getLogger(LoggingExample1.class.getName());

    public static void main(String args[]) {

        // add log messages of different log levels
        logger.info("Info message");
        logger.severe("Severe message");
        logger.warning("Warning Message");
        logger.severe("Another Severe message");

        int a = 5;
        int b = 0;

        // we induce an error
        try {
            int c = a / b;
            System.out.println("result:" + c);
        } catch (ArithmeticException ex) {
            logger.log(Level.SEVERE, "Arithmetic Exception occured. Cannot divide by zero!", ex);
        }
    }
}
```

In this example, we purposely generate an exception so that it is caught by the logger and printed on the console.

The output generated in this case is as follows:

```
Console    Problems  @ Javadoc  Declaration  Annotations  Call Hierarchy
<terminated> LoggingExample1 [Java Application] C:\Program Files\java\jdk1.8.0_92\bin\javaw.exe
Oct 04, 2017 2:13:23 PM com.java.loggingExamples.LoggingExample1 main
INFO: Info message
Oct 04, 2017 2:13:23 PM com.java.loggingExamples.LoggingExample1 main
SEVERE: Severe message
Oct 04, 2017 2:13:23 PM com.java.loggingExamples.LoggingExample1 main
WARNING: Warning Message
Oct 04, 2017 2:13:23 PM com.java.loggingExamples.LoggingExample1 main
SEVERE: Another Severe message
Oct 04, 2017 2:13:23 PM com.java.loggingExamples.LoggingExample1 main
SEVERE: Arithmetic Exception occured. Cannot divide by zero!
java.lang.ArithmeticException: / by zero
        at com.java.loggingExamples.LoggingExample1.main(LoggingExample1.java:24)
```

Example 2: Custom configuration file example

In this example, we use a custom configuration file to load the logging configuration. In this case, we configure it to display log messages that have only the level SEVERE.

The properties file:

```
logging.properties ⌧
# This is the properties file used for configuring the java logging facility

handlers=java.util.logging.ConsoleHandler

#Default Logging Level: This level may be overridden by Loggers and Handlers

.level= INFO

#Loggers
#----------------------------------------------------------------
com.java.loggingExamples.level=ALL


# Handlers
#----------------------------------------------------------------

#------Console Handler--------------
#Override the global logging level
java.util.logging.ConsoleHandler.level = SEVERE
java.util.logging.ConsoleHandler.formatter = java.util.logging.SimpleFormatter
```

The java class:

```
LoggingExample1.java ⌧
package com.java.loggingExamples;

import java.util.logging.Level;
import java.util.logging.Logger;

public class LoggingExample1 {

    // Instantiate the logger object
    private static final Logger logger = Logger.getLogger(LoggingExample1.class.getName());

    public static void main(String args[]) {

        // add log messages of different log levels
        logger.info("Info message");
        logger.severe("Severe message");
        logger.warning("Warning Message");
        logger.severe("Another Severe message");

        int a = 5;
        int b = 0;

        // we induce an error
        try {
            int c = a / b;
            System.out.println("result:" + c);
        } catch (ArithmeticException ex) {
            logger.log(Level.SEVERE, "Arithmetic Exception occured. Cannot divide by zero!", ex);
        }
    }
}
```

To execute the java class, we provide the java.util.logging.config.file parameter in the arguments section as explained previously.

The output is:

```
Console ⌧   Problems  @ Javadoc  Declaration  Annotations  Call Hierarchy
<terminated> LoggingExample1 [Java Application] C:\Program Files\java\jdk1.8.0_92\bin\javaw.exe
Oct 04, 2017 2:27:10 PM com.java.loggingExamples.LoggingExample1 main
SEVERE: Severe message
Oct 04, 2017 2:27:10 PM com.java.loggingExamples.LoggingExample1 main
SEVERE: Another Severe message
Oct 04, 2017 2:27:10 PM com.java.loggingExamples.LoggingExample1 main
SEVERE: Arithmetic Exception occured. Cannot divide by zero!
java.lang.ArithmeticException: / by zero
        at com.java.loggingExamples.LoggingExample1.main(LoggingExample1.java:24)
```

Example 3: File Handler with default Java configuration

In this example, we demonstrate the use of a file Handler. This example outputs the log messages to only a file and not on the console. In the java. util.logging package, the default configuration doesn't declare a file Handler. But, it does provide default properties such as output file pattern, rotation, and size. The configuration file used is the default file that has been provided by Java.

```
logging.properties ⊠
############################################################
#    Default Logging Configuration File
#
# You can use a different file by specifying a filename
# with the java.util.logging.config.file system property.
# For example java -Djava.util.logging.config.file=myfile
############################################################

############################################################
#    Global properties
############################################################

# "handlers" specifies a comma separated list of log Handler
# classes.  These handlers will be installed during VM startup.
# Note that these classes must be on the system classpath.
# By default we only configure a ConsoleHandler, which will only
# show messages at the INFO and above levels.
handlers= java.util.logging.ConsoleHandler

# To also add the FileHandler, use the following line instead.
#handlers= java.util.logging.FileHandler, java.util.logging.ConsoleHandler

# Default global logging level.
# This specifies which kinds of events are logged across
# all loggers.  For any given facility this global level
# can be overriden by a facility specific level
# Note that the ConsoleHandler also has a separate level
# setting to limit messages printed to the console.
.level= INFO
############################################################
# Handler specific properties.
# Describes specific configuration info for Handlers.
############################################################

# default file output is in user's home directory.
java.util.logging.FileHandler.pattern = %h/java%u.log
java.util.logging.FileHandler.limit = 50000
java.util.logging.FileHandler.count = 1
java.util.logging.FileHandler.formatter = java.util.logging.XMLFormatter

# Limit the message that are printed on the console to INFO and above.
java.util.logging.ConsoleHandler.level = INFO
java.util.logging.ConsoleHandler.formatter = java.util.logging.SimpleFormatter

# Example to customize the SimpleFormatter output format
# to print one-line log message like this:
#     <level>: <log message> [<date/time>]
#
# java.util.logging.SimpleFormatter.format=%4$s: %5$s [%1$tc]%n

############################################################
# Facility specific properties.
# Provides extra control for each logger.
############################################################

# For example, set the com.xyz.foo logger to only log SEVERE
# messages:
com.xyz.foo.level = SEVERE
```

In order to use the default properties of the file Handler provided by the logging API, we can programmatically create and invoke a FileHandler object. This is shown by the class LoggingExample2 below:

```java
package com.java.loggingExamples;

import java.io.IOException;
import java.util.logging.FileHandler;
import java.util.logging.Level;
import java.util.logging.LogManager;
import java.util.logging.Logger;

public class LoggingExample2 {

    // Instantiate the logger object
    private static final Logger logger = Logger.getLogger(LoggingExample2.class.getName());

    // get an instance of the LogManager
    static LogManager logManager = LogManager.getLogManager();

    public static void main(String args[]) throws SecurityException, IOException {

        // create a FileHandler
        // this fileHandler without arguments constructs a default FileHandler
        // object
        FileHandler fileHandler = new FileHandler();
        // add the handler to the logger
        logger.addHandler(fileHandler);

        // log messages

        logger.info("Info Message");
        logger.finer("Finer Message");
        logger.warning("Warning Message");

        int arr[] = { 1, 2 };
        try {
            for (int i = 3; i > 0; i--) {
                System.out.println(arr[i]);
            }
        } catch (ArrayIndexOutOfBoundsException e) {
            logger.log(Level.SEVERE, "Array Index is out of bounds.", e);
        }
    }
}
```

The output is as follows:

```
Console 🔳    Problems    @ Javadoc    Declaration    Annotations    Call Hierarchy
<terminated> LoggingExample2 [Java Application] C:\Program Files\java\jdk1.8.0_92\bin\javaw.exe
Oct 05, 2017 10:35:08 AM com.java.loggingExamples.LoggingExample2 main
INFO: Info Message
Oct 05, 2017 10:35:08 AM com.java.loggingExamples.LoggingExample2 main
WARNING: Warning Message
Oct 05, 2017 10:35:08 AM com.java.loggingExamples.LoggingExample2 main
SEVERE: Array Index is out of bounds.
java.lang.ArrayIndexOutOfBoundsException: 3
        at com.java.loggingExamples.LoggingExample2.main(LoggingExample2.java:35)
```

As we can see from the output, only messages above a certain level are displayed. This is because the default level is INFO and it is configured in the properties file. Hence, log messages of level Finer that have been added in our program are not displayed on the console.

The File Handler generates a file in the USER.HOME directory named java0.log.

The contents of this file are as follows:

```
java0.log ⋈
<?xml version="1.0" encoding="windows-1252" standalone="no"?>
<!DOCTYPE log SYSTEM "logger.dtd">
<log>
<record>
  <date>2017-10-05T10:35:08</date>
  <millis>1507192508159</millis>
  <sequence>0</sequence>
  <logger>com.java.loggingExamples.LoggingExample2</logger>
  <level>INFO</level>
  <class>com.java.loggingExamples.LoggingExample2</class>
  <method>main</method>
  <thread>1</thread>
  <message>Info Message</message>
</record>
<record>
  <date>2017-10-05T10:35:08</date>
  <millis>1507192508205</millis>
  <sequence>1</sequence>
  <logger>com.java.loggingExamples.LoggingExample2</logger>
  <level>WARNING</level>
  <class>com.java.loggingExamples.LoggingExample2</class>
  <method>main</method>
  <thread>1</thread>
  <message>Warning Message</message>
</record>
<record>
  <date>2017-10-05T10:35:08</date>
  <millis>1507192508205</millis>
  <sequence>2</sequence>
  <logger>com.java.loggingExamples.LoggingExample2</logger>
  <level>SEVERE</level>
  <class>com.java.loggingExamples.LoggingExample2</class>
  <method>main</method>
  <thread>1</thread>
  <message>Array Index is out of bounds.</message>
  <exception>
    <message>java.lang.ArrayIndexOutOfBoundsException: 3</message>
    <frame>
      <class>com.java.loggingExamples.LoggingExample2</class>
      <method>main</method>
      <line>35</line>
    </frame>
  </exception>
</record>
</log>
```

The File Handler output file too doesn't log messages of levels that are lower than INFO. This is because, in the default configuration, no level has been specified for the default file handler. Hence, it inherits the LEVEL from its parent which is the Logger instance. This instance holds the default level INFO that has been set in the properties file.

But, if we want to change this level, it can be done easily programmatically. This is demonstrated by the class LoggingExample2 which has been modified to take log messages of all levels.

```
LoggingExample2.java ⋈
package com.java.loggingExamples;

import java.io.IOException;

public class LoggingExample2 {
    // Instantiate the logger object
    private static final Logger logger = Logger.getLogger(LoggingExample2.class.getName());

    // get an instance of the LogManager
    static LogManager logManager = LogManager.getLogManager();

    public static void main(String args[]) throws SecurityException, IOException {

        // create a FileHandler
        // this FileHandler without arguments constructs a default FileHandler
        // object
        FileHandler fileHandler = new FileHandler();

        // add the handler to the logger
        logger.addHandler(fileHandler);
        // change the level to accept all messages
        logger.setLevel(Level.ALL);
        // log messages

        logger.info("Info Message");
        logger.finer("Finer Message");
        logger.warning("Warning Message");

        int arr[] = { 1, 2 };
        try {
            for (int i = 3; i > 0; i--) {
                System.out.println(arr[i]);
            }

        } catch (ArrayIndexOutOfBoundsException e) {
            logger.log(Level.SEVERE, "Array Index is out of bounds.", e);
        }
    }
}
```

The console output doesn't change, but the file handler output changes and now logs all types of messages. The contents of this file are as follows:

```
java0.log
<?xml version="1.0" encoding="windows-1252" standalone="no"?>
<!DOCTYPE log SYSTEM "logger.dtd">
<log>
<record>
  <date>2017-10-05T12:05:23</date>
  <millis>1507197923932</millis>
  <sequence>0</sequence>
  <logger>com.java.loggingExamples.LoggingExample2</logger>
  <level>INFO</level>
  <class>com.java.loggingExamples.LoggingExample2</class>
  <method>main</method>
  <thread>1</thread>
  <message>Info Message</message>
</record>
<record>
  <date>2017-10-05T12:05:23</date>
  <millis>1507197923979</millis>
  <sequence>1</sequence>
  <logger>com.java.loggingExamples.LoggingExample2</logger>
  <level>FINER</level>
  <class>com.java.loggingExamples.LoggingExample2</class>
  <method>main</method>
  <thread>1</thread>
  <message>Finer Message</message>
</record>
<record>
  <date>2017-10-05T12:05:23</date>
  <millis>1507197923979</millis>
  <sequence>2</sequence>
  <logger>com.java.loggingExamples.LoggingExample2</logger>
  <level>WARNING</level>
  <class>com.java.loggingExamples.LoggingExample2</class>
  <method>main</method>
  <thread>1</thread>
  <message>Warning Message</message>
</record>
<record>
  <date>2017-10-05T12:05:23</date>
  <millis>1507197923979</millis>
  <sequence>3</sequence>
  <logger>com.java.loggingExamples.LoggingExample2</logger>
  <level>SEVERE</level>
  <class>com.java.loggingExamples.LoggingExample2</class>
  <method>main</method>
  <thread>1</thread>
  <message>Array Index is out of bounds.</message>
  <exception>
    <message>java.lang.ArrayIndexOutOfBoundsException: 3</message>
    <frame>
      <class>com.java.loggingExamples.LoggingExample2</class>
      <method>main</method>
      <line>36</line>
    </frame>
  </exception>
</record>
</log>
```

Note that in the above file, the FINER log message has been displayed and this shows that now messages of all Levels are being logged.

Example 4: File Handler with custom configuration

In this example, we use a separate configuration file for creation of a File Handler. In this example, only a single Handler has been defined.

The Configuration file is as follows:

```
logging2.properties

# This is the properties file used for configuring the java logging facility

handlers=java.util.logging.ConsoleHandler

#Default Logging Level: This level may be overridden by Loggers and Handlers

.level= INFO

#Loggers
#---------------------------------------------------------------
com.java.loggingExamples.level=ALL


# Handlers
# ------------------------------------------------
# --- FileHandler ---
# Override the global logging level INFO
java.util.logging.FileHandler.level=ALL
#provide the location and pattern of the output log file
java.util.logging.FileHandler.pattern=myFile.log
#provide the size limit of the log file
java.util.logging.FileHandler.limit=50000
#provide the count in case of rotations
java.util.logging.FileHandler.count=1
#provide the formatter to be used
java.util.logging.FileHandler.formatter=java.util.logging.XMLFormatter
```

We define a simple File Handler with a custom pattern and Simple Formatter. The java class is as follows:

```
LoggingExample2.java

package com.java.loggingExamples;

+ import java.io.IOException;

public class LoggingExample2 {

    // Instantiate the logger object
    private static final Logger logger = Logger.getLogger(LoggingExample2.class.getName());

    public static void main(String args[]) throws SecurityException, IOException {

        // add log messages of different log levels
        logger.info("Info Message");
        logger.finer("Finer Message");
        logger.warning("Warning Message");

        int arr[] = { 1, 2 };
        try {
            for (int i = 3; i>0; i--) {
                System.out.println(arr[i]);
            }

        } catch (ArrayIndexOutOfBoundsException e) {
            logger.log(Level.SEVERE, "Array Index is out of bounds.", e);
        }
    }
}
```

As we have defined a single handler (File Handler) for this logger, there is no output displayed on the console. But, in the project directory, a new log file is created as shown below:

The contents of this output file are as follows:

```xml
myFile.log
<?xml version="1.0" encoding="windows-1252" standalone="no"?>
<!DOCTYPE log SYSTEM "logger.dtd">
<log>
<record>
  <date>2017-10-04T15:15:12</date>
  <millis>1507122912272</millis>
  <sequence>0</sequence>
  <logger>com.java.loggingExamples.LoggingExample2</logger>
  <level>INFO</level>
  <class>com.java.loggingExamples.LoggingExample2</class>
  <method>main</method>
  <thread>1</thread>
  <message>Info Message</message>
</record>
<record>
  <date>2017-10-04T15:15:12</date>
  <millis>1507122912334</millis>
  <sequence>1</sequence>
  <logger>com.java.loggingExamples.LoggingExample2</logger>
  <level>FINER</level>
  <class>com.java.loggingExamples.LoggingExample2</class>
  <method>main</method>
  <thread>1</thread>
  <message>Finer Message</message>
</record>
<record>
  <date>2017-10-04T15:15:12</date>
  <millis>1507122912334</millis>
  <sequence>2</sequence>
  <logger>com.java.loggingExamples.LoggingExample2</logger>
  <level>WARNING</level>
  <class>com.java.loggingExamples.LoggingExample2</class>
  <method>main</method>
  <thread>1</thread>
  <message>Warning Message</message>
</record>
<record>
  <date>2017-10-04T15:15:12</date>
  <millis>1507122912334</millis>
  <sequence>3</sequence>
  <logger>com.java.loggingExamples.LoggingExample2</logger>
  <level>SEVERE</level>
  <class>com.java.loggingExamples.LoggingExample2</class>
  <method>main</method>
  <thread>1</thread>
  <message>Array Index is out of bounds.</message>
  <exception>
    <message>java.lang.ArrayIndexOutOfBoundsException: 3</message>
    <frame>
      <class>com.java.loggingExamples.LoggingExample2</class>
      <method>main</method>
      <line>25</line>
    </frame>
  </exception>
</record>
</log>
```

As we can see, log messages of all Log levels have been displayed as configured in the properties file.

Example 5: Custom configuration with File Handler and Console Handler

This example demonstrates the use of a custom configuration file that defines two Handlers: File and Console.

The config file is as follows:

```
logging2.properties
# This is the properties file used for configuring the java logging facility

handlers=java.util.logging.ConsoleHandler

#Default Logging Level: This level may be overridden by Loggers and Handlers

.level= INFO

#Loggers
#-----------------------------------------------------------------
com.java.loggingExamples.level=ALL

# Handlers
#-----------------------------------------------------------------
#------Console Handler--------------
#Override the global logging level
java.util.logging.ConsoleHandler.level = ALL
java.util.logging.ConsoleHandler.formatter = java.util.logging.SimpleFormatter

# ---------------------------------------
# --- FileHandler ---
# Override the global logging level INFO
java.util.logging.FileHandler.level=SEVERE
#provide the location and pattern of the output log file
java.util.logging.FileHandler.pattern=myFile.log
#provide the size limit of the log file
java.util.logging.FileHandler.limit=50000
#provide the count in case of rotations
java.util.logging.FileHandler.count=1
#provide the formatter to be used
java.util.logging.FileHandler.formatter=java.util.logging.XMLFormatter
```

The Java Class LoggingExample3 is as follows:

```
LoggingExample3.java
package com.java.loggingExamples;

import java.io.IOException;

public class LoggingExample3 {

    // Instantiate the logger object
    private static final Logger logger = Logger.getLogger(LoggingExample3.class.getName());

    public static void main(String args[]) throws SecurityException, IOException {

        logger.info("Info Message");
        logger.finer("Finer Message");
        logger.warning("Warning Message");
        logger.finer("Severe Message");

        int arr[] = { 1, 2 };
        try {
            for (int i = 3; i > 0; i--) {
                System.out.println(arr[i]);
            }
        } catch (ArrayIndexOutOfBoundsException e) {
            logger.log(Level.SEVERE, "Array Index is out of bounds.", e);
        }
    }
}
```

The output on the console is as follows:

```
Console ⊠    Problems   @ Javadoc   Declaration   @ Annotations   Call Hierarchy
<terminated> LoggingExample3 [Java Application] C:\Program Files\java\jdk1.8.0_92\bin\javaw.exe
Oct 05, 2017 1:27:07 PM com.java.loggingExamples.LoggingExample3 main
INFO: Info Message
Oct 05, 2017 1:27:08 PM com.java.loggingExamples.LoggingExample3 main
FINER: Finer Message
Oct 05, 2017 1:27:08 PM com.java.loggingExamples.LoggingExample3 main
WARNING: Warning Message
Oct 05, 2017 1:27:08 PM com.java.loggingExamples.LoggingExample3 main
FINER: Severe Message
Oct 05, 2017 1:27:08 PM com.java.loggingExamples.LoggingExample3 main
SEVERE: Array Index is out of bounds.
java.lang.ArrayIndexOutOfBoundsException: 3
        at com.java.loggingExamples.LoggingExample3.main(LoggingExample3.java:23)
```

As the logger has been configured to accept all types of messages for the console handler, all log messages have been displayed.

But, on the other hand, the file handler has been configured to only output messages of level SEVERE, which is shown from the output file 'myFile.log' that is generated.

The contents of this file are:

```
myFile.log ⊠
<?xml version="1.0" encoding="windows-1252" standalone="no"?>
<!DOCTYPE log SYSTEM "logger.dtd">
<log>
<record>
  <date>2017-10-05T13:27:08</date>
  <millis>1507202828047</millis>
  <sequence>4</sequence>
  <logger>com.java.loggingExamples.LoggingExample3</logger>
  <level>SEVERE</level>
  <class>com.java.loggingExamples.LoggingExample3</class>
  <method>main</method>
  <thread>1</thread>
  <message>Array Index is out of bounds.</message>
  <exception>
    <message>java.lang.ArrayIndexOutOfBoundsException: 3</message>
    <frame>
      <class>com.java.loggingExamples.LoggingExample3</class>
      <method>main</method>
      <line>23</line>
    </frame>
  </exception>
</record>
</log>
```

Example 6: Formatters

This example demonstrates the use of the 2 Formatters that have been provided to us by the java.util.logging package namely: Simple Formatter and XML Formatter.

In the class Log Formatter Example, we make use of the default logging configuration to display the log message in XML Format and then programmatically override the value for the Formatter of the FileHandler and set it to the Simple Formatter.

```java
package com.java.loggingExamples;

+ import java.io.IOException;

public class LogFormatterExample {

    private static final Logger LOGGER = Logger.getLogger(LogFormatterExample.class.getName());

    public static void main(String[] args) throws SecurityException, IOException {
        // Create a FileHandler object
        Handler fileHandler = new FileHandler("./myFormatter.log");

        // Creating SimpleFormatter
        SimpleFormatter simpleFormatter = new SimpleFormatter();

        // Assigning-adding the handler to the logger
        LOGGER.addHandler(fileHandler);

        /* Log a message of Level INFO which will be published using the default
        // Formatter: XMLFormatter
        LOGGER.warning("WARNING message: default XML Formatter");

        // apply the SimpleFormatter to the Handler object
        fileHandler.setFormatter(simpleFormatter);

        // Setting the Levels for the logger and the FileHandler
        fileHandler.setLevel(Level.INFO);
        LOGGER.setLevel(Level.ALL);

        // Log a message of level WARNING which will now be published using the
        // Simple Formatter
        LOGGER.info("INFO message: Simple Formatter");
    }
}
```

We configure the File Handler to output to a file named myFormatter. log. The contents of this file are as follows:

```xml
<?xml version="1.0" encoding="windows-1252" standalone="no"?>
<!DOCTYPE log SYSTEM "logger.dtd">
<log>
<record>
  <date>2017-10-05T13:53:58</date>
  <millis>1507204438011</millis>
  <sequence>0</sequence>
  <logger>com.java.loggingExamples.LogFormatterExample</logger>
  <level>WARNING</level>
  <class>com.java.loggingExamples.LogFormatterExample</class>
  <method>main</method>
  <thread>1</thread>
  <message>WARNING message: default XML Formatter</message>
</record>
Oct 05, 2017 1:53:58 PM com.java.loggingExamples.LogFormatterExample main
INFO: INFO message: Simple Formatter
```

As we can see from the above image, the first log message of level WARNING is displayed in XML format whereas the second log message of type INFO has been logged using the Simple Format.

The console output is as follows:

```
🖥 Console ⊠  ❗ Problems  @ Javadoc  🔍 Declaration  🗔 Annotations  ⅔ Call Hierarch
<terminated> LogFormatterExample [Java Application] C:\Program Files\java\jdk1.8.0_92\bin\java
Oct 05, 2017 1:53:58 PM com.java.loggingExamples.LogFormatterExample main
WARNING: WARNING message: default XML Formatter
Oct 05, 2017 1:53:58 PM com.java.loggingExamples.LogFormatterExample main
INFO: INFO message: Simple Formatter
```

Here, both the log messages have been logged as both their levels are higher than INFO.

Example 7: Adding and Removing Handlers

In this example, we illustrate the use of the add Handler() and remove Handler() methods.

```java
LoggingHandlerExample.java
package com.java.loggingExamples;

+ import java.io.IOException;

public class LoggingHandlerExample {

    private static final Logger logger = Logger.getLogger(LoggingHandlerExample.class.getName());

    public static void main(String[] args) throws SecurityException, IOException {

        // Create a FileHandler
        Handler fileHandler = new FileHandler("./LoggingHandler.log");

        // Assign the handlers to the Logger object
        logger.addHandler(fileHandler);

        // Set the log levels for the handler
        fileHandler.setLevel(Level.ALL);

        // set the log level for the logger object
        logger.setLevel(Level.ALL);

        logger.warning("Warning message logged");

        // Remove the File handler
        logger.removeHandler(fileHandler);

        // log a message (this message won't appear in the output log file)
        logger.info("Info Message logged");

        // add the file handler again
        logger.addHandler(fileHandler);

        // log another message (this message will appear in the output log file)
        logger.severe("Severe Message logged");
    }
}
```

The console output is:

```
Console    Problems   @ Javadoc   Declaration   Annotations   Call Hierarchy
<terminated> LoggingHandlerExample [Java Application] C:\Program Files\java\jdk1.8.0_92\bin\java
Oct 05, 2017 2:44:50 PM com.java.loggingExamples.LoggingHandlerExample main
WARNING: Warning message logged
Oct 05, 2017 2:44:51 PM com.java.loggingExamples.LoggingHandlerExample main
INFO: Info Message logged
Oct 05, 2017 2:44:51 PM com.java.loggingExamples.LoggingHandlerExample main
SEVERE: Severe Message logged
```

As the default java configuration has been used for the logger, all the log messages have been logged as they have a level of INFO or higher (INFO is the default level defined in the logging.properties file in JDK_HOME).

But, as we add and remove the File Handler, its contents are different as shown below:

```
LoggingHandler.log
<?xml version="1.0" encoding="windows-1252" standalone="no"?>
<!DOCTYPE log SYSTEM "logger.dtd">
<log>
<record>
  <date>2017-10-05T14:46:02</date>
  <millis>1507207562174</millis>
  <sequence>0</sequence>
  <logger>com.java.loggingExamples.LoggingHandlerExample</logger>
  <level>WARNING</level>
  <class>com.java.loggingExamples.LoggingHandlerExample</class>
  <method>main</method>
  <thread>1</thread>
  <message>Warning message logged</message>
</record>
<record>
  <date>2017-10-05T14:46:02</date>
  <millis>1507207562205</millis>
  <sequence>2</sequence>
  <logger>com.java.loggingExamples.LoggingHandlerExample</logger>
  <level>SEVERE</level>
  <class>com.java.loggingExamples.LoggingHandlerExample</class>
  <method>main</method>
  <thread>1</thread>
  <message>Severe Message logged</message>
</record>
</log>
```

As we can see, only two log messages have been logged in the File Handler output file 'LoggingHandler.log.'

Example 8: Filters that filter a specific log level

This example implements a Filter that filters out log messages of level INFO. Any messages with this level are rejected by the logger.

To filter the log output, we need to implement the Filter interface and implement the is Loggable() method.

```java
LoggingFilterExample.java
package com.java.loggingExamples;

import java.util.logging.Filter;

public class LoggingFilterExample implements Filter {

    private static final Logger LOGGER = Logger.getLogger(LoggingFilterExample.class.getName());

    public static void main(String[] args) {

        // set the filter for the logger
        LOGGER.setFilter(new LoggingFilterExample());

        // This log message will get published as its level is not INFO
        LOGGER.severe("Severe message");

        // log a message
        // Since this is a log message of level WARNING it will be ignored by
        // the logger
        LOGGER.info("Information message");

        // This log message will get published as its level is not INFO
        LOGGER.warning("Warning message");

    }

    // Override the isLoggable() method to filter messages of level INFO
    @Override
    public boolean isLoggable(LogRecord record) {

        // return false if the Level is INFO (this message won't be logged)
        if (record.getLevel() == Level.INFO)
            return false;

        // else return false
        return true;
    }

}
```

As seen from the output below, only the messages with level SEVERE and WARNING have been displayed.

```
🖳 Console ⌗  🔲 Problems  @ Javadoc  🔍 Declaration  🗔 Annotations  🔧 Call Hierarchy
<terminated> LoggingFilterExample [Java Application] C:\Program Files\java\jdk1.8.0_92\bin\javaw.
Oct 05, 2017 3:06:25 PM com.java.loggingExamples.LoggingFilterExample main
SEVERE: Severe message
Oct 05, 2017 3:06:25 PM com.java.loggingExamples.LoggingFilterExample main
WARNING: Warning message
```

Example 9: Filters filtering specific content within the log message

In this example, we implement a filter that filters out any log message that contain the text 'Information' or 'Debug.'

```
LoggingFilterExample1.java ⌗
  package com.java.loggingExamples;

  import java.util.logging.Filter;
  import java.util.logging.LogRecord;
  import java.util.logging.Logger;

  public class LoggingFilterExample1 implements Filter {

    private static final Logger logger = Logger.getLogger(LoggingFilterExample1.class.getName());

    public static void main(String[] args) {

      // set the filter for the logger
      logger.setFilter(new LoggingFilterExample1());

      // This log message will get published as its level is not INFO
      logger.severe("Severe message");

      // log a message
      // Since this is a log message of level WARNING it will be ignored by
      // the logger
      logger.info("Information message");

      // This log message will get published as its level is not INFO
      logger.warning("Warning message");

      // This log message will get published as its level is not INFO
      logger.warning("Debug message");

    }

    // Override the isLoggable() method to filter messages that contain particular words
    @Override
    public boolean isLoggable(LogRecord record) {

      // return false if the LogRecord contains the word 'information' or 'debug'  (this message won't be logged)
      if (record.getMessage().contains("Information")|| record.getMessage().contains("Debug"))
        return false;

      // else return false
      return true;
    }

  }
```

The output below shows that only the messages that do not contain the text 'Information' or 'Debug' have been logged.

```
🖳 Console ⌗  🔲 Problems  @ Javadoc  🔍 Declaration  🗔 Annotations  🔧 Call Hierarchy
<terminated> LoggingFilterExample1 [Java Application] C:\Program Files\java\jdk1.8.0_92\bin\javaw.e
Oct 05, 2017 5:05:44 PM com.java.loggingExamples.LoggingFilterExample1 main
SEVERE: Severe message
Oct 05, 2017 5:05:45 PM com.java.loggingExamples.LoggingFilterExample1 main
WARNING: Warning message
```

Example 10: Custom Logger

In this example, we implement a custom Logger by extending the Logger class. The class CustomLogger.java implementing the logger is as follows:

```
CustomLogger.java
    package com.java.logging.loggerExamples;

  + import java.util.logging.ConsoleHandler;

    //extend the logger class
    public class CustomLogger extends Logger {

        protected CustomLogger(String name, String resourceBundleName) {

            super(name, resourceBundleName);
        }

        public static void main(String[] args) {

            //get the global logger
            Logger logger = Logger.getGlobal();
            //get the resource bundle
            String resourceBundleName= logger.getResourceBundleName();

            //instantiate your custom logger
            CustomLogger customLogger = new CustomLogger("com.java.logging", resourceBundleName);

            //add a handler
            customLogger.addHandler(new ConsoleHandler());

            //add log messages
            customLogger.info("Information Message");
            customLogger.warning("Warning Message");
        }

    }
```

In the above class, we create a logger named 'com.java.logging' and configure it with a console handler. We use this newly created logger to log messages.

The output generated is:

```
Console ⊠   Problems   @ Javadoc   Declaration   Annotations   Call Hierarchy
<terminated> CustomLogger [Java Application] C:\Program Files\java\jdk1.8.0_92\bin\javaw.exe
Oct 06, 2017 1:53:32 PM com.java.logging.loggerExamples.CustomLogger main
INFO: Information Message
Oct 06, 2017 1:53:32 PM com.java.logging.loggerExamples.CustomLogger main
WARNING: Warning Message
```

As we have not set any specific log level for the logger or the handled, the log level is set to INFO by default.

Example 11: Custom Handler and Formatter

In this example, we implement a formatter and use this formatter in a class that adds a Handler programmatically. The formatter class is as follows:

```
[J] MyLogFormatter.java ⛋
    package com.java.logging.loggerExamples;

 + import java.text.DateFormat;□

    //extend the Formatter class
    public class MyLogFormatter extends Formatter {

        //define the format that you wish to display the logs in
        private static final DateFormat dateFormat = new SimpleDateFormat("yyyy/dd/MM hh:mm:ss");

        //override the format method as per your logging needs
        public String format(LogRecord logRecord) {

            StringBuilder logMessage = new StringBuilder();
            //add date
            logMessage.append(dateFormat.format(new Date(logRecord.getMillis()))).append(" - ");
            //add log level
            logMessage.append("[").append(logRecord.getLevel()).append("] - ");
            //add source class and method name of the class that issued the log
            logMessage.append("[").append(logRecord.getSourceClassName()).append(".");
            logMessage.append(logRecord.getSourceMethodName()).append("] - ");
            //display the log message
            logMessage.append(formatMessage(logRecord));
            logMessage.append("\n");
            // return the formatted string
            return logMessage.toString();
        }
    }
```

We extend the Formatter class and override the format () message to specify the log format of our choice.

Now we write a class to that uses a logger and creates a handler that uses the custom format.

```
[J] CustomLoggingFormatter.java ⛋
    package com.java.logging.loggerExamples;

 + import java.util.logging.ConsoleHandler;□

    public class CustomLoggingFormatter {
        public static void main(String[] args) {
            // get the logger object
            Logger logger = Logger.getLogger(CustomLoggingFormatter.class.getName());
            logger.setUseParentHandlers(false);

            // create a formatter object
            MyLogFormatter myLogFormatter = new MyLogFormatter();
            // create a handler
            ConsoleHandler consoleHandler = new ConsoleHandler();
            // configure the handler to use the custom formatter
            consoleHandler.setFormatter(myLogFormatter);

            // add the handler to the logger
            logger.addHandler(consoleHandler);

            // log messages to the console
            logger.info("A customized Information message ");
            logger.info(" The application is working fine");
            logger.severe("A customized severe message.");
            logger.warning("A customized warning message.");
        }
    }
```

The output is as follows:

```
Console ⌧  Problems  @ Javadoc  Declaration  Annotations  Call Hierarchy
<terminated> CustomLoggingFormatter [Java Application] C:\Program Files\java\jdk1.8.0_92\bin\javaw.exe
2017/06/10 03:43:34 - [INFO] - [com.java.logging.loggerExamples.CustomLoggingFormatter.main] - A customized Information message
2017/06/10 03:43:34 - [INFO] - [com.java.logging.loggerExamples.CustomLoggingFormatter.main] -  The application is working fine
2017/06/10 03:43:34 - [SEVERE] - [com.java.logging.loggerExamples.CustomLoggingFormatter.main] - A customized severe message.
2017/06/10 03:43:34 - [WARNING] - [com.java.logging.loggerExamples.CustomLoggingFormatter.main] - A customized warning message.
```

Example 12: HTML file

In this example, we implement a custom formatter that logs records in the HTML format. The custom formatter implementation is as follows:

```java
// MyCustomFormatter.java

package com.java.logging.loggerExamples;

+ import java.util.logging.*;

// This class is a custom formatter class
//It formats the logs into an HTML based format

//To create a Custom Formatter extend the Formatter class
class MyCustomFormatter extends Formatter {

    // override the format() method to provide the format in which your logs
    // will be displayed
    public String format(LogRecord logRecord) {

        StringBuffer logMessage = new StringBuffer();

        // assign a color according to the log level
        if (logRecord.getLevel().intValue() >= Level.SEVERE.intValue()) {
            logMessage.append("<font color=\"red\">");
            logMessage.append(logRecord.getLevel());
            logMessage.append("</font>");
        } else if (logRecord.getLevel().intValue() >= Level.WARNING.intValue()) {
            logMessage.append("<font color=\"orange\">");
            logMessage.append(logRecord.getLevel());
            logMessage.append("</font>");
        } else {
            logMessage.append("<font color=\"green\">");
            logMessage.append(logRecord.getLevel());
            logMessage.append("</font>");
        }

        logMessage.append(' ');
        logMessage.append(formatMessage(logRecord));
        logMessage.append('\n');
        return logMessage.toString();
    }

    // this method is called on handler creation
    // we provide the html header here
    public String getHead(Handler h) {
        return "<HTML><HEAD> Customized Logs " + (new Date()) + "</HEAD><BODY><H2>The logs</H2><PRE>\n";
    }

    // This method is called on closing of the handler
    public String getTail(Handler h) {
        return "</PRE></BODY></HTML>\n";
    }
}
```

We now write a class that uses the custom formatter. The following class implements the custom formatter:

```
CustomLogFormatter.java
   package com.java.logging.loggerExamples;

 + import java.io.*;

   public class CustomLogFormatter {

       public static void main(String[] args) {
           // get the logger object
           Logger logger = Logger.getLogger("com.java.logging.loggerExamples.CustomLogFormatter");

           try {
               // Create a file handler that uses the custom formatter
               FileHandler fileHandler = new FileHandler("myCustomLogPage.html");
               fileHandler.setFormatter(new MyCustomFormatter());
               logger.addHandler(fileHandler);
           } catch (IOException e) {
               System.out.println(e);
           }

           // log messages of different levels
           logger.info("Simple information message");
           logger.info("Another information message");
           logger.warning(" Warning, a property has not been set properly!");
           logger.severe(" Application not working ");
           logger.severe(" Application crashed! ");

       }
   }
```

The above class implements 2 handlers, a console handler by default and a file handler that outputs the log records to an HTML file.

On running the java class, the console output is:

```
Console    Problems  @ Javadoc  Declaration  Annotations  Call Hierarchy
<terminated> CustomLogFormatter [Java Application] C:\Program Files\java\jdk1.8.0_92\bin\javaw.exe
Oct 06, 2017 6:08:38 PM com.java.logging.loggerExamples.CustomLogFormatter main
INFO: Simple information message
Oct 06, 2017 6:08:38 PM com.java.logging.loggerExamples.CustomLogFormatter main
INFO: Another information message
Oct 06, 2017 6:08:38 PM com.java.logging.loggerExamples.CustomLogFormatter main
WARNING:  Warning, a property has not been set properly!
Oct 06, 2017 6:08:38 PM com.java.logging.loggerExamples.CustomLogFormatter main
SEVERE:  Application not working
Oct 06, 2017 6:08:38 PM com.java.logging.loggerExamples.CustomLogFormatter main
SEVERE:  Application crashed!
```

A new html file is created as shown below:

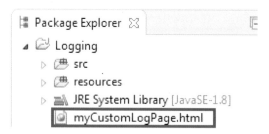

The contents of this file are:

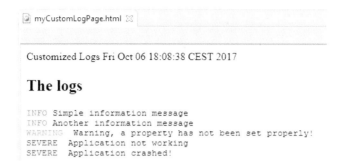

Example 17: Simple formatter variations

In this example, we use the configuration file to set formatting style of the logs

There are 3 pre-defined styles provided the by the java.util.logging package. They are as follows:

1. java.util.logging. Simple Formatter.format="%4$s: %5$s [%1$tc]%n"

    This prints 1 line with the log level (4$), the log message (5$) and the timestamp (1$) in a square bracket.

2. java.util.logging. Simple Formatter. format="%1$tc %2$s%n%4$s: %5$s%6$s%n"

This prints 2 lines where the first line includes the timestamp (1$) and the source (2$); the second line includes the log level (4$) and the log message (5$) followed with the throwable and its back trace (6$), if any:

Tue Mar 22 13:11:31 PDT 2011 My Class fatal

SEVERE: several message with an exception
java. Lang. Illegal Argument Exception: invalid argument

at MyClass.mash(MyClass.java:9)

at MyClass.crunch(MyClass.java:6)

at MyClass.main(MyClass.java:3)

3. java.util.logging. Simple Formatter. Format = "%1$tb %1$td, %1$tY %1$tl:%1$tM:%1$tS %1$Tp %2$s%n%4$s: %5$s%n"

This prints the same format as before but doesn't output the stack trace.

The class that we use to print the logs is as follows:

```
FormatterExample1.java
package com.java.logging.loggerExamples;

import java.io.IOException;
import java.io.InputStream;
import java.util.logging.LogManager;
import java.util.logging.Logger;

public class FormatterExample1 {

    public static void main(String[] args) {
        // declare the logger object
        Logger logger = null;

        // read the logging configuration file in an input stream
        InputStream stream = FormatterExample1.class.getClassLoader().getResourceAsStream("myLogging.properties");
        try {
            // update the logging configuration with the new file
            LogManager.getLogManager().readConfiguration(stream);
            // create the logger object
            logger = Logger.getLogger(FormatterExample1.class.getName());

        } catch (IOException e) {
            System.out.println("Exception:" + e);
        }

        // add log messages
        logger.warning("Logging Warning");
        logger.info("Logging Info");
    }
}
```

To set the format, we need to configure it via the logging.properties file. This is done as follows:

```
myLogging.properties
handlers= java.util.logging.ConsoleHandler
.level= INFO
java.util.logging.ConsoleHandler.level = INFO
java.util.logging.ConsoleHandler.formatter = java.util.logging.SimpleFormatter
#Setting a custom log format
java.util.logging.SimpleFormatter.format=%4$s: %5$s [%1$tc]%n
```

We configure the file to print the logs in the first format.

The output is:

```
Console    Problems   @ Javadoc   Declaration   Annotatic
<terminated> FormatterExample1 [Java Application] C:\Program Files\java\jc
WARNING: Logging Warning [Mon Oct 09 10:26:01 CEST 2017]
INFO: Logging Info [Mon Oct 09 10:26:01 CEST 2017]
```

With class name and package name:

```
FormatterExample2.java
package com.java.logging.loggerExamples;

import java.io.IOException;

public class FormatterExample2 {

    public static void main(String[] args) {
        // declare the logger object
        Logger logger = null;

        // read the logging configuration file in an input stream
        InputStream stream = FormatterExample2.class.getClassLoader().getResourceAsStream("myLogging.properties");
        try {
            // update the logging configuration with the new file
            LogManager.getLogManager().readConfiguration(stream);
            // create the logger object
            logger = Logger.getLogger(FormatterExample2.class.getName());

        } catch (IOException e) {
            System.out.println("Exception:" + e);
        }

        // add log messages
        logger.warning("Logging Warning");
        logger.info("Logging Info");

        // we generate an exception
        try {
            int a = 0, b = 0;
            int c = a / b;
            System.out.println("result:" + c);
        } catch (ArithmeticException ex) {
            logger.log(Level.SEVERE, "Arithmetic Exception occured. Cannot divide by zero!", ex);
        }
    }
}
```

```
myLogging.properties
handlers= java.util.logging.ConsoleHandler
.level= INFO
java.util.logging.ConsoleHandler.level = INFO
java.util.logging.ConsoleHandler.formatter = java.util.logging.SimpleFormatter
#Setting a custom log format
java.util.logging.SimpleFormatter.format=%1$tc %2$s%n%4$s: %5$s%6$s%n
```

The output is as follows:

```
Console    Problems   @ Javadoc   Declaration   Annotations   Call Hierarchy
<terminated> FormatterExample2 [Java Application] C:\Program Files\java\jdk1.8.0_92\bin\javaw.exe
Mon Oct 09 10:33:42 CEST 2017 com.java.logging.loggerExamples.FormatterExample2 main
WARNING: Logging Warning
Mon Oct 09 10:33:42 CEST 2017 com.java.logging.loggerExamples.FormatterExample2 main
INFO: Logging Info
Mon Oct 09 10:33:42 CEST 2017 com.java.logging.loggerExamples.FormatterExample2 main
SEVERE: Arithmetic Exception occured. Cannot divide by zero!
java.lang.ArithmeticException: / by zero
        at com.java.logging.loggerExamples.FormatterExample2.main(FormatterExample2.java:35)
```

This is the default format of java.util.logging. Simple Formatter.

Third part:

```
FormatterExample3.java
    package com.java.logging.loggerExamples;

  + import java.io.IOException;

    public class FormatterExample3 {

        public static void main(String[] args) {

            // declare the logger object
            Logger logger = null;

            // read the logging configuration file in an input stream
            InputStream stream = FormatterExample3.class.getClassLoader().getResourceAsStream("myLogging.properties");
            try {
                // update the logging configuration with the new file
                LogManager.getLogManager().readConfiguration(stream);
                // create the logger object
                logger = Logger.getLogger(FormatterExample3.class.getName());

            } catch (IOException e) {
                System.out.println("Exception:" + e);
            }

            // add log messages
            logger.warning("Logging Warning");
            logger.info("Logging Info");

            // we generate an exception
            try {
                int a = 0, b = 0;
                int c = a / b;
                System.out.println("result:" + c);
            } catch (ArithmeticException ex) {
                logger.log(Level.SEVERE, "Arithmetic Exception occured. Cannot divide by zero!", ex);
            }
        }
    }
```

The log configuration file:

```
myLogging.properties
handlers= java.util.logging.ConsoleHandler
.level= INFO
java.util.logging.ConsoleHandler.level = INFO
java.util.logging.ConsoleHandler.formatter = java.util.logging.SimpleFormatter
#Setting a custom log format
java.util.logging.SimpleFormatter.format=%1$tb %1$td, %1$tY %1$tl:%1$tM:%1$tS %1$Tp %2$s%n%4$s: %5$s%n
```

The output is as follows:

```
🖥 Console ⊠  ⁝ Problems  @ Javadoc  🔖 Declaration  🗔 Annotations  ⠂◦ Call Hierarchy
<terminated> FormatterExample2 [Java Application] C:\Program Files\java\jdk1.8.0_92\bin\javaw.exe
Oct 09, 2017 10:35:43 AM com.java.logging.loggerExamples.FormatterExample2 main
WARNING: Logging Warning
Oct 09, 2017 10:35:43 AM com.java.logging.loggerExamples.FormatterExample2 main
INFO: Logging Info
Oct 09, 2017 10:35:43 AM com.java.logging.loggerExamples.FormatterExample2 main
SEVERE: Arithmetic Exception occured. Cannot divide by zero!
```

We can implement the same functionality programmatically. This is shown in the next example.

Example 18: Simple Formatter programmatically

Consider the following Java class:

```java
📄 FormatterExample4.java ⊠
    package com.java.logging.loggerExamples;

+ import java.util.logging.ConsoleHandler;

    public class FormatterExample4 {

        public static void main(String[] args) {

            // Programmatic configuration of the format using system properties
            System.setProperty("java.util.logging.SimpleFormatter.format",
                "%1$tY-%1$tm-%1$td %1$tH:%1$tM:%1$tS.%1$tL %4$-7s [%3$s] (%2$s) %5$s %6$s%n");

            // declare a handler
            final ConsoleHandler consoleHandler = new ConsoleHandler();
            // set its level
            consoleHandler.setLevel(Level.FINER);
            // set the formatter
            consoleHandler.setFormatter(new SimpleFormatter());

            // get the logger object
            final Logger logger = Logger.getLogger(FormatterExample4.class.getName());
            logger.setUseParentHandlers(false);
            // set the logger level and add the handler
            logger.setLevel(Level.FINER);
            logger.addHandler(consoleHandler);

            /// log message on to the console
            logger.log(Level.WARNING, "Warning Message");
            logger.finer("Finer Message");
            logger.info("Information Message");
            logger.severe("Severe Message");

        }
    }
```

Here we set the format of the Simple Formatter class using a system property.

The output generated on execution of the above example is as follows:

```
🖥 Console ⊠  ⁝ Problems  ⊜ Javadoc  🔖 Declaration  🗔 Annotations  ⠂◦ Call Hierarchy                    ◼ ✖ 🗙  🔲 ⏷  🖭 🖭  🔁 ⏷
<terminated> FormatterExample4 [Java Application] C:\Program Files\java\jdk
2017-11-29 14:22:15.652 WARNING [com.java.logging.loggerExamples.FormatterExample4] (com.java.logging.loggerExamples.FormatterExample4 main) Warning Message
2017-11-29 14:22:15.652 FINER   [com.java.logging.loggerExamples.FormatterExample4] (com.java.logging.loggerExamples.FormatterExample4 main) Finer Message
2017-11-29 14:22:15.652 INFO    [com.java.logging.loggerExamples.FormatterExample4] (com.java.logging.loggerExamples.FormatterExample4 main) Information Message
2017-11-29 14:22:15.652 SEVERE  [com.java.logging.loggerExamples.FormatterExample4] (com.java.logging.loggerExamples.FormatterExample4 main) Severe Message
```

Example 19: Setting the Log Format Programmatically with stack trace

```java
FormatterExample5.java
package com.java.logging.loggerExamples;

import java.util.logging.ConsoleHandler;

public class FormatterExample5 {

    public static void main(String[] args) {
        // Programmatic configuration of the format using system properties
        System.setProperty("java.util.logging.SimpleFormatter.format",
                "%1$tb %1$td, %1$tY %1$tl:%1$tM:%1$tS %1$Tp %2$s%n%4$s: %5$s%6$s%n");

        // declare a handler
        final ConsoleHandler consoleHandler = new ConsoleHandler();
        // set its level
        consoleHandler.setLevel(Level.FINE);
        // set the formatter
        consoleHandler.setFormatter(new SimpleFormatter());

        // get the logger object
        final Logger logger = Logger.getLogger(FormatterExample5.class.getName());
        logger.setUseParentHandlers(false);
        // set the logger level and add the handler
        logger.setLevel(Level.FINE);
        logger.addHandler(consoleHandler);

        /// log message on to the console
        logger.log(Level.WARNING, "Warning Message");
        logger.log(Level.FINER, "Finer Message");
        logger.severe("Severe Message");
        // induce exceptions and log errors
        try {
            Integer x = null;
            x.doubleValue();
        } catch (NullPointerException e) {
            logger.log(Level.SEVERE, "Value is null!", e);
        } catch (Exception e) {
            logger.severe("Exception thrown! ");
        }

    }
}
```

The output generated on the console is as follows:

```
Console   Problems  @ Javadoc  Declaration  Annotations  Call Hierarchy
<terminated> FormatterExample5 [Java Application] C:\Program Files\java\
Nov 29, 2017 2:59:52 PM com.java.logging.loggerExamples.FormatterExample5 main
WARNING: Warning Message
Nov 29, 2017 2:59:52 PM com.java.logging.loggerExamples.FormatterExample5 main
SEVERE: Severe Message
Nov 29, 2017 2:59:52 PM com.java.logging.loggerExamples.FormatterExample5 main
SEVERE: Value is null!
java.lang.NullPointerException
        at com.java.logging.loggerExamples.FormatterExample5.main(FormatterExample5.java:37)
```

2.5.1. The Formatter class

The java.util.logging. Formatter class is basically a formatter that takes printf or C-style arguments as an input. This class provides support for layout justification and alignment, common formats for numeric, string, and date/time data, and locale-specific output (java.util.logging (Java Platform SE 7, 2017).

This is formatted printing which is completely inspired by the traditional C language's printf statements.

For formatting the log message, we call the format message. But if we want to customize this message, a format String along with a list of arguments is provided. This string contains text (the log message) and one or more **format specifiers**.

In general, the syntax for general, character, and numerical format specifiers is as follows:

% [index_ of_ argument$] [flags] [width of argument] [. precision] conversion

Here, the index, width, precision, and flags are all optional. The index is a decimal integer which specifies the position of the argument in the list of arguments.

The flags are nothing but a set of characters that modify the output. Precision is used to limit the number of characters. Conversion is another character that indicates how the argument should be formatted. A *conversion* is applied to an argument. This is a character element that indicates what content should be inserted in the log output. This may be of different types.

Additionally, the format specifiers for date and time are different and have the following syntax: %[index_ of_ argument $][flags][width]conversion

Like for general format specifiers, the parameters index of the argument, flags, width, and conversion are optional.

In this case, the **conversion** that is required a sequence of two characters. The first character in the sequence is 't' or 'T.' The second character indicates the format to be used (java.util.logging (Java Platform SE 7), 2017).

There exist 6 categories of conversions. They are:

- General: Applicable to any argument;
- Character: Applicable to Unicode characters char, byte, short and their respective Wrapper classes;
- Numeric: Applicable to Integer and Floating-point values such as int, float, double, Big Decimal, Big Integer, and their respective wrapper classes;
- Date/Time: Applicable to Date, time classes in Java;
- Percent: this produces the literal '%'; and
- Line Separator: This produces a line separator that is specific to the platform.

Some of the various conversions that are used are described in the table below.

Table 2.13: Date and Time conversions (java.util.logging (Java Platform SE 7, 2017)

Conversion	Category	Description
c or C	Character	This conversion gives a Unicode character as a result
D	Integer	This conversion returns a formatted decimal integer as output
O	Integer	This conversion returns a formatted octal integer as output
X or X	Integer	This conversion returns a formatted hexadecimal integer as output
F	Floating Point	This conversion returns a formatted decimal integer as output
e or E	Floating Point	This conversion returns a formatted decimal integer in a scientific notation as output
g or G	Floating Point	This conversion returns a formatted decimal integer/computerized scientific notation as output
a or A	Floating Point	This conversion returns a formatted hexadecimal floating point with an exponent and a significant.
b or B	General	If the provided argument is null, then false is returned. If the provided argument has a Boolean value, the result is the same as the return value of String. Value Of(argument). If the argument is of any other type true is returned.
h or H	General	If the provided argument is null, then null is returned. Else, the result returned is the same as the output returned by calling the Integer. To Hex String (argument.hashCOde()).
s or S	General	If the provided argument is null, then null is returned. If the provided argument implements Formattable, then the result given is the result of invoking arg.formatTo. Else, arg.toString() is invoked.
t or T	Date/Time	It serves as the prefix for conversions of Date or Time
n	Line Separator	This conversion returns a platform specific line separator

Date/Time Conversions

Time Conversions

Table 2.14: Time Conversions (java.util.logging (Java Platform SE 7, 2017)

Conversion	Description
H	Hour of the day (00-23)
I	Hour for the clock of 12 hours (01-12)
K	Hour for the clock of 24 hours (01-24)

L	Hour for the clock of 12 hours (unformatted: 1-12)
M	Minute of the hour (00-59)
S	Seconds of the minute (00-59)
L	Millisecond of the second (000-999)
N	Nanosecond of the second (000000000 – 999999999)
P	Locale-specific AM/PM
Z	Numeric Time zone offset as calculated from GMT. E.g., –0900
Z	String that represents an abbreviation of the time zone
S	Seconds elapsed since 1st January 1970
Q	Milliseconds elapsed since 1st January 1970

Date Conversions:

Table 2.15: Date Conversions (java.util.logging (Java Platform SE 7, 2017)

Conversion	Description
B	Full month name
b or h	Abbreviated month name
A	Full name of the day of the week
A	Abbreviated name of the day of the week
C or y	Four digit year divided by 100 (00-99)
Y	Year formatted with the last four digits
J	Day of the year (001- 366)
M	Month in numbers (01-12)
D	Day of the month (00-31)
E	Day of the month (unformatted: 1-31)

Date and Time Conversions:

Table 2.16: Date and Time Conversions (java.util.logging (Java Platform SE 7), 2017)

Conversion	Description
R	This represents the time formatted for the 24 hour clock: %tH:%tM
T	This represents the time formatted for the 24 hour clock: "%tH:%tM:%tS"
R	This represents the time formatted for the 12 hour clock: %tI:%tM:%tS %Tp
D	This represents the date formatted as the standard date month year format: %tm/%td/%ty
F	This represents the ISO 8601 date format: %tY-%tm-%td
c	This represents the Date and time formatted as words with the locale: %ta %tb %td %tT %tZ %tY," e.g. "Sun Jul 20 16:17:00 EDT 1969

Table: Date and time conversions (java.util.logging (Java Platform SE 7), 2017)

Consider the example below:

String format = "[%1$tF %1$tT] [%2$s] %3$s %n";

public synchronized String format(LogRecord logRecord) {

  return String.*format*(**format**, **new** Date(logRecord.getMillis()), logRecord. getLevel(),

logRecord.getMessage());

                    }

The very first input parameter is the format string. This format String has the following format specifiers: "%1$tF, %1$tT, %2$s and %3$s. These specifiers indicate the manner in which the arguments should be processed and at which position in the text they should be inserted.

Here, tF displays the date in the format tY-%tm-%td (YYYY/MM/DD)

tT displays the time in the format "%tH:%tM:%tS HH:MM:SS)

%2$s and %3$s display the log level and log message respectively

%n introduces a new line after every log message

Some examples that describe the implementation of formatters using format specifiers have been provided below.

Consider the class FormatterExample below:

```
[J] FormatterExample4.java ⊠
    package com.java.logging.loggerExamples;

  ─ import java.util.Date;
    import java.util.logging.ConsoleHandler;
    import java.util.logging.Level;
    import java.util.logging.LogRecord;
    import java.util.logging.Logger;
    import java.util.logging.SimpleFormatter;

    public class FormatterExample4 {

        public static void main(String[] args) {

            // create the logger object
            Logger logger = Logger.getLogger("com.java.logging.loggerExamples");

            // disable use of default parent handlers
            logger.setUseParentHandlers(false);

            // define a new console handler
            ConsoleHandler consoleHandler = new ConsoleHandler();

            // define a custom formatter programmatically
            consoleHandler.setFormatter(new SimpleFormatter() {
                // set the log output format
                // tF  - ISO standard %tY-%tm-%td  (YYYY-MM-DD)
                // tT  - time formatted as the hour clock %tH:%tM:%tS  (HH:MM:SS)
                // %2$s - Log Level
                // %3$s -Log Message
                // %n -new line
                private static final String format = "[%1$tF %1$tT] [%2$s] %3$s %n";

                // override the format message and provide the custom format
                @Override
                public synchronized String format(LogRecord logRecord) {
                    return String.format(format, new Date(logRecord.getMillis()), logRecord.getLevel(),
                            logRecord.getMessage());
                }
            });

            // add the new handler to the logger
            logger.addHandler(consoleHandler);
            consoleHandler.setLevel(Level.FINE);
            logger.setLevel(Level.FINE);

            // add log messages
            logger.warning("A warning message");
            logger.info("An information message");
            logger.fine("A fine message");

        }
    }
```

We define a new SimpleFormatter class directly in the setFormatter method as shown above. We override the format() method to provide a custom format and then proceed to add a handler and log messages.

The output is:

```
Console ⊠   Problems   @ Javadoc   Declaration   A
<terminated> FormatterExample4 [Java Application] C:\Program File
[2017-10-09 11:39:59] [WARNING] A warning message
[2017-10-09 11:39:59] [INFO] An information message
[2017-10-09 11:39:59] [FINE] A fine message
```

Another way to set the format is to use a system property as shown below:

```
J FormatterExample5.java ⋈
    package com.java.logging.loggerExamples;

    import java.util.logging.Level;
    import java.util.logging.Logger;

    public class FormatterExample5 {

        public static void main(String[] args) {

            // create the logger object
            Logger logger = Logger.getLogger("com.java.logging.loggerExamples");

            // set the log output format
            // %1$tc - Date and time formatted as %ta %tb %td %tT %tZ %tY", like
            // "Mon Jul 21 16:17:00 EDT 1969"
            // %2$s - Class and method that is logging the message
            // %3$s - Root/Parent logger
            // %4$s - Log Level
            // %5$s - Log Message
            // %n -new line
            System.setProperty("java.util.logging.SimpleFormatter.format", "[%1$tc] [%2$s] [%3$s] [%4$-8s] %5$s %n");

            logger.setLevel(Level.FINE);

            // add log messages
            logger.warning("A warning message");
            logger.info("An information message");
            logger.severe("A severe message");

        }
    }
```

The output is:

```
Console ⋈  Problems  Javadoc  Declaration  Annotations  Call Hierarchy
<terminated> FormatterExample5 [Java Application] C:\Program Files\java\jdk1.8.0_92\bin\javaw.exe
[Mon Oct 09 11:55:00 CEST 2017] [com.java.logging.loggerExamples.FormatterExample5 main] [com.java.logging.loggerExamples] [WARNING ] A warning message
[Mon Oct 09 11:55:00 CEST 2017] [com.java.logging.loggerExamples.FormatterExample5 main] [com.java.logging.loggerExamples] [INFO    ] An information message
[Mon Oct 09 11:55:00 CEST 2017] [com.java.logging.loggerExamples.FormatterExample5 main] [com.java.logging.loggerExamples] [SEVERE  ] A severe message
```

An additional way to provide the format without adding it or configuring it programmatically is via the runtime jvm argument.

This is done as follows:

```
J FormatterExample6.java ⋈
    package com.java.logging.loggerExamples;

    import java.util.logging.Level;
    import java.util.logging.Logger;

    public class FormatterExample6 {

        public static void main(String[] args) {

            // create the logger object
            Logger logger = Logger.getLogger("com.java.logging.loggerExamples");

            // add log messages
            logger.warning("A warning message");
            logger.info("An information message");
            logger.severe("A severe message");

            //generate an exception
            Throwable ex = new IllegalArgumentException("Illegal Argument Exception thrown");
            logger.log(Level.SEVERE, "Exception thrown", ex);

        }
    }
```

The jvm property can be set by right-click on the class, selecting the Run as->Run Configurations.option. The following window is displayed:

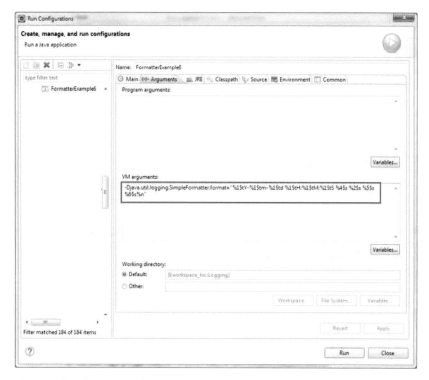

We set the format and run the class. The output is as follows:

```
Console ⊠   Problems  @ Javadoc  Declaration   Annotations   Call Hierarchy
<terminated> FormatterExample6 [Java Application] C:\Program Files\java\jdk1.8.0_92\bin\javaw.exe
2017-10-09 12:15:08 WARNING com.java.logging.loggerExamples.FormatterExample6 main A warning message
2017-10-09 12:15:08 INFO com.java.logging.loggerExamples.FormatterExample6 main An information message
2017-10-09 12:15:08 SEVERE com.java.logging.loggerExamples.FormatterExample6 main A severe message
2017-10-09 12:15:08 SEVERE com.java.logging.loggerExamples.FormatterExample6 main Exception thrown
java.lang.IllegalArgumentException: Illegal Argument Exception thrown
        at com.java.logging.loggerExamples.FormatterExample6.main(FormatterExample6.java:19)
```

As seen by the output, the format provided by the VM argument has been used to format the log messages.

Example 20: Custom Log Handler

In this example, we implement a custom log handler by extending the handler class. We override the publish() method to specify the way in which we want to publish the logs. This class is as shown below:

```
J MyCustomLogHandler.java ⊠
  package com.java.logging.loggerExamples;

+ import java.text.DateFormat;

  //extend the Handler class
  public class MyCustomLogHandler extends Handler {

      //define the format that you wish to display the logs in
      private static final DateFormat dateFormat = new SimpleDateFormat("yyyy/dd/MM hh:mm:ss");

      //override the publish method
      @Override
      public void publish(LogRecord logRecord) {
          StringBuilder logMessage = new StringBuilder();
          logMessage.append(dateFormat.format(new Date(logRecord.getMillis())))
              .append(" - ")
              .append(logRecord.getSourceClassName())
              .append(" ")
              .append(logRecord.getSourceMethodName())
              .append(" - ")
              .append(logRecord.getLevel())
              .append(" - ")
              .append(logRecord.getMessage());

          System.out.println(logMessage.toString());
      }

      @Override
      public void flush() {

      }

      @Override
      public void close() throws SecurityException {
      }
  }
```

We now proceed to write another java class that will make use of the custom handler.

The class implementing this handler is as follows:

```
J CustomHandler2.java ⊠
  package com.java.logging.loggerExamples;
+ import java.util.logging.LogManager;

  public class CustomHandler2 {

    public static void main(String[] args) {
        //get the logger object
        Logger rootLogger = LogManager.getLogManager().getLogger("");

        //remove all the existing handlers using reset()
        LogManager.getLogManager().reset();

        //add the custom handler
        rootLogger.addHandler(new MyCustomLogHandler());

        //log messages
        rootLogger.info("A simple Information Message");
    }
  }
```

The output on the console is:

```
Console ⊠  Problems  Javadoc  Declaration  Annotations  Call Hierarchy
<terminated> CustomHandler2 [Java Application] C:\Program Files\java\jdk1.8.0_92\bin\javaw.exe
2017/06/10 06:39:00 - java.util.logging.LogManager$RootLogger log - INFO - A simple Information Message
```

As the output clearly shows, the log record has been published in the way that was defined in the custom handler.

Example 20: Localization

In this example, we implement a locale that is different from the default one. Here, we set the locale to the French language as shown by the class below:

```java
LocaleExample1.java ⅍

package com.java.logging.loggerExamples;

+import java.util.Locale;

public class LocaleExample1 {

    public static void main(String[] args) {

        //set the locale
        //Here we set it to French
        Locale.setDefault(new Locale("fr"));

        //get the logger object
        Logger logger = Logger.getLogger("com.java.logging.loggerExamples.LocaleExample1");

        // add log messages
        logger.warning("A warning message");
        logger.info("An information message");
        logger.severe("A severe message");
    }
}
```

On executing the class, the output is as follows:

```
Console ⅍   Problems   @ Javadoc   Declaration   Annotations   Call Hierarchy
<terminated> LocaleExample1 [Java Application] C:\Program Files\java\jdk1.8.0_92\bin\javaw.exe
oct. 09, 2017 4:50:50 PM com.java.logging.loggerExamples.LocaleExample1 main
AVERTISSEMENT: A warning message
oct. 09, 2017 4:50:50 PM com.java.logging.loggerExamples.LocaleExample1 main
INFOS: An information message
oct. 09, 2017 4:50:50 PM com.java.logging.loggerExamples.LocaleExample1 main
GRAVE: A severe message
```

As the output shows, the log messages have been displayed in French.

The locale can be set via the VM arguments as well. We implement this now.

The contents of the java class change as follows:

```java
LocaleExample2.java ⅍

package com.java.logging.loggerExamples;

import java.util.logging.Logger;

public class LocaleExample2 {

    public static void main(String[] args) {

        //get the logger object
        Logger logger = Logger.getLogger("com.java.logging.loggerExamples.LocaleExample2");

        // add log messages
        logger.warning("A warning message");
        logger.info("An information message");
        logger.severe("A severe message");
    }
}
```

We remove the statement where we have set the locale.

The parameters are now set in the run configuration as follows:

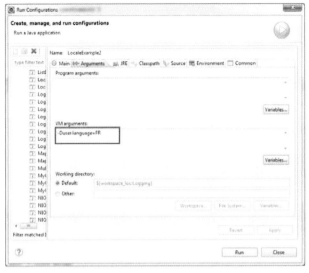

```
Console 🔲  Problems  @ Javadoc  Declaration  Annotations  Call Hierarchy
<terminated> LocaleExample2 [Java Application] C:\Program Files\java\jdk1.8.0_92\bin\javaw.exe
oct. 09, 2017 4:59:38 PM com.java.logging.loggerExamples.LocaleExample2 main
AVERTISSEMENT: A warning message
oct. 09, 2017 4:59:38 PM com.java.logging.loggerExamples.LocaleExample2 main
INFOS: An information message
oct. 09, 2017 4:59:38 PM com.java.logging.loggerExamples.LocaleExample2 main
GRAVE: A severe message
```

The output is the same as that of the previous example.

Example 21: Using Lambda Expressions

```java
LambdaExample.java

  package com.java.logging.loggerExamples;

+ import java.util.logging.Level;

  public class LambdaExample {
      public static void main(String[] args) {

          // get the logger
          Logger logger = Logger.getLogger(LambdaExample.class.getName());

          // set log level to INFO
          logger.setLevel(Level.FINEST);

          // log messages using lambda expressions
          logger.info(() -> "Information Log: " + getValue());
          logger.severe(() -> "Severe Log: " + getValue());
      }

      // method that returns a value
      private static String getValue() {
          String value = "Hello";
          return value;
      }
  }
```

```
Console ☒ | Problems  @ Javadoc  Declaration  Annotations  Call Hierarchy
<terminated> LoggerTest [Java Application] C:\Program Files\java\
Nov 29, 2017 4:14:58 PM com.java.logging.loggerExamples.LoggerTest main
INFO: Information Log: Hello
Nov 29, 2017 4:14:58 PM com.java.logging.loggerExamples.LoggerTest main
SEVERE: Severe Log: Hello
```

Example 22: Lambda Expressions Example using interface

In this example, we take a look at how to log messages using lambda expressions with the use of interfaces.

We declare interfaces and provide their functional implementations in our class as shown below:

```java
LambdaExample1.java ☒
    package com.java.logging.loggerExamples;

    import java.util.logging.Level;
    import java.util.logging.Logger;

    //declare an interface
    interface MyInterface {

        public String getValue();
    }

    public class LambdaExample1 {

        public static void main(String[] args) {

            // get the logger
            Logger logger = Logger.getLogger(LambdaExample1.class.getName());

            // set log level to INFO
            logger.setLevel(Level.FINEST);

            // Provide functional implementation of the interface method
            // MyInterface()
            MyInterface int1 = () -> {
                return "The application is stable. No issues to report";
            };

            // log a simple message
            logger.info(int1.getValue());

            // Provide another functional implementation of the interface method
            // MyInterface()
            MyInterface int2 = () -> {
                return "Error! The application is unstable.";
            };

            // log message using lambda expressions
            logger.severe(() -> int2.getValue());

            // Provide a third functional implementation of the interface method
            // MyInterface()
            MyInterface int3 = () -> {
                return "Warning! The application is running with Errors.";
            };

            // log a message using lambda expressions and a log message
            logger.warning(() -> "Warning Message:" + int3.getValue());
        }
    }
```

```
Console ☒ | Problems  @ Javadoc  Declaration  Annotations  Call Hierarchy
<terminated> LambdaExample1 [Java Application] C:\Program Files\java
Nov 29, 2017 4:42:20 PM com.java.logging.loggerExamples.LambdaExample1 main
INFO: The application is stable. No issues to report
Nov 29, 2017 4:42:20 PM com.java.logging.loggerExamples.LambdaExample1 main
SEVERE: Error! The application is unstable.
Nov 29, 2017 4:42:20 PM com.java.logging.loggerExamples.LambdaExample1 main
WARNING: Warning Message:Warning! The application is running with Errors.
```

2.6. MISCELLANEOUS FEATURES

2.6.1. Security Issues

In the java.util.logging package security issues within logging have not been considered in too much detail. Although logging is not considered to be the most important part of an application, a mechanism has been provided to ensure the protection of the configuration.

The Logging Permission class provides security that prevents unauthorized class to change the log configuration. It is a security permission that needs to be defined which controls access to the updating of the configuration file. In this way, the untrustworthy code is not allowed to make changes and impede the functioning of the logger. Using this mechanism only trusted/registered applications are handed the required permissions to modify and update the logging configuration. So, the applications that do not have the appropriate permissions will only be able to create loggers and log messages, but not add or remove loggers or handlers.

But, a security breach present in the logging package is that untrusted applications still have the right to create, define and use their very own anonymous loggers that are not registered anywhere in the logger namespace tree. These loggers are not checked for permissions and hence any class can modify the configuration of the logs using these loggers (Java Logging Overview, 2017).

Another security threat is that spoofing is not prevented. This means that the source of calls for logging cannot be determined. The source may or may not be fake. The XML formatter is susceptible to injection threats.

Furthermore, the Java logging framework is vulnerable to DOS (Denial of Service) attacks. It is possible for any client to flood the application with dozens of meaningless log messages and attempt to mask an important log message.

2.6.2. Remote Access and Serialization

Although the java logging framework has been defined for use in a single address space and the calls to the logging methods are local. But we have the possibility of logging to remote locations. The Socket Handler is capable of writing data to machines on another network using messages in an XML format. XML format is a standard format that can be processed on many different types of systems.

Another way to do logging remotely is the ability of a handler to write a Log Record over the network using RMI. But this class is not serializable which may pose problems.

It is important to note that many of the classes in the java.util.logging package is not serializable. They were not created with an intention of Serialization. Handlers and Loggers are classes that are stateful that are linked to a fixed machine.

The logger and handler classes can be thought to be analogous to java. io. Input Stream classes which are not serializable.

Security and remote logging is not part of the scope of this book. But for additional information, you can reference the book *Logging in Java with the JDK 1.4 Logging API and Apache log4j* by Samudra Gupta.

CHAPTER
3

LOG4J

CONTENTS

3.1. INTRODUCTION

Log4j is another logging framework based on the Java language owned and released by Apache. It was written by Ceki Gülcü. It is a part of the logging services project of the entity Apache Software Foundation. It was first released in 1996. It was developed by the European Union SEMPER (Secure Electronic Marketplace for Europe) project that year as the project wished to have a tracing API of its own like most large applications (Goers, 2017).

Then, after several enhancements and evolutions, this API gradually became log4j which is now an extremely popular logging framework for Java. The package for this framework is now distributed under the *Apache Software License* which is an open source certified license.

As mentioned earlier, logging has many advantages and log4j tries to provide a complete, easy and fast logging mechanism. Log4j is a flexible framework that is written completely in Java but can also be used in other languages such as C++, C#, Perl, Python, Ruby, etc. An excellent feature of log4j is its ability of dynamic configuration via external files at runtime. Additionally, it provides good methods of remote logging. Using this framework, logs can easily be written to various targets such as Databases, Remote files, Syslog and so on.

The latest version of log4j is Apache log4j 2.9.1 which was released in September 2017. All the examples provided in this book are based on this version.

3.2. LOG4J VERSIONS

Log4j has several versions that were released over the years. The very first version that was released after the initial package was log4j 0.5 which was released in 1999. Post this release, another 60 versions of log4j 1.x were released; each version with some modifications and features. 1.2 was the last version released in this series. Details of the changes related to this version can be found at the following link.

https://logging.apache.org/log4j/1.2/changes-report.html

In 2015, Apache announced that the log4j 1.x series has reached its end and will be discontinued.

The successor version log4j 2.0-alpha1was released in 2012. Since then several versions of log4j 2.x have been released. The latest version is log4j 2.9.1. The release history can be found at the following link: https://logging. apache.org/log4j/2.x/changes-report.html#a2.9.1

3.3. LOG4J FEATURES

Log4j offers several advanced features for simplifying logging as follows (Gülcü, 2003):

1. Log4j offers fast, thread-safe logging services.
2. Log4j offers a dynamic configuration of properties at runtime.
3. Log4j offers its own version of garbage free logging which saves memory.
4. Multiple appender outputs along with internationalization is provided.
5. It is based on a plugin type system which makes it easy to extend the existing framework.
6. It is fairly easy to customize different components such as log levels, handlers, and loggers.
7. It can be used as an auditing framework due to its transparency and extended exception handling capabilities.
8. It supports the Java 8 feature of lambda expressions which makes it easy to construct log messages.
9. The way the log is formatted can be changed by providing custom layouts which is easier to manipulate using the Layout class.
10. TCP and UDP support is provided by the Syslog appender.
11. Log4j is open source software and has a wide support community.
12. It is not restrictive to a specific set of classes that one needs to build open. The configuration in log4j is simple and not always bound to specific classes, packages or methods.

3.4. COMPONENTS OF LOG4J

The log4j framework is built upon the following components:

1. *Loggers*

These objects are the central objects for this framework. They are the objects that capture the information to be logged. Like we have already seen in the Java logging framework, the loggers are stored in a namespace hierarchy.

2. *Appenders*

These objects are another important part of the framework. They handle the publishing aspect of logging. They take the log records and publish them to the required destination.

3. *Layouts*

The layouts' main function is to format the log output. Many different ways of configuring and formatting the log output are provided via the use of Layout classes. Appenders use layout objects before they publish the log information. The layouts help render the log easily readable by humans.

3.5. AXILLARY COMPONENTS

In addition to the above three important components, the log4j framework has auxiliary components that help these core components. Although these components are not the main objects, they help the core objects to a great extent. They are the following:

3.5.1. Log Manager

This object, as its name, manages the complete logging configuration. It reads the configuration file and sets the parameters via a configuration file or class. This configuration is applicable at a system level. It handles and manages the namespace hierarchy for the loggers.

3.5.2. Object Renderer

This component is used to provide a String representation of log objects that are passed to the framework. This method is similar to the to String () method in Java String class.

3.5.3. Filter Object

Similar to the filter as we have studied in Chapter 2, this filter is used to analyze the log records and decide which information should be logged and which information should be discarded. Each appender can have one or more filters added to it. When a log is sent to the Appender, all the filter objects must approve the log before it could be published to its destination. Hence, filters serve to be extremely useful to remove unwanted logging information based on properties of the system.

3.5.4. Level Object

This object defines the priority and granularity of the logging information (Apache Log4j API 2.9.1, 2017). It is also called the priority object. Seven logging levels have been provided: OFF, DEBUG, INFO, ERROR, WARN, FATAL and all. Similar to the java logging framework, each level has an integer value assigned to it.

3.6. WORKING OF LOG4J

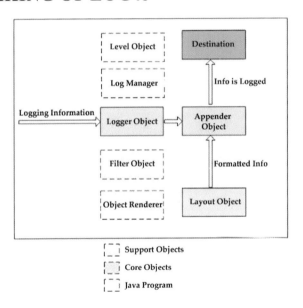

Figure 3.1: Log4j architecture (Tutorialspoint.com, 2017).

As we can see from the above figure, the architecture of log4j is simple and easy to follow. (Figure 3.1).

The core components are compulsory to enable logging in any application. The logging information is taken from the application/Java program that wishes to enable logging and given to the logger defined by the configuration. The logger forwards it to the Appender which formats the log record with the help of the Layout object. After formatting the log information, the appender publishes the logs to the appropriate destination.

The axillary objects may or may not be connected to the core objects depending on the configuration.

Now that we have seen the basic architecture of log4j we see how they interact with one another. A sample sequence of events that takes place once a logger object is invoked is shown below (Figure 3.2).

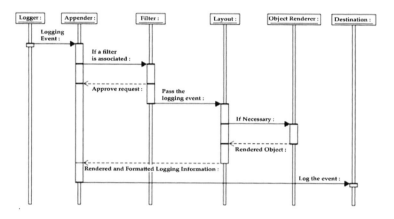

Figure 3.2: Log4j overview (Gülcü, 2003).

The application creates a logger object and provides it with logging information. Whenever an application instantiates a Logger object, a logging event is invoked. The logger has a Log Level associated with it and it will log messages that possess a level that is either equal to or greater than its set level.

If this condition is met, then the Logger forwards the log data to the Appender. This data is sent to all its Appender objects and the appender objects of its parent as well. This is done in a recursive manner up the hierarchy tree. The Appender checks the associated level threshold and if this condition is met, moves on to the next check.

It checks if a filter has been defined. If there are any filters defined, the log data is passed through all the filters for approval. Once the log data is approved by the filters, the appender then makes use of the Layout object associated to it to format the log message. If a Renderer is defined for the given layout, it is consulted in the formatting of the message. Once, the rendering has been done, the control is passed to the Layout object which then passes the control back to the Appender object. Now, the appender holds the rendered and formatted log information. After this, the Appender publishes the logs to its respective destination.

3.7. LOG4J API

This section covers the basic API classes provided by the log4j framework.

3.7.1. Logger

Loggers are the central unit of the log4j framework. Loggers are nothing but named entities (Gülcü, 2003).

The loggers in log4j are named using the named hierarchy rule.

This rule is as follows:

"A logger is said to be an ancestor of another logger if its name is followed by a dot is a prefix of the descendant logger name. A logger which is an immediate ancestor of a descendant is said to be a parent logger and the immediate descendant is the child logger." (Apache Log4j API 2.9.1, 2017).

To explain this with a simple example the named "com.abc" is a parent of "com.abc.package1."

The default root logger is parent logger of all the loggers. This logger is a special logger that always exists and whose level cannot be null. Additionally, it doesn't possess a name and hence cannot be retrieved by its name.

Programmatically, to retrieve the logger object, we use the static get Logger () method of the class Log Manager class. Some of the important methods of this class are as shown in the table below:

Methods of the Log Manager class: (Apache Log4j API 2.9.1, 2017)

Method	Description
static Logger get Logger ()	This method returns a logger object with the name of the class that calls this method
static Logger get Logger (String name)	This method returns a logger object with the specified name
static Logger get Root Logger ()	This method returns the root Logger
Static Logger get Formatted Logger (String name)	This method returns a logger that is formatted with the specified name

| static Boolean exists (String name) | This method checks if the logger with the specified name exists |
| Static Logger Context get Context () | This method returns the current Logger Context |

In log4j2, the Logger class provides several methods that are used to add logging functionality in Java applications. Some of these methods are described below: (Table 3.1).

Table 3.1: Logger class methods (Apache Log4j API 2.9.1, 2017)

Method	Description
void debug(Message message)	This method logs a message of level DEBUG.
void info(Message message)	This method logs a message of level INFO.
void warn(Message message)	This method logs a message of level WARN.
void error(Message message)	This method logs a message of level ERROR.
void fatal(Message message)	This method logs a message of level FATAL.
void trace(Message message)	This method logs a message of level TRACE.
Level get Level()	These methods return the level associated with the logger.
String get Name()	This method returns the name of the logger.
void log (Level level, Object message)	This method logs a log message with the specified level.
void log (Level level, Object message, Throwable t)	This method logs a message with the specified level and also the stack trace of the Throwable parameter

3.7.2. Level

In log4j several different values for the Log Level can be set. These levels are provided by the **org. apache. log4j.Level class.** The available options have been described in the table below. (Table 3.2).

Table 3.2: Log4j Level Class (Apache Log4j API 2.9.1, 2017)

Log Level	Description
TRACE	This log level permits all log information
DEBUG	This log level provides detailed informational logs that are useful for debugging an application.
INFO	This log level is for log messages that provide coarse-grained level logging. Progress and state information is provided.
WARN	This level serves as a high priority level and gives warnings about unexpected events taking place within the application.

ERROR	This log level indicates a serious issue within the application which may potentially destabilize the application.
FATAL	This log level indicates a log message of the highest priority. It usually indicates that the application will be aborted.
ALL	This log level permits messages of all the log levels to be logged.
OFF	This log level indicates that the logging has been turned off.

The ranking of all the levels is as follows (Apache Log4j API 2.9.1, 2017):

ALL <TRACE< DEBUG < INFO < WARN < ERROR < FATAL < OFF

The following table demonstrates which levels are permitted for which log level. For instance, for the log level WARN, messages of this level are visible only for levels WARN, ERROR, FATAL and ALL.

Table 3.3: Log Levels and Their Access (Apache Log4j API 2.9.1, 2017)

Levels	ALL	FATAL	ERROR	WARN	INFO	DEBUG	TRACE
ALL	Y	Y	Y	Y	Y	Y	Y
FATAL	Y	Y	N	N	N	N	N
ERROR	Y	Y	Y	N	N	N	N
WARN	Y	Y	Y	Y	N	N	N
INFO	Y	Y	Y	Y	Y	N	N
DEBUG	Y	Y	Y	Y	Y	Y	N
TRACE	Y	Y	Y	Y	Y	Y	Y

3.7.3. Appenders

Appenders are objects that help write logs to multiple destinations such as console, remote sockets, files, swing components, JMS, loggers for events and Unix syslog's (remote or local). Attaching multiple appenders is possible in log4j. Additionally, this is configurable. Appenders can be added and removed at any point of time in an application.

Log4j provides several different appenders that print to one or more destinations.

Some of the Appender classes are as follows:

1.   Console Appender: This appender writes the log output to console (System. out or System. out)

2. File Appender: This appender writes to a file. It is an output Stream appender and writes to the filename specified in the configuration.

3. Rolling File Appender: This is another output Sream based File Appender that writes to a file and also rolls/rotates the file depending on the rollover and triggering policies.

4. Random Access File Appender: This appender is like the standard File Appender but it is always buffered using a Buffered Output Stream.

5. JDBC Appender: This appender writes logs to an RDBMS (Relational Database) table using jdbc connection.

6. JMS Appender: This appender sends the log event to a Java Messaging Service queue destination.

7. Async Appender: This is called the Asynchronous appender and it contains references to other different appenders. Log messages are written to the Appenders it contains on a separate thread. This is extremely useful in case of multithreaded applications.

8. SMTP Appender: This appender is used to send emails when a specific type of event in case of logging takes place such as fatal errors.

9. Socket Appender: This is another output Stream appender that writes the log to a remote destination accepting a host and a port as input parameters.

10. Syslog Appender: This is an extension of the Socket Appender which conforms to a specific Syslog format. (BSD or RFC 4524).

11. Writer Appender: This appender appends log information in the form of strings to a writer.

Each Appender object has different properties associated with it, and these properties indicate the behavior of that object.

*   Target: This is the destination of the log message. It can be a file, console or another network location.

*   Level: Each appender has an associated level which is used to filter the outgoing log messages

*   Layout: The appender classes use a layout to format the log information.

Additionally, am appender may optionally have a Threshold and a Filter associated to it. A threshold is used to set a minimum log level that is permitted to be sent to its destination. All messages with a Level equal or higher to the threshold level are allowed. An appender can also have a filter defined that accepts log messages based on various criteria such as level, size, key-value pairs, etc.

Some of the important methods from the Appender interface are listed below:

Table 3.4: Methods of the Appender class (Apache Log4j API 2.9.1, 2017)

Method	Description
void append (LogEvent e)	This method log the LogEvent to the specified destination
String getName()	This method returns the name of the appender.
Layout<? Extends Serializable> getLayout()	This method returns the Layout used by the appender.
ErroHandler getHandler()	This method returns the ErrorHandler that is used for handling the exceptions
void setHandler(ErrorHandler handler)	This method sets the given parameter as the ErrorHandler for the appender.

3.7.4. Filters

Filters are the components that determine which log messages will reach their target destination. If and when a filter is invoked, it calls its filter method and returns an Enumeration result value which has 3 possibilities: ACCEPT, DENY or NEUTRAL. They can be configured at Logger, Appender or Context level.

Log4j provides the following types of filters:

1. Threshold Filter: This filter defines a threshold level and allows the log event to pass if the log event has a level that is either equal or higher than the current threshold.

2. Time Filter: This filter is used to limit the logging for a particular time period. It accepts a start and end time that can be configured.

3. Burst Filter: This filter provides a limit on the number of possible logging events. Using this filter the rate, speed and processing of the logging can be controlled. It has a parameter that maintains

the maximum number of events that can take place (maxBurst). Once this number is reached, the filter quietly discards the log events.

4. Composite Filter: This filter allows the use of multiple filters in the same context.

5. Map Filter: This is a unique filter that allows the log messages to be filtered on the basis of a Map that contains key-value pairs. Based on the key-value pairs being present in the log message, the logs are accepted or rejected.

6. Regex Filter: This filter allows the log information to be filter against a regular expression. It takes in a pattern and filters the log messages based on the pattern.

7. Structured Data Filter: This is an advanced Map Filter that is used to filter log information on the basis of the event id, type of message/event and the message itself.

8. Marker Filter: This filter filters the logging event Marker against a Marker value. Each event's Marker is compared with the marker value in the filter and based on the result, the log event is accepted or rejected.

9. Thread Context Map Filter: This filter is used to filter log events based on the elements present in the Thread Context Map. Key-value pairs are used.

10. Dynamic Threshold Filter: This filter provides the possibility of filtering logging information based on different properties such as log level, user id, context, etc.

We shall now see some of the methods of the Filter interface.

Table 3.5: Methods of the Filter Interface (Apache Log4j API 2.9.1, 2017)

Method	Description
Filter. Result filter (Log Event event)	This method filters the given log event.
Filter. Result get On Match ()	This method returns the value that should be returned if there is a match.
Filter. Result get On Mismatch ()	This method returns the value that should be returned if there is not a match.

Note that the Filter. Result in the above table is an Enumeration that returns either one of the following values: ACCEPT, DENY or NEUTRAL.

3.7.5. Layouts

Layouts are used by appenders to format the contents of the logging information. Several different types of layouts are provided by log4j to format the log information. Some of the layouts are as follows:

1. Pattern Layout: This is the most commonly used layout which is easily configurable using a string pattern. This layout is used to format the contents of a log events based on the string pattern. The formatting of the log event is completely dependent on the conversion pattern. Log4j provides many conversion patterns that help format the log events. Some of the most common conversions formats are as follows

    a. c{precision} logger{precision}: outputs the logger name

    b. d{pattern}/date{pattern}: outputs the date with the specified pattern

    c. m/msg/message: outputs the log message

    d. p/level: outputs the level of the log message

    e. r/relative: gives the number of milliseconds elapsed since the JVM started until the log was created.

    f. t/thread: this gives the thread which generated the log event.

2. JSON Layout: This layout is another well-used layout that appends JSON strings serialized as bytes.

3. HTML Layout: This layout is used to generate the log information in an html format that can be opened in any web browser. Each log event is considered to be a row in this layout.

4. XML Layout: This layout is used to append a list of events and output it as a well-formed XML document, the namespace by default being the log4j namespace.

5. Syslog Layout: This layout conforms to the BSD Syslog record and formats the logging information/event as per the standards of the BSD Syslog protocol

6. RFC5424 layout: This layout formats the logging data as per the RFC 5424 specifications, which are an advanced/enhanced syslog specification.

7. Serialized Layout: This layout performs serialization of the log event into a byte array.

8.   GELF Layout: This layout formats the log event in the Gray log Extended log format. It has the ability to compress the JSON log data if its size is greater than 1024 bytes.

A few important methods of the layout interface are shown below:

Table 3.6: Methods of the layout interface (Apache Log4j API 2.9.1, 2017)

Method	Description
byte[] get Header()	This method returns the header for the format of the layout
Byte [] get Footer ()	This method returns the footer for the format of the layout
Byte [] to Byte Array (Log Event event)	This method formats the given log event to a byte array.
T to Serializable (Log Event event)	This method formats the given log event into a serializable object.
String get Context Type ()	This method returns the content type of the log message that is being formatted by the layout.
Map<String, String> get Content Format ()	This method returns a map containing the format of the content.

3.8. THE LOG4J.PROPERTIES/XML FILE

The previous section covered the various log4j classes in detail. This section covers the log4j configuration.

In log4j, the configuration file can be of two types: either a properties file or an XML file.

The **configuration** file is a simple file that holds the log4j configuration properties in key-value pairs. In the earlier version (log4j1.x.x) this file was called log4j.properties. Starting from the next version log4j2 (log4 2.x.x), this file is now called as log4j2.properties. Although the name has been changed, this file contains the same information as before which is the logging configuration.

This file is used to configure the core log4j components using a configuration file (either properties or XML). This configuration involves defining the Appender, specifying the level and setting Layout objects in this configuration file.

The syntax for both the files is provided below.

log4j2.properties file

```
log4j2.properties ⊠

#define the root logger level
rootLogger.level = INFO

#define the appenders
appenders = console
appender.console.type = Console
appender.console.name = STDOUT

#set the layout and pattern
appender.console.layout.type = PatternLayout
appender.console.layout.pattern = %d %5p [%t] (%F:%L) - %m%n

#add the appenders to the logger
rootLogger.appenderRefs = console
rootLogger.appenderRef.console.ref = STDOUT
```

log4j2.xml:

```
<?xml version="1.0" encoding="UTF-8"?>
<Configuration>
 <Appenders>
  <Console name="STDOUT" target="SYSTEM_OUT">
   <PatternLayout pattern="%-5p | %d{yyyy-MM-dd HH:mm:ss} | [%t] %C{2} (%F:%L) - %m%n"/>
  </Console>
 </Appenders>
 <Loggers>
  <Root level="debug">
  <AppenderRef ref="STDOUT"/>
  </Root>
 </Loggers>
</Configuration>
```

Both the files show the basic configuration for a simple console appender that prints the logs to the console.

The default behavior of log4j is that at startup the Log Manager will look for a properties/XML file named log4j2.properties/XML in the classpath.

The log4j jars need to be added to the classpath which has been discussed in the next section.

3.9. LOG4J INSTALLATION

The API package of log4j is an open source packager that is distributed by Apache.

To install and run log4j, the log4j2 package needs to be downloaded on to your machine and installed in your local environment. The latest package is available for download purposes at the Apache download sit as follows:

https://logging.apache.org/log4j/2.0/download.html

To install and then configure log4j 2 on your system, download the latest version 2.9.1 from the Downloads page. Download the binary zip files.

Unzip the files on your local machine (preferably in a folder within your workspace).

If you are compiling and executing your java classes via a command prompt, add the path of the log4j-api-2.x.x.jar and log4j-core-2.x.x.jar jars to your classpath. This can be done as follows:

set CLASSPATH =.; <path to bin log4j bin folder>

If you are using an editor such as Eclipse for your Java applications, this is very easy to install and configure.

Open the Eclipse IDE and create a new project. Right click on your project and go to the option Build Path -> Configure Build Path. Click on Add External JARs.

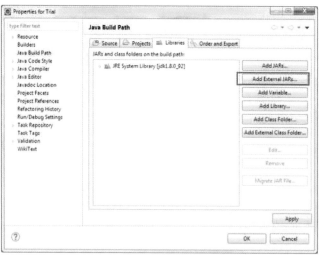

Navigate to the path where your jar files are present and select the following 2 jars to add to your build path:

-log4j-api-2.9.1.jar

-log4j-core-2.9.1.jar

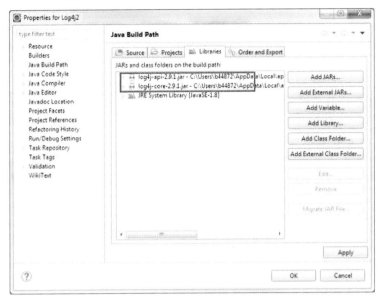

Now your local environment installation setup is done.

Once this basic setup is done, we now write a simple class that uses log4j for adding logs.

First, we create a new folder called as the resources folder in the project. In this folder, we create a log4j2.properties file.

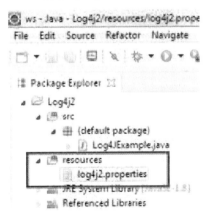

The contents of this file are as follows:

```
log4j2.properties ⊠
    #define the root logger level
    rootLogger.level = INFO
    #add appender
    appenders = console
    appender.console.type = Console
    appender.console.name = STDOUT
    #set a pattern
    appender.console.layout.type = PatternLayout
    appender.console.layout.pattern = %d %5p [%t] - %m%n
    #add appender to the root logger
    rootLogger.appenderRefs = console
    rootLogger.appenderRef.console.ref = STDOUT
```

The java class log4jExample below demonstrates the use of the log4j api for logging:

```
Log4JExample.java ⊠
  import org.apache.logging.log4j.LogManager;
  import org.apache.logging.log4j.Logger;

  public class Log4JExample {

      //get the logger object from the LogManager
      private static final Logger LOG = LogManager.getLogger(Log4JExample.class);

      public static void main(String args[]) {

          //add log statements
          LOG.debug("Debug message");
          LOG.info("Info message");
          LOG.warn("Warn message");
          LOG.error("Error message");
          LOG.fatal("Fatal message");

      }
  }
```

The output generated by the class is the following:

```
Console ⊠    Problems   @ Javadoc   Declaration   Annoti
<terminated> Log4JExample (2) [Java Application] C:\Program Files\java\j
2017-09-12 15:25:51,021  INFO [main] - Info message
2017-09-12 15:25:51,021  WARN [main] - Warn message
2017-09-12 15:25:51,021 ERROR [main] - Error message
2017-09-12 15:25:51,021 FATAL [main] - Fatal message
```

This section described a simple example demonstrating the use of log4j in a small Java application. The next section provides additional examples that use XML configuration, different appenders, filters, layouts, etc.

3.10. EXAMPLES

Example1: File Appender Example

In this example, we demonstrate a simple FileAppender that has been configured using the log4j2.properties file.

The configuration file is as follows:

```
log4j2.properties

#define the root logger level
rootLogger.level = INFO
#add appender
appenders = File

#define the File Appender
appender.File.type = File
appender.File.name = File
#provide the output log file and path
appender.File.fileName = logFile.log

#set a pattern for the output
appender.File.layout.type = PatternLayout
appender.File.layout.pattern = %d{yyyy-MM-dd HH:mm:ss} %c{1} [%p] %m%n

#add file appender to the root logger
rootLogger.appenderRefs = File
rootLogger.appenderRef.File.ref = File
```

In the above configuration file, we configure the java application to use log4 and use a file appender to log the messages in a file named logFile.log and the pattern of the log entries to be in the yyyy-mm-dd –logger name- level- message format.

The Java class used to test this configuration is shown below:

```
Log4JExample1.java

import org.apache.logging.log4j.LogManager;

public class Log4JExample1 {

    //get the logger object from the LogManager
    private static final Logger LOG = LogManager.getLogger(Log4JExample1.class);

    public static void main(String args[]) {

        //add log statements
        LOG.debug("A Debug message");
        LOG.info("An Info message");
        LOG.warn("A Warn message");
        LOG.error("An Error message");
        LOG.fatal("A Fatal message");

    }
}
```

When we run this class, a new file is created in the java project:

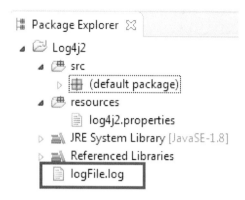

The contents of this file are as follows:

```
logFile.log ⌧

2017-09-12 15:50:32 Log4JExample1 [INFO] Info message
2017-09-12 15:50:32 Log4JExample1 [WARN] Warn message
2017-09-12 15:50:32 Log4JExample1 [ERROR] Error message
2017-09-12 15:50:32 Log4JExample1 [FATAL] Fatal message
```

Example 2: Multiple Appenders

In this example, we demonstrate a log4j configuration that makes use of multiple appenders. We now configure log4 to use two appenders: console and file as shown below:

```
log4j2.properties ⌧

#define the root logger level
rootLogger.level = WARN
#add appender
appenders = File, console

#define the Console appender
appender.console.type = Console
appender.console.name = STDOUT
#set a pattern
appender.console.layout.type = PatternLayout
appender.console.layout.pattern = %d %5p [%t] [%F:%L] - %m%n

#define the File Appender
appender.File.type = File
appender.File.name = File
#provide the output log file and path
appender.File.fileName = logFile.log
#set a pattern for the output
appender.File.layout.type = PatternLayout
appender.File.layout.pattern = %d{yyyy-MM-dd HH:mm:ss} %c{1} [%p] %m%n

#add file appender to the root logger
rootLogger.appenderRefs = File, console
rootLogger.appenderRef.File.ref = File
rootLogger.appenderRef.console.ref = STDOUT
```

The java class that will be used to test the configuration is as follows:

```
J Log4JExample2.java ⊠
 ⊕ import org.apache.logging.log4j.LogManager;

  public class Log4JExample2 {

      // get the logger object from the LogManager
      private static final Logger LOG = LogManager.getLogger(Log4JExample2.class);

      public static void main(String args[]) {

          // add log statements
          LOG.warn("A Warn message");
          LOG.error("An Error message");
          LOG.fatal("A Fatal message");

          // induce an exception
          try {
              int a = 5/0;
              System.out.println(a);
          } catch (ArithmeticException e) {
              // log the exception
              LOG.error("Cannot divide by zero!");
          }

      }
  }
```

When we run this class, the log output is sent to two different destinations: the console and a file named myLogFile.log.

The console output generated on execution of the above class is as follows:

```
□ Console ⊠    Problems    Javadoc    Declaration    Annotations    Call Hierarchy
<terminated> Log4JExample2 [Java Application] C:\Program Files\java\jdk1.8.0_92\bin\javaw.exe
2017-09-12 16:26:39,702  WARN  [main] [Log4JExample2.java:12] - A Warn message
2017-09-12 16:26:39,702 ERROR  [main] [Log4JExample2.java:13] - An Error message
2017-09-12 16:26:39,702 FATAL  [main] [Log4JExample2.java:14] - A Fatal message
2017-09-12 16:26:39,702 ERROR  [main] [Log4JExample2.java:22] - Cannot divide by zero!
```

The file output is as follows:

```
📄 logFile.log ⊠
    2017-09-12 16:26:39 Log4JExample2 [WARN] A Warn message
    2017-09-12 16:26:39 Log4JExample2 [ERROR] An Error message
    2017-09-12 16:26:39 Log4JExample2 [FATAL] A Fatal message
    2017-09-12 16:26:39 Log4JExample2 [ERROR] Cannot divide by zero!
```

Example 3: Rolling File Appender

In the previous 2 examples, we studied how to implement the console and file Appender. Now we shall see how to configure log4j2 logging to use a rolling file appender.

The configuration file used is as follows:

```
log4j2.properties

#define the root logger level
rootLogger.level = DEBUG

property.filename = myLogFile.log

#add appenders
appenders = R, console

#define the Console appender
appender.console.type = Console
appender.console.name = STDOUT
#set a pattern
appender.console.layout.type = PatternLayout
appender.console.layout.pattern = %d %5p [%t] [%F:%L] - %m%n

#define the File Appender
appender.R.type = RollingFile
appender.R.name = File
appender.R.fileName = ${filename}
appender.R.filePattern = ${filename}-%i.log
appender.R.layout.type = PatternLayout
appender.R.layout.pattern = %d{yyyy-MM-dd HH:mm:ss} %c{1} [%p] %m%n
appender.R.policies.type = Policies
appender.R.policies.time.type = SizeBasedTriggeringPolicy
appender.R.policies.time.interval = 1

#add file appender to the root logger
rootLogger.appenderRefs = R, console
rootLogger.appenderRef.File.ref = File
rootLogger.appenderRef.console.ref = STDOUT
```

In the above configuration, we used two appenders, the console, and the rolling file appender. We define the policy to be based on size and roll files when the size of the log file reaches 1 KB.

The java class is as follows:

```java
Log4JExample3.java

+ import org.apache.logging.log4j.LogManager;

public class Log4JExample3 {

    // get the logger object from the LogManager
    private static final Logger LOG = LogManager.getLogger(Log4JExample3.class);

    public static void main(String args[]) {

        // add log statements
        for (int i = 0; i < 50; i++) {
            LOG.debug("i:" + (i+1));
        }

        int[] myIntArray = new int[] { 1, 2, 3 };

        // induce an exception
        try {
            int c = myIntArray[3];
            System.out.println(c);
        } catch (ArrayIndexOutOfBoundsException e) {
            // log the exception
            LOG.error("Array Index is not within bounds!");
        }

    }
}
```

On execution, 3 files are created as shown below:

```
Package Explorer ☒                    ▣
  ▲ 🗁 Log4j2
    ▲ 🎹 src
      ▲ ⊞ (default package)
        ▷ 🗎 Log4JExample.java
        ▷ 🗎 Log4JExample1.java
        ▷ 🗎 Log4JExample2.java
        ▷ 🗎 Log4JExample3.java
    ▷ 🎹 resources
    ▷ ➦ JRE System Library [JavaSE-1.8]
    ▷ ➦ Referenced Libraries
      🗎 myLogFile-1.log
      🗎 myLogFile-2.log
      🗎 myLogFile-3.log
```

The contents are as follows:

```
🗎 myLogFile-1.log ☒
   2017-09-12 17:09:11 Log4JExample3 [DEBUG] i:1
   2017-09-12 17:09:11 Log4JExample3 [DEBUG] i:2
   2017-09-12 17:09:11 Log4JExample3 [DEBUG] i:3
   2017-09-12 17:09:11 Log4JExample3 [DEBUG] i:4
   2017-09-12 17:09:11 Log4JExample3 [DEBUG] i:5
   2017-09-12 17:09:11 Log4JExample3 [DEBUG] i:6
   2017-09-12 17:09:11 Log4JExample3 [DEBUG] i:7
   2017-09-12 17:09:11 Log4JExample3 [DEBUG] i:8
   2017-09-12 17:09:11 Log4JExample3 [DEBUG] i:9
   2017-09-12 17:09:11 Log4JExample3 [DEBUG] i:10
   2017-09-12 17:09:11 Log4JExample3 [DEBUG] i:11
   2017-09-12 17:09:11 Log4JExample3 [DEBUG] i:12
   2017-09-12 17:09:11 Log4JExample3 [DEBUG] i:13
   2017-09-12 17:09:11 Log4JExample3 [DEBUG] i:14
   2017-09-12 17:09:11 Log4JExample3 [DEBUG] i:15
   2017-09-12 17:09:11 Log4JExample3 [DEBUG] i:16
   2017-09-12 17:09:11 Log4JExample3 [DEBUG] i:17
   2017-09-12 17:09:11 Log4JExample3 [DEBUG] i:18
   2017-09-12 17:09:11 Log4JExample3 [DEBUG] i:19
   2017-09-12 17:09:11 Log4JExample3 [DEBUG] i:20
   2017-09-12 17:09:11 Log4JExample3 [DEBUG] i:21
   2017-09-12 17:09:11 Log4JExample3 [DEBUG] i:22

🗎 myLogFile-2.log ☒
   2017-09-12 17:09:11 Log4JExample3 [DEBUG] i:23
   2017-09-12 17:09:11 Log4JExample3 [DEBUG] i:24
   2017-09-12 17:09:11 Log4JExample3 [DEBUG] i:25
   2017-09-12 17:09:11 Log4JExample3 [DEBUG] i:26
   2017-09-12 17:09:11 Log4JExample3 [DEBUG] i:27
   2017-09-12 17:09:11 Log4JExample3 [DEBUG] i:28
   2017-09-12 17:09:11 Log4JExample3 [DEBUG] i:29
   2017-09-12 17:09:11 Log4JExample3 [DEBUG] i:30
   2017-09-12 17:09:11 Log4JExample3 [DEBUG] i:31
   2017-09-12 17:09:11 Log4JExample3 [DEBUG] i:32
   2017-09-12 17:09:11 Log4JExample3 [DEBUG] i:33
   2017-09-12 17:09:11 Log4JExample3 [DEBUG] i:34
   2017-09-12 17:09:11 Log4JExample3 [DEBUG] i:35
   2017-09-12 17:09:11 Log4JExample3 [DEBUG] i:36
   2017-09-12 17:09:11 Log4JExample3 [DEBUG] i:37
   2017-09-12 17:09:11 Log4JExample3 [DEBUG] i:38
   2017-09-12 17:09:11 Log4JExample3 [DEBUG] i:39
   2017-09-12 17:09:11 Log4JExample3 [DEBUG] i:40
   2017-09-12 17:09:11 Log4JExample3 [DEBUG] i:41
   2017-09-12 17:09:11 Log4JExample3 [DEBUG] i:42
   2017-09-12 17:09:11 Log4JExample3 [DEBUG] i:43
   2017-09-12 17:09:11 Log4JExample3 [DEBUG] i:44
```

```
myLogFile-3.log

2017-09-12 17:09:11 Log4JExample3 [DEBUG] i:45
2017-09-12 17:09:11 Log4JExample3 [DEBUG] i:46
2017-09-12 17:09:11 Log4JExample3 [DEBUG] i:47
2017-09-12 17:09:11 Log4JExample3 [DEBUG] i:48
2017-09-12 17:09:11 Log4JExample3 [DEBUG] i:49
2017-09-12 17:09:11 Log4JExample3 [DEBUG] i:50
2017-09-12 17:09:11 Log4JExample3 [ERROR] Array Index is not within bounds!
```

The console output is as follows:

```
Console    Problems    Javadoc    Declaration    Annotations    Call Hierarchy
<terminated> Log4JExample3 [Java Application] C:\Program Files\java\jdk1.8.0_92\bin\javaw.exe (12 oct. 2017 à 17:10:11)
2017-09-12 17:10:11,777 DEBUG [main] (Log4JExample3.java:13) - i:1
2017-09-12 17:10:11,793 DEBUG [main] (Log4JExample3.java:13) - i:2
2017-09-12 17:10:11,793 DEBUG [main] (Log4JExample3.java:13) - i:3
2017-09-12 17:10:11,793 DEBUG [main] (Log4JExample3.java:13) - i:4
2017-09-12 17:10:11,793 DEBUG [main] (Log4JExample3.java:13) - i:5
2017-09-12 17:10:11,793 DEBUG [main] (Log4JExample3.java:13) - i:6
2017-09-12 17:10:11,793 DEBUG [main] (Log4JExample3.java:13) - i:7
2017-09-12 17:10:11,793 DEBUG [main] (Log4JExample3.java:13) - i:8
2017-09-12 17:10:11,793 DEBUG [main] (Log4JExample3.java:13) - i:9
2017-09-12 17:10:11,793 DEBUG [main] (Log4JExample3.java:13) - i:10
2017-09-12 17:10:11,793 DEBUG [main] (Log4JExample3.java:13) - i:11
2017-09-12 17:10:11,793 DEBUG [main] (Log4JExample3.java:13) - i:12
2017-09-12 17:10:11,793 DEBUG [main] (Log4JExample3.java:13) - i:13
2017-09-12 17:10:11,793 DEBUG [main] (Log4JExample3.java:13) - i:14
2017-09-12 17:10:11,793 DEBUG [main] (Log4JExample3.java:13) - i:15
2017-09-12 17:10:11,793 DEBUG [main] (Log4JExample3.java:13) - i:16
2017-09-12 17:10:11,793 DEBUG [main] (Log4JExample3.java:13) - i:17
2017-09-12 17:10:11,793 DEBUG [main] (Log4JExample3.java:13) - i:18
2017-09-12 17:10:11,793 DEBUG [main] (Log4JExample3.java:13) - i:19
2017-09-12 17:10:11,793 DEBUG [main] (Log4JExample3.java:13) - i:20
2017-09-12 17:10:11,793 DEBUG [main] (Log4JExample3.java:13) - i:21
2017-09-12 17:10:11,793 DEBUG [main] (Log4JExample3.java:13) - i:22
2017-09-12 17:10:11,793 DEBUG [main] (Log4JExample3.java:13) - i:23
2017-09-12 17:10:11,793 DEBUG [main] (Log4JExample3.java:13) - i:24
2017-09-12 17:10:11,793 DEBUG [main] (Log4JExample3.java:13) - i:25
2017-09-12 17:10:11,793 DEBUG [main] (Log4JExample3.java:13) - i:26
2017-09-12 17:10:11,793 DEBUG [main] (Log4JExample3.java:13) - i:27
2017-09-12 17:10:11,793 DEBUG [main] (Log4JExample3.java:13) - i:28
2017-09-12 17:10:11,793 DEBUG [main] (Log4JExample3.java:13) - i:29
2017-09-12 17:10:11,793 DEBUG [main] (Log4JExample3.java:13) - i:30
2017-09-12 17:10:11,793 DEBUG [main] (Log4JExample3.java:13) - i:31
2017-09-12 17:10:11,793 DEBUG [main] (Log4JExample3.java:13) - i:32
2017-09-12 17:10:11,793 DEBUG [main] (Log4JExample3.java:13) - i:33
2017-09-12 17:10:11,793 DEBUG [main] (Log4JExample3.java:13) - i:34
2017-09-12 17:10:11,793 DEBUG [main] (Log4JExample3.java:13) - i:35
2017-09-12 17:10:11,793 DEBUG [main] (Log4JExample3.java:13) - i:36
2017-09-12 17:10:11,793 DEBUG [main] (Log4JExample3.java:13) - i:37
2017-09-12 17:10:11,793 DEBUG [main] (Log4JExample3.java:13) - i:38
2017-09-12 17:10:11,793 DEBUG [main] (Log4JExample3.java:13) - i:39
2017-09-12 17:10:11,793 DEBUG [main] (Log4JExample3.java:13) - i:40
2017-09-12 17:10:11,793 DEBUG [main] (Log4JExample3.java:13) - i:41
2017-09-12 17:10:11,793 DEBUG [main] (Log4JExample3.java:13) - i:42
2017-09-12 17:10:11,793 DEBUG [main] (Log4JExample3.java:13) - i:43
2017-09-12 17:10:11,793 DEBUG [main] (Log4JExample3.java:13) - i:44
2017-09-12 17:10:11,793 DEBUG [main] (Log4JExample3.java:13) - i:45
2017-09-12 17:10:11,809 DEBUG [main] (Log4JExample3.java:13) - i:46
2017-09-12 17:10:11,809 DEBUG [main] (Log4JExample3.java:13) - i:47
2017-09-12 17:10:11,809 DEBUG [main] (Log4JExample3.java:13) - i:48
2017-09-12 17:10:11,809 DEBUG [main] (Log4JExample3.java:13) - i:49
2017-09-12 17:10:11,809 DEBUG [main] (Log4JExample3.java:13) - i:50
2017-09-12 17:10:11,809 ERROR [main] (Log4JExample3.java:24) - Array Index is not within bounds!
```

Example 4: Rolling File Appender based on Size and Time

In the previous example, we have seen a rolling file appender that is configured on the basis of size. In this example, we configure the rolling file appender on the basis of size and time. This is done with the use of a TimeBasedTriggeringPolicy in addition to a SizeBasedTriggeringPolicy.

We set the configuration to log files at intervals of 1 minute as shown below:

```
log4j2.properties

#define the root logger level
property.filename = logFile.log
rootLogger.level = DEBUG

#add appender
appenders = rolling, console

#define the Console appender
appender.console.type = Console
appender.console.name = STDOUT
#set a pattern
appender.console.layout.type = PatternLayout
appender.console.layout.pattern = %d %5p [%t] [%F:%L] - %m%n

appender.rolling.type = RollingFile
appender.rolling.name = RollingFile
appender.rolling.fileName = ${filename}
appender.rolling.filePattern = debug-backup-%d{MM-dd-yy-HH-mm-ss}-%i.log.zip
appender.rolling.layout.type = PatternLayout
appender.rolling.layout.pattern = %d{yyyy-MM-dd HH:mm:ss} %-5p %c{1}:%L - %m%n
appender.rolling.policies.type = Policies
appender.rolling.policies.time.type = TimeBasedTriggeringPolicy
appender.rolling.policies.time.interval = 1
appender.rolling.policies.time.modulate = true
appender.rolling.policies.size.type = SizeBasedTriggeringPolicy
appender.rolling.policies.size.size=2KB
appender.rolling.strategy.type = DefaultRolloverStrategy
appender.rolling.strategy.max = 10

#add file appender to the root logger
rootLogger.appenderRefs = rolling, console
rootLogger.appenderRef.File.ref = RollingFile
rootLogger.appenderRef.console.ref = STDOUT
```

The java class is as follows:

```java
Log4JExample4.java

package com.logging;
+ import org.apache.logging.log4j.LogManager;

public class Log4JExample4 {

    // get the logger object from the LogManager
    private static final Logger LOG = LogManager.getLogger(Log4JExample4.class);

    public static void main(String args[]) throws InterruptedException {

        // add log statements
        for (int i = 0; i < 15; i++) {
            Thread.sleep(200);
            LOG.debug("i:" + (i + 1));
        }
    }
}
```

When we run this class, zip files are created in the project structure as follows:

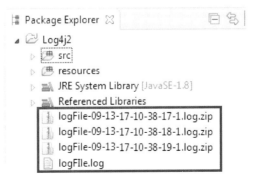

The contents of these files are as follows:

Up until now, we have seen samples of log4j configuration using a properties file. We now take a look at examples that used the XML based which is most used type of configuration with log4j2.

Example 5: Simple console appender using log42.xml file

This example shows the log4 configuration using an XML file. The following configuration file is used to configure your application with a simple console appender as shown below:

```xml
<?xml version="1.0" encoding="UTF-8"?>
<Configuration status="WARN">
    <Appenders>
        <Console name="consoleAppender" target="SYSTEM_OUT">
            <PatternLayout pattern="%-5p | %d{yyyy-MM-dd HH:mm:ss} | [%t] %C{2} (%F:%L) - %m%n" />
        </Console>
    </Appenders>
    <Loggers>
        <Root level="debug">
            <AppenderRef ref="consoleAppender" />
        </Root>
    </Loggers>
</Configuration>
```

The java class used is as follows:

```
J Log4JExample5.java ⊠
  + import org.apache.logging.log4j.LogManager;

   public class Log4JExample5 {

       //get the logger object from the LogManager
       private static final Logger LOG = LogManager.getLogger(Log4JExample5.class);

       public static void main(String args[]) {

           //add log statements
           LOG.debug("Debug message");
           LOG.info("Info message");
           LOG.warn("Warn message");
           LOG.error("Error message");
           LOG.fatal("Fatal message");

       }
   }
```

The console output is the following:

```
Console ⊠  Problems  @ Javadoc  Declaration  Annotations  Call Hierarchy
<terminated> Log4JExample5 [Java Application] C:\Program Files\java\jdk1.8.0_92\bin\javaw.exe
DEBUG | 2017-09-13 13:17:46 | [main] Log4JExample5 (Log4JExample5.java:12) - Debug message
INFO  | 2017-09-13 13:17:46 | [main] Log4JExample5 (Log4JExample5.java:13) - Info message
WARN  | 2017-09-13 13:17:46 | [main] Log4JExample5 (Log4JExample5.java:14) - Warn message
ERROR | 2017-09-13 13:17:46 | [main] Log4JExample5 (Log4JExample5.java:15) - Error message
FATAL | 2017-09-13 13:17:46 | [main] Log4JExample5 (Log4JExample5.java:16) - Fatal message
```

Example 6: File Appender with xml-based configuration

In example 5, we saw the XML configuration for a console appender. Here, we take a look at an XML based log4j2 configuration that log to a file using the file appender.

```
X log4j2.xml ⊠
   <?xml version="1.0" encoding="UTF-8"?>
   <Configuration status="WARN">
       <Appenders>
           <File name="myAppender" fileName="myLogFile.log" append="false">
               <PatternLayout pattern="%t %-5p %c{2} - %m%n" />
           </File>
       </Appenders>
       <Loggers>
           <Root level="info">
               <AppenderRef ref="myAppender" />
           </Root>
       </Loggers>
   </Configuration>
```

The test Java class is as follows:

```java
Log4JExample6.java ⊠
⊕ import org.apache.logging.log4j.LogManager;⬚

    public class Log4JExample6 {

        //get the logger object from the LogManager
        private static final Logger LOG = LogManager.getLogger(Log4JExample6.class);

        public static void main(String args[]) {

            //add log statements
            LOG.debug("Debug message");
            LOG.info("Info message");
            LOG.warn("Warn message");
            LOG.error("Error message");
            LOG.fatal("Fatal message");

            Object obj = null;
            if(obj== null)
                LOG.fatal("Object is null!");
        }
    }
```

On execution of the java class, a log file is generated in the project structure.

The log file contents are as follows:

```
myLogFile.log ⊠
    main INFO   Log4JExample6 - Info message
    main WARN   Log4JExample6 - Warn message
    main ERROR  Log4JExample6 - Error message
    main FATAL  Log4JExample6 - Fatal message
    main FATAL  Log4JExample6 - Object is null!
```

Example 7: Multiple appenders

In the previous 2 appenders, we observed the console and file appender independently. We shall now see the XML based configuration for multiple appenders.

```xml
log4j2.xml ⊠
    <?xml version="1.0" encoding="UTF-8"?>
    <Configuration>
        <Appenders>
            <Console name="STDOUT" target="SYSTEM_OUT">
                <PatternLayout
                    pattern="%-5p | %d{yyyy-MM-dd HH:mm:ss} | [%t] %C{2} (%F:%L) - %m%n" />
            </Console>

            <File name="myAppender" fileName="myLogFile.log" append="false">
                <PatternLayout pattern="%t %-5p %c{2} - %m%n" />
            </File>
        </Appenders>
        <Loggers>
            <Root level="info">
                <AppenderRef ref="myAppender" />
                <AppenderRef ref="STDOUT" />
            </Root>
        </Loggers>
    </Configuration>
```

We have configured our application to use the console and the file appender.

The java class is as follows:

```
Log4JExample7.java

+ import org.apache.logging.log4j.LogManager;

    public class Log4JExample7 {

        // get the logger object from the LogManager
        private static final Logger LOG = LogManager.getLogger(Log4JExample7.class);

        public static void main(String args[]) {

            // add log statements
            LOG.debug("Debug message");
            LOG.info("Info message");
            LOG.warn("Warn message");
            LOG.error("Error message");
            LOG.fatal("Fatal message");

            Object obj = null;
            if (obj == null)
                LOG.fatal("Object is null!");

            // induce an exception
            try {
                int a = 5 / 0;
                System.out.println(a);
            } catch (ArithmeticException e) {
                // log the exception
                LOG.error("Cannot divide by zero!");
            }
        }
    }
```

On running the java class, we get two outputs: one on the console and another one in a file named myLogFile.log.

The log file output is:

```
myLogFile.log

    main INFO  Log4JExample7 - Info message
    main WARN  Log4JExample7 - Warn message
    main ERROR Log4JExample7 - Error message
    main FATAL Log4JExample7 - Fatal message
    main FATAL Log4JExample7 - Object is null!
    main ERROR Log4JExample7 - Cannot divide by zero!
```

The console output is:

```
Console    Problems  @ Javadoc  Declaration  Annotations  Call Hierarchy
<terminated> Log4JExample7 [Java Application] C:\Program Files\java\jdk1.8.0_92\bin\javaw.exe
INFO  | 2017-09-13 13:43:22 | [main] Log4JExample7 (Log4JExample7.java:13) - Info message
WARN  | 2017-09-13 13:43:22 | [main] Log4JExample7 (Log4JExample7.java:14) - Warn message
ERROR | 2017-09-13 13:43:22 | [main] Log4JExample7 (Log4JExample7.java:15) - Error message
FATAL | 2017-09-13 13:43:22 | [main] Log4JExample7 (Log4JExample7.java:16) - Fatal message
FATAL | 2017-09-13 13:43:22 | [main] Log4JExample7 (Log4JExample7.java:20) - Object is null!
ERROR | 2017-09-13 13:43:22 | [main] Log4JExample7 (Log4JExample7.java:28) - Cannot divide by zero!
```

Example 8: DailyRollingFileAppender

In this example, we configure the application so that it logs messages to a file that rotates on a daily basis.

```xml
x log4j2.xml

<?xml version="1.0" encoding="UTF-8"?>
<Configuration status="info">
    <Appenders>
        <!-- Rolling File Appender -->
        <RollingFile name="RollingFile">
            <FileName>mylog.log</FileName>
            <FilePattern>%d{yyyy-MM-dd-hh-mm}.log.zip
            </FilePattern>
            <PatternLayout>
                <Pattern>%d{yyyy-MMM-dd HH:mm:ss a} [%t] %-5level %logger{36} - %msg%n</Pattern>
            </PatternLayout>
            <Policies>
                <TimeBasedTriggeringPolicy interval="1"
                    modulate="true" />
            </Policies>
            <DefaultRolloverStrategy max="5" />
        </RollingFile>

        <Console name="console" target="SYSTEM_OUT">
            <PatternLayout
                pattern="%-5p | %d{yyyy-MM-dd HH:mm:ss} | [%t] %C{2} (%F:%L) - %m%n" />
        </Console>
    </Appenders>
    <Loggers>
        <Root level="info" additivity="false">
            <appender-ref ref="console" />
            <appender-ref ref="RollingFile" />
        </Root>
    </Loggers>
</Configuration>
```

The java class is the following:

```java
J Log4JExample8.java

+ import org.apache.logging.log4j.LogManager;

public class Log4JExample8 {

    // get the logger object from the LogManager
    private static final Logger LOG = LogManager.getLogger(Log4JExample8.class);

    public static void main(String args[]) {

        // add log statements
        LOG.debug("Debug message");
        LOG.info("Info message");
        LOG.warn("Warn message");
        LOG.error("Error message");
        LOG.fatal("Fatal message");

        Object obj = null;
        if (obj == null)
            LOG.fatal("Object is null!");

        // induce an exception
        try {
            int a = 5 / 0;
            System.out.println(a);
        } catch (ArithmeticException e) {
            // log the exception
            LOG.error("Cannot divide by zero!");
        }
    }
}
```

The output generated on the console is as follows:

```
Console 23   Problems   @ Javadoc   Declaration   Annotations   Call Hierarchy
<terminated> Log4JExample8 [Java Application] C:\Program Files\java\jdk1.8.0_92\bin\javaw.exe
INFO  | 2017-09-13 14:34:16 | [main] Log4JExample8 (Log4JExample8.java:13) - Info message
WARN  | 2017-09-13 14:34:16 | [main] Log4JExample8 (Log4JExample8.java:14) - Warn message
ERROR | 2017-09-13 14:34:16 | [main] Log4JExample8 (Log4JExample8.java:15) - Error message
FATAL | 2017-09-13 14:34:16 | [main] Log4JExample8 (Log4JExample8.java:16) - Fatal message
FATAL | 2017-09-13 14:34:16 | [main] Log4JExample8 (Log4JExample8.java:20) - Object is null!
ERROR | 2017-09-13 14:34:16 | [main] Log4JExample8 (Log4JExample8.java:28) - Cannot divide by zero!
```

The output generated in the log file is as follows:

The contents of the file are as follows:

```
mylog.log 23
2017-Sep-13 14:34:16 PM [main] INFO  Log4JExample8 - Info message
2017-Sep-13 14:34:16 PM [main] WARN  Log4JExample8 - Warn message
2017-Sep-13 14:34:16 PM [main] ERROR Log4JExample8 - Error message
2017-Sep-13 14:34:16 PM [main] FATAL Log4JExample8 - Fatal message
2017-Sep-13 14:34:16 PM [main] FATAL Log4JExample8 - Object is null!
2017-Sep-13 14:34:16 PM [main] ERROR Log4JExample8 - Cannot divide by zero!
```

Example 9: Rolling FileAppender based on size

In this example, we see the implementation of a rolling file appender that rolls over log files based on size. Once the size reaches 5KB it is rolled over and zipped.

```xml
log4j2.xml 23
<?xml version="1.0" encoding="UTF-8"?>
<Configuration status="info">
    <Appenders>
        <!-- Rolling File Appender -->
        <RollingFile name="RollingFile">
            <FileName>mylog.log</FileName>
            <FilePattern>%d{yyyy-MM-dd-hh-mm}.log.zip</FilePattern>
            <PatternLayout>
                <Pattern>%d{yyyy-MMM-dd HH:mm:ss a} [%t] %-5level %logger{36} - %msg%n</Pattern>
            </PatternLayout>
            <Policies>
                <TimeBasedTriggeringPolicy interval="1"
                    modulate="true" />
                    <SizeBasedTriggeringPolicy size="5 KB"/>
            </Policies>
            <DefaultRolloverStrategy max="5" />
        </RollingFile>

        <Console name="console" target="SYSTEM_OUT">
            <PatternLayout
                pattern="%-5p | %d{yyyy-MM-dd HH:mm:ss} | [%t] %C{2} (%F:%L) - %m%n" />
        </Console>
    </Appenders>
    <Loggers>
        <Root level="info" additivity="false">
            <appender-ref ref="console" />
            <appender-ref ref="RollingFile" />
        </Root>
    </Loggers>
</Configuration>
```

The java class is as follows:

```java
Log4JExample9.java
+ import org.apache.logging.log4j.LogManager;

public class Log4JExample9 {
    // get the logger object from the LogManager
    private static final Logger LOG = LogManager.getLogger(Log4JExample9.class);

    public static void main(String args[]) {
        // add log statements
        LOG.debug("Debug message");
        LOG.error("Error message");
        LOG.fatal("Fatal message");

        for(int i=0; i< 100; i++)
        {
            LOG.info("Info: " + i);
        }
        //checked exceptions
        Object obj = null;
        if (obj == null)
            LOG.fatal("Object is null!");

        // induce an exception
        try {
            int a = 5 / 0;
            System.out.println(a);
        } catch (ArithmeticException e) {
            // log the exception
            LOG.error("Cannot divide by zero!");
        }
    }
}
```

The zip files are created as shown in the explorer package:

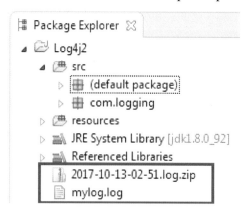

Example 10: Async Appender

This appender is used in a multithreaded environment, where the sync appender accepts multiple log requests and writes to different appenders via many threads. This appender can hold many appenders within it. All the appenders held by this appender will be invoked in an asynchronous manner. A simple configuration of this appender is as shown below:

```xml
x log4j2.xml

    <?xml version="1.0" encoding="UTF-8"?>
    <Configuration status="info" name = "MyApp" packages= "">
        <Appenders>
            <File name="MyFile" fileName="myLogFile.log">
                <PatternLayout pattern="%d %p %c{1.} [%t] %m%n" />
            </File>
            <Async name="Async">
                <AppenderRef ref="MyFile" />
            </Async>
        </Appenders>
        <Loggers>
            <Root level="info">
                <AppenderRef ref="Async" />
            </Root>
        </Loggers>
    </Configuration>
```

We configure the file appender to be invoked asynchronously.

The Java class is:

```java
J Log4JExample10.java

+ import org.apache.logging.log4j.LogManager;

   public class Log4JExample10 {

        // get the logger object from the LogManager
        private static final Logger LOG = LogManager.getLogger(Log4JExample10.class);

        public static void main(String args[]) throws InterruptedException {

            // add log statements
            LOG.info("Info message");
            LOG.error("Error message");
            LOG.fatal("Fatal message");
            LOG.warn("Warning Message ");
            LOG.debug("Debug Message");

        }
    }
```

The output generated in the output file my Logfile is as follows:

```
myLogFile.log

2017-09-17 14:07:41,778 INFO Log4JExample10 [main] Info message
2017-09-17 14:07:41,783 ERROR Log4JExample10 [main] Error message
2017-09-17 14:07:41,783 FATAL Log4JExample10 [main] Fatal message
2017-09-17 14:07:41,783 WARN Log4JExample10 [main] Warning Message
```

Example 11: Random Access File Appender

This example shows a simple log4j configuration for a random-access file appender.

```
x  log4j2.xml

<?xml version="1.0" encoding="UTF-8"?>
<Configuration>
    <Appenders>
        <RandomAccessFile name="myFileAppender" fileName="myLogFile.log">
            <PatternLayout>
                <Pattern>%d %p %c{1.} [%t] %m%n</Pattern>
            </PatternLayout>
        </RandomAccessFile>
    </Appenders>

    <Loggers>
        <Root level="info">
            <AppenderRef ref="myFileAppender" />
        </Root>
    </Loggers>
</Configuration>
```

This appender is fast as the log requests are buffered in this case. It uses a byte buffer internally to store the log events and hence processes them faster.

The Java class used to test this appender is as follows:

```
J  Log4JExample11.java
import org.apache.logging.log4j.LogManager;

public class Log4JExample11 {

    // get the logger object from the LogManager
    private static final Logger LOG = LogManager.getLogger(Log4JExample11.class);

    public static void main(String args[]) throws InterruptedException {

        // add log statements
        LOG.info("Info message");
        LOG.error("Error message");
        LOG.fatal("Fatal message");
        LOG.warn("Warning Message ");
        LOG.debug("Debug Message");

        // checked exceptions
        Object obj = null;
        if (obj == null)
            LOG.fatal("Object is null!");

    }
}
```

The output generated in the log file is as follows:

```
myLogFile.log
2017-09-17 14:26:09,268 INFO Log4JExample11 [main] Info message
2017-09-17 14:26:09,271 ERROR Log4JExample1 [main] Error message
2017-09-17 14:26:09,271 FATAL Log4JExample11 [main] Fatal message
2017-09-17 14:26:09,272 WARN Log4JExample11 [main] Warning Message
2017-09-17 14:26:09,272 DEBUG Log4JExample11 [main] Debug Message
```

As we have used the parameter "status=debug" in the configuration file, the internal logs of the log4j logger are printed on the console as well.

This is shown below:

Example 12: Custom Logger

In this example, we take a look at a simple way to create a user-defined logger.

We simply add the new logger name and level in the configuration file as follows:

```xml
 log4j2.xml

<?xml version="1.0" encoding="UTF-8"?>
<Configuration>
    <Appenders>
    <Console name="console" target="SYSTEM_OUT">
            <PatternLayout
                pattern="%d{HH:mm:ss.SSS} [%t] %-5level %Logger{36} - %msg%n" />
        </Console>
    </Appenders>
    <Loggers>
        <logger name="com.myLogger" level="DEBUG">
            <AppenderRef ref="console"/>
        </logger>
    </Loggers>
</Configuration>
```

We then call this logger in our test class shown below:

```java
 Log4JExample12.java

import org.apache.logging.log4j.LogManager;

public class Log4JExample12 {

    // get the logger object from the LogManager
    private static final Logger LOG = LogManager.getLogger("com.myLogger");

    public static void main(String args[]) throws InterruptedException {

        // add log statements
        LOG.info("Info message");
        LOG.error("Error message");
        LOG.fatal("Fatal message");
        LOG.warn("Warning Message ");
        LOG.debug("Debug Message");
    }
}
```

The output generated is as follows:

```
🖥 Console ⊠   ⚹ Markers   ⬜ Properties   ⚿ Servers   ▦ Data Source
<terminated> Log4JExample12 [Java Application] C:\Program Files\java\jdk1.
18:24:00.518 [main] INFO   com.myLogger - Info message
18:24:00.518 [main] ERROR  com.myLogger - Error message
18:24:00.518 [main] FATAL  com.myLogger - Fatal message
18:24:00.518 [main] WARN   com.myLogger - Warning Message
18:24:00.518 [main] DEBUG  com.myLogger - Debug Message
```

Example 13: Custom Log Level

Log4j2 has provided us with an excellent feature of creating our own custom log levels. This case be easily done with the help of the <CustomLevels> parameter as shown below:

```xml
x log4j2.xml ⊠
    <?xml version="1.0" encoding="UTF-8"?>
  <Configuration>
      <CustomLevels>
          <CustomLevel name="NOTIFICATION" intLevel="350" />
          <CustomLevel name="DIAGNOSE" intLevel="450" />
          <CustomLevel name="ADVANCED" intLevel="550" />
      </CustomLevels>
      <Appenders>
          <Console name="STDOUT" target="SYSTEM_OUT">
              <PatternLayout
                    pattern="%-5p | %d{yyyy-MM-dd HH:mm:ss} | [%t] %C{2} (%F:%L) - %m%n" />
          </Console>
      </Appenders>
      <Loggers>
          <Root level="trace">
              <AppenderRef ref="STDOUT"/>
          </Root>
      </Loggers>
  </Configuration>
```

We have added three new levels: NOTIFICATION, DIAGNOSE and ADVANCED.

We now proceed to make use of these levels in our program as follows:

```java
J Log4JExample14.java ⊠
 + import org.apache.logging.log4j.Level;

  public class Log4JExample14 {

      // get the logger object from the LogManager
      private static final Logger LOG = LogManager.getLogger(Log4JExample14.class);

      public static void main(String args[]) throws InterruptedException {

          // add standard log statements
          LOG.error("Error message");
          LOG.fatal("Fatal message");
          LOG.warn("Warning Message ");
          LOG.debug("Debug Message");

          //add log messages with custom log levels
          LOG.log(Level.forName("NOTIFICATION", 350), "Custom Log level Notification message");
          LOG.log(Level.forName("DIAGNOSE", 450), "Custom Log level Diagnose message");
          LOG.log(Level.forName("ADVANCED", 550), "Custom Log level Advanced message");
          LOG.log(Level.forName("NOTIFICATION", 350), "Another Custom Log level Notification message");
      }
  }
```

The generated output is:

```
Console ☒  ↑ Marking   Properties  Servers  Data Source Explorer  Snippets  Annotations       ▪ ✖ ✖ ↓
<terminated> Log4JExample14 [Java Application] C:\Program Files\java\jdk1.8.0_92\bin\javaw.exe
ERROR | 2017-09-18 09:30:32 | [main] Log4JExample14 (Log4JExample14.java:13) - Error message
FATAL | 2017-09-18 09:30:32 | [main] Log4JExample14 (Log4JExample14.java:14) - Fatal message
WARN  | 2017-09-18 09:30:32 | [main] Log4JExample14 (Log4JExample14.java:15) - Warning Message
DEBUG | 2017-09-18 09:30:32 | [main] Log4JExample14 (Log4JExample14.java:16) - Debug Message
NOTIFICATION | 2017-09-18 09:30:32 | [main] Log4JExample14 (Log4JExample14.java:19) - Custom Log level Notification message
DIAGNOSE | 2017-09-18 09:30:32 | [main] Log4JExample14 (Log4JExample14.java:20) - Custom Log level Diagnose message
ADVANCED | 2017-09-18 09:30:32 | [main] Log4JExample14 (Log4JExample14.java:21) - Custom Log level Advanced message
NOTIFICATION | 2017-09-18 09:30:32 | [main] Log4JExample14 (Log4JExample14.java:22) - Another Custom Log level Notification message
```

Example 15: Regex Filter Example

In this example, we show the use of a regex filter. We configure a regex to accept log messages that contain the string pattern *message*. If the log messages match this condition, they are accepted; else they are rejected.

```xml
X  log4j2.xml ☒

    <?xml version="1.0" encoding="UTF-8"?>
    <Configuration>
        <Appenders>
            <Console name="consoleAppender">
                <RegexFilter regex=".*message.*" onMatch="ACCEPT"
                    onMismatch="DENY" />
                <PatternLayout pattern="[%logger{36}] %message %n" />
            </Console>
        </Appenders>
        <Loggers>
            <Root level="trace">
                <AppenderRef ref="consoleAppender" />
            </Root>
        </Loggers>
    </Configuration>
```

The test java class is as follows:

```java
J  Log4JExample15.java ☒

+ import org.apache.logging.log4j.LogManager;

  public class Log4JExample15 {

      // get the logger object from the LogManager
      private static final Logger LOG = LogManager.getLogger(Log4JExample15.class);

      public static void main(String args[]) throws InterruptedException {

          // add standard log statements
          LOG.error("Error message");
          LOG.fatal("Fatal message");
          LOG.warn("Warning message ");
          LOG.debug("Debug message");
          LOG.trace("Trace message");

          // This message will not be displayed as it does not conatin the string
          // 'message'
          LOG.info("Info msg");
      }
  }
```

As we can see from the output, all the log messages that contain the word 'message' have been printed whereas the last log statement, the info message has been discarded based on the filter.

```
🖵 Console ⌕  ▣ Markers  ☐ Properties
<terminated> Log4JExample15 [Java Applicat
[Log4JExample15] Error message
[Log4JExample15] Fatal message
[Log4JExample15] Warning message
[Log4JExample15] Debug message
[Log4JExample15] Trace message
```

Example 16: Threshold Filter

This example demonstrates the use of the threshold filter. We set up two appenders that use this filter. We set up the rolling file appender to accept log messages of level debug and above. We set up the console appender to accept log messages of level info and above as shown below:

```xml
X log4j2.xml ⌕
  <?xml version="1.0" encoding="UTF-8"?>
  <Configuration>
    <Appenders>
      <Console name="STDOUT" target="SYSTEM_OUT">
        <ThresholdFilter level="INFO" onMatch="ACCEPT" onMismatch="DENY" />
        <PatternLayout
            pattern="%-5p | %d{yyyy-MM-dd HH:mm:ss} | [%t] %C{2} (%F:%L) - %m%n" />
      </Console>

      <RollingFile name="RollingFileAppender" fileName="myLogFile.log"
          filePattern="myLogFile-%d{MM-dd-yyyy}.log.gz">
        <ThresholdFilter level="DEBUG" onMatch="ACCEPT" onMismatch="DENY" />
        <PatternLayout>
          <pattern>%d %p %c{1.} [%t] %m%n</pattern>
        </PatternLayout>
        <TimeBasedTriggeringPolicy />
      </RollingFile>
    </Appenders>
    <Loggers>
      <Root level="trace">
        <AppenderRef ref="RollingFileAppender" />
        <AppenderRef ref="STDOUT" />
      </Root>
    </Loggers>
  </Configuration>
```

The java class is as follows:

```java
J Log4JExample16.java ⌕
 + import org.apache.logging.log4j.LogManager;

public class Log4JExample16 {

    // get the logger object from the LogManager
    private static final Logger LOG = LogManager.getLogger(Log4JExample16.class);

    public static void main(String args[]) throws InterruptedException {

        // add standard log statements
        LOG.error("Error message");
        LOG.fatal("Fatal message");
        LOG.warn("Warning message ");
        LOG.info("Information message");

        // This message will not be displayed on the console as it of
        // the type 'DEBUG'
        // But, it will be displayed in the log file as the threshold for the
        // Rolling File Appender is DEBUG
        LOG.debug("Debug message");

        // this message will not be displayed in either the console or the log
        // file as the threshold for both is set to a level higher that trace
        LOG.trace("Trace message");

    }
}
```

The console output is as follows:

```
Console 23    Markers   Properties   Servers   Data Source Explorer   Snippets   Annotations
<terminated> Log4JExample16 [Java Application] C:\Program Files\java\jdk1.8.0_92\bin\javaw.exe
ERROR | 2017-09-12 13:34:25 | [main] Log4JExample16 (Log4JExample16.java:12) - Error message
FATAL | 2017-09-12 13:34:25 | [main] Log4JExample16 (Log4JExample16.java:13) - Fatal message
WARN  | 2017-09-12 13:34:25 | [main] Log4JExample16 (Log4JExample16.java:14) - Warning message
INFO  | 2017-09-12 13:34:25 | [main] Log4JExample16 (Log4JExample16.java:15) - Information message
```

The debug message is not displayed as the console is configured at the threshold INFO.

The file output is as follows:

```
myLogFile.log 23
2017-09-18 13:45:57,170 ERROR Log4JExample16 [main] Error message
2017-09-18 13:45:57,177 FATAL Log4JExample16 [main] Fatal message
2017-09-18 13:45:57,177 WARN Log4JExample16 [main] Warning message
2017-09-18 13:45:57,178 INFO Log4JExample16 [main] Information message
2017-09-18 13:45:57,179 DEBUG Log4JExample16 [main] Debug message
```

The Trace message is not logged as the file appender is configured to have a threshold of level debug.

Example 17: Programmatically configuring logging functionality

The following class shows how to configure log4j using the API:

```java
Log4JExample17.java 23
import org.apache.logging.log4j.Level;
import org.apache.logging.log4j.Logger;
import org.apache.logging.log4j.core.Filter;
import org.apache.logging.log4j.core.LoggerContext;
import org.apache.logging.log4j.core.appender.ConsoleAppender;
import org.apache.logging.log4j.core.config.Configurator;
import org.apache.logging.log4j.core.config.builder.api.AppenderComponentBuilder;
import org.apache.logging.log4j.core.config.builder.api.ConfigurationBuilder;
import org.apache.logging.log4j.core.config.builder.api.ConfigurationBuilderFactory;
import org.apache.logging.log4j.core.config.builder.impl.BuiltConfiguration;

public class Log4JExample17 {

    public static void main(String args[]) throws InterruptedException {

        ConfigurationBuilder<BuiltConfiguration> builder = ConfigurationBuilderFactory.newConfigurationBuilder();

        builder.setStatusLevel(Level.WARN);
        builder.setConfigurationName("MyConfig");

        // add a threshold filter that filters out messages of Level INFO and
        // above
        builder.add(builder.newFilter("ThresholdFilter", Filter.Result.ACCEPT, Filter.Result.NEUTRAL)
            .addAttribute("level", Level.DEBUG));

        // add a new appender using the AppenderComponentBuilder class
        AppenderComponentBuilder appenderComponent = builder.newAppender("Stdout", "CONSOLE").addAttribute("target",
            ConsoleAppender.Target.SYSTEM_OUT);

        // set the Layout for the appender
        appenderComponent.add(
            builder.newLayout("PatternLayout").addAttribute("pattern", "%d [%t] (%c) %-5level: %msg%n%throwable"));

        // add appender to the builder
        builder.add(appenderComponent);

        // add the root logger to builder
        builder.add(builder.newRootLogger(Level.ERROR).add(builder.newAppenderRef("Stdout")));

        // initialize the LoggerContext
        LoggerContext ctx = Configurator.initialize(builder.build());

        // get the logger instance and log messages
        Logger LOG = ctx.getRootLogger();

        // add standard log statements
        LOG.error("Error message");
        LOG.fatal("Fatal message");
        LOG.warn("Warning message");
        LOG.info("Information message");
        LOG.debug("Debug message");

        // this message will not be displayed on the console as we have
        // programmatically set the threshold level to DEBUG
        LOG.trace("Trace message");
    }
}
```

Here, we configure log4j for our application with a console appender that has a threshold filter of level debug.

On executing the above class, the logging is configured and messages are logged to console as follows:

Example 18: Adding Custom Logger programmatically

In this example, we configure our program to add a custom logger using the log4j2 api.

As we can see in the above class, we add the logger 'com. logging. my logger' to the context and then use it to log messages.

The console output generated on executing the above class is as follows:

As no root logger is configured, we get a warning message saying that a default root logger will be created.

Example 19: Multiple Loggers

In this example, we configure multiple loggers programmatically. We create two logger named 'com. logging.my logger' and 'com. logging. Second Logger' and add it to the context and use them to log messages:

```java
☑ Log4JExample19.java ⋈
+ import org.apache.logging.log4j.Level;

public class Log4JExample19 {

    public static void main(String args[]) throws InterruptedException {

        ConfigurationBuilder<BuiltConfiguration> builder = ConfigurationBuilderFactory.newConfigurationBuilder();

        builder.setStatusLevel(Level.WARN);
        builder.setConfigurationName("MyConfig");

        // add a new appender using the AppenderComponentBuilder class
        AppenderComponentBuilder appenderComponent = builder.newAppender("Stdout", "CONSOLE").addAttribute("target",
                ConsoleAppender.Target.SYSTEM_OUT);

        // set the layout for the appender
        appenderComponent.add(
                builder.newLayout("PatternLayout").addAttribute("pattern", "%d [%t] (%c) %-5level: %msg%n%throwable"));

        // add appender to the builder
        builder.add(appenderComponent);

        // add a new custom logger and add the new appender to this logger
        builder.add(builder.newLogger("com.logging.myLogger", Level.DEBUG).add(builder.newAppenderRef("Stdout"))
                .addAttribute("additivity", true));

        // add a another custom logger with level WARN and add the console
        // appender to this logger
        builder.add(builder.newLogger("com.logging.SecondLogger", Level.WARN).add(builder.newAppenderRef("Stdout"))
                .addAttribute("additivity", true));

        // add the root logger to builder
        builder.add(builder.newRootLogger(Level.ERROR).add(builder.newAppenderRef("Stdout")));

        // initialize the LoggerContext
        LoggerContext ctx = Configurator.initialize(builder.build());

        // get the logger instances
        Logger LOG = ctx.getRootLogger();
        Logger myLogger = ctx.getLogger("com.logging.myLogger");
        Logger secondLogger = ctx.getLogger("com.logging.SecondLogger");

        // add standard log statements using the different loggers
        LOG.warn("Warning message ");
        LOG.info("Information message");
        LOG.debug("Debug message");

        myLogger.info("Another Information Message");
        myLogger.error("Another Error Message ");

        secondLogger.warn("A simple Warning Message");
        secondLogger.fatal("A simple Fatal Message");

    }
}
```

The console output is as follows:

```
📺 Console ⋈  🔎 Markers  ☐ Properties  ⛁ Servers  🔲 Data Source Explorer  📄 Snippets  🗀 Annotations
<terminated> Log4JExample19 [Java Application] C:\Program Files\java\jdk1.8.0_92\bin\javaw.exe
2017-09-18 17:25:52,185 [main] (com.logging.myLogger) INFO : Another Information Message
2017-09-18 17:25:52,185 [main] (com.logging.myLogger) INFO : Another Information Message
2017-09-18 17:25:52,200 [main] (com.logging.myLogger) ERROR: Another Error Message
2017-09-18 17:25:52,200 [main] (com.logging.myLogger) ERROR: Another Error Message
2017-09-18 17:25:52,200 [main] (com.logging.SecondLogger) WARN : A simple Warning Message
2017-09-18 17:25:52,200 [main] (com.logging.SecondLogger) WARN : A simple Warning Message
2017-09-18 17:25:52,200 [main] (com.logging.SecondLogger) FATAL: A simple Fatal Message
2017-09-18 17:25:52,200 [main] (com.logging.SecondLogger) FATAL: A simple Fatal Message
```

Example 20: Loading the configuration file programmatically

We now see a simple way to load the configuration file programmatically. Consider the following configuration file located at the location: c:\temp

```
X log4j2.xml ⋈
    <?xml version="1.0" encoding="UTF-8"?>
  - <Configuration status="WARN">
        <Appenders>
            <Console name="consoleAppender" target="SYSTEM_OUT">
                <PatternLayout pattern="%-5p | %d{yyyy-MM-dd HH:mm:ss} | [%t] %C{2} (%F:%L) - %m%n" />
            </Console>
        </Appenders>
        <Loggers>
            <Root level="trace">
                <AppenderRef ref="consoleAppender" />
            </Root>
        </Loggers>
    </Configuration>
```

To load the configuration file from the specified path, we make used of the ConfigurationSource class as shown below:

```
J Log4JExample20.java ⋈
+ import java.io.File;

public class Log4JExample20 {

    public static void main(String args[]) throws InterruptedException, FileNotFoundException, IOException {

        // specify the configuration file location
        // create an object of type ConfigurationSource with the specified
        // InputStream
        ConfigurationSource source = new ConfigurationSource(new FileInputStream(new File("C:\\TEMP\\log4j2.xml")));

        // initialize the logging context using the source
        Configurator.initialize(null, source);

        // get the logger object
        Logger LOG = LogManager.getLogger(Log4JExample20.class);

        // add standard log statements
        LOG.error("Error message");
        LOG.fatal("Fatal message");
        LOG.warn("Warning message ");
        LOG.info("Information message");
        LOG.debug("Debug message");
        LOG.trace("Trace message");

    }

}
```

On execution, the console output is as follows:

```
□ Console ⋈    Marker    Properties    Servers    Data Source Explorer    Snippets    Annotations
<terminated> Log4JExample20 [Java Application] C:\Program Files\java\jdk1.8.0_92\bin\javaw.exe
ERROR | 2017-10-18 18:32:29 | [main] Log4JExample20 (Log4JExample20.java:27) - Error message
FATAL | 2017-10-18 18:32:29 | [main] Log4JExample20 (Log4JExample20.java:28) - Fatal message
WARN  | 2017-10-18 18:32:29 | [main] Log4JExample20 (Log4JExample20.java:29) - Warning message
INFO  | 2017-10-18 18:32:29 | [main] Log4JExample20 (Log4JExample20.java:30) - Information message
DEBUG | 2017-10-18 18:32:29 | [main] Log4JExample20 (Log4JExample20.java:31) - Debug message
TRACE | 2017-10-18 18:32:29 | [main] Log4JExample20 (Log4JExample20.java:32) - Trace message
```

As we can see from the result, the configuration file that was provided by us has been implemented and used by our class.

Example 21: HTML output

In this example, we generated a file output of type HTML. The configuration used is as follows:

```
X log4j2.xml
    <?xml version="1.0" encoding="UTF-8"?>
    <Configuration status="WARN">
        <Appenders>
            <File name="fileAppender" fileName="Log.html">
                <HTMLLayout charset = "UTF-8" title="Log Information" locationInfo="true"></HTMLLayout>
            </File>
        </Appenders>
        <Loggers>
            <Root level="trace">
                <AppenderRef ref="fileAppender" />
            </Root>
        </Loggers>
    </Configuration>
```

The test java class is as shown below:

```
J Log4jExample21.java
    + import org.apache.logging.log4j.LogManager;

    public class Log4jExample21 {

        // get the logger object
        private static final Logger logger = LogManager
        .getLogger(Log4jExample21.class);

        public static void main(String args[]) throws InterruptedException {

            // log standard log messages
            logger.trace("A trace message");
            logger.debug("A debug message");
            logger.error("An error message");
            logger.fatal("A fatal message");

        }

    }
```

On execution, a new file called as log.html is created. The html output generated on execution of the above class is as follows:

Log session start time Tue Sep 19 02:18:54 CEST 2017

Time	Thread	Level	Logger	File:Line	Message
553	main	TRACE	Log4jExample21	Log4jExample21.java:13	A trace message
557	main	DEBUG	Log4jExample21	Log4jExample21.java:14	A debug message
557	main	ERROR	Log4jExample21	Log4jExample21.java:15	An error message
557	main	FATAL	Log4jExample21	Log4jExample21.java:16	A fatal message

Example 22: Rolling File Appender programmatically

In this example, we programmatically configure our application to use a rolling file appender with a rolling policy based on size.

```
Log4JExample22.java
import java.io.FileNotFoundException;
import java.io.IOException;

import org.apache.logging.log4j.Level;
import org.apache.logging.log4j.Logger;
import org.apache.logging.log4j.core.LoggerContext;
import org.apache.logging.log4j.core.config.Configurator;
import org.apache.logging.log4j.core.config.builder.api.AppenderComponentBuilder;
import org.apache.logging.log4j.core.config.builder.api.ComponentBuilder;
import org.apache.logging.log4j.core.config.builder.api.ConfigurationBuilder;
import org.apache.logging.log4j.core.config.builder.api.ConfigurationBuilderFactory;
import org.apache.logging.log4j.core.config.builder.api.LayoutComponentBuilder;
import org.apache.logging.log4j.core.config.builder.impl.BuiltConfiguration;

public class Log4JExample22 {

    public static void main(String args[]) throws InterruptedException, FileNotFoundException, IOException {

        // get a ConfigurationBuilder object
        ConfigurationBuilder<BuiltConfiguration> builder = ConfigurationBuilderFactory.newConfigurationBuilder();

        // set the level and name for the builder object
        builder.setStatusLevel(Level.INFO);
        builder.setConfigurationName("MyRollingFileAppenderConfig");

        // Define a layout component to format the rolling file appender output
        LayoutComponentBuilder layoutBuilder = builder.newLayout("PatternLayout").addAttribute("pattern",
            "%d [%t] %-5level: %msg%n");

        // Define the Rolling Policy for the appender
        // Here we use SizeBasedTriggeringPolicy
        ComponentBuilder triggeringPolicy = builder.newComponent("Policies")
            .addComponent(builder.newComponent("SizeBasedTriggeringPolicy").addAttribute("size", "1KB"));

        // Define the rolling file appender with the triggering policy, pattern
        // and output file details
        AppenderComponentBuilder appenderComponent = builder.newAppender("rolling", "RollingFile")
            .addAttribute("fileName", "myRollingFile.log")
            .addAttribute("filePattern", "rolling-%d{MM-dd-yy}.log.gz").addComponent(layoutBuilder)
            .addComponent(triggeringPolicy);
        builder.add(appenderComponent);

        // add the root logger to builder
        builder.add(builder.newRootLogger(Level.TRACE).add(builder.newAppenderRef("rolling")));

        // initialize the LoggerContext
        LoggerContext ctx = Configurator.initialize(builder.build());
        // get the root logger instance
        Logger LOG = ctx.getRootLogger();

        // add standard log statements using the root logger
        LOG.warn("Warning message ");
        LOG.info("Information message");
        LOG.debug("Debug message");
    }
}
```

On execution, a file named myRollingFile.log is generated, the contents of which are as follows:

```
myRollingLogFile.log
2017-09-19 10:18:42,611 [main] WARN : Warning message
2017-09-19 10:18:42,611 [main] INFO : Information message
2017-09-19 10:18:42,611 [main] DEBUG: Debug message
```

Example 23: JSON layout

In this example, we configure our application to output the logs using the JSON layout for a file appender. In order to configure this layout, we need to add the following jars in the classpath:

-     jackson-core.jar

-     jackson-databind.jar

Once we have added the above jars to our classpath, we configure our project as follows:

```
log4j2.xml
<?xml version="1.0" encoding="UTF-8"?>
<Configuration status = "info">
    <Appenders>
        <File name="fileAppender" fileName="myJSONLogFile.json">
            <JSONLayout />
        </File>
    </Appenders>

    <Loggers>
        <Root level="info">
            <AppenderRef ref="fileAppender" />
        </Root>
    </Loggers>
</Configuration>
```

The test java class is as follows:

```java
🗋 Log4JExample23.java ⊠
+ import org.apache.logging.log4j.LogManager;

public class Log4JExample23 {

    // get the logger object from the LogManager
    private static final Logger LOG = LogManager.getLogger(Log4JExample23.class);

    public static void main(String args[]) throws InterruptedException {

        // add standard log statements
        LOG.error("Error message");
        LOG.fatal("Fatal message");
        LOG.warn("Warning message ");
        LOG.info("Information message");
        LOG.debug("Debug message");

    }
}
```

On execution, the output that we get is as follows:

```json
🗋 myJSONLogFile.json ⊠
{
    "timeMillis" : 1508405427036,
    "thread" : "main",
    "level" : "ERROR",
    "loggerName" : "Log4JExample23",
    "message" : "Error message",
    "endOfBatch" : false,
    "loggerFqcn" : "org.apache.logging.log4j.spi.AbstractLogger",
    "threadId" : 1,
    "threadPriority" : 5
}
{
    "timeMillis" : 1508405427161,
    "thread" : "main",
    "level" : "FATAL",
    "loggerName" : "Log4JExample23",
    "message" : "Fatal message",
    "endOfBatch" : false,
    "loggerFqcn" : "org.apache.logging.log4j.spi.AbstractLogger",
    "threadId" : 1,
    "threadPriority" : 5
}
{
    "timeMillis" : 1508405427161,
    "thread" : "main",
    "level" : "WARN",
    "loggerName" : "Log4JExample23",
    "message" : "Warning message ",
    "endOfBatch" : false,
    "loggerFqcn" : "org.apache.logging.log4j.spi.AbstractLogger",
    "threadId" : 1,
    "threadPriority" : 5
}
{
    "timeMillis" : 1508405427161,
    "thread" : "main",
    "level" : "INFO",
    "loggerName" : "Log4JExample23",
    "message" : "Information message",
    "endOfBatch" : false,
    "loggerFqcn" : "org.apache.logging.log4j.spi.AbstractLogger",
    "threadId" : 1,
    "threadPriority" : 5
}
```

Example 24: CSV Layout

We see how to output our logs in a CSV format in this example. We make use of the CSV layout to generate csv style log output. But, in order to use this format, we need to have the apache-commons.jar on our classpath. Once we download and add it to our classpath, we configure our rolling file appender to output the logs to a csv format by using the spirometer layout element as shown below:

```
X log4j2.xml ☒
    <?xml version="1.0" encoding="UTF-8"?>
    <Configuration status="INFO">
        <Properties>
            <Property name="file-header">column1,column2</Property>
        </Properties>
        <Appenders>
            <RollingFile name="csvFileAppender"
                        fileName="myCSVLogFile.csv"
                        filePattern="myCSVLogFile-%d{MM-dd-yyyy}-%i.csv" >
                <CsvParameterLayout delimiter="," header="${file-header}\n"/>
                <Policies>
                    <TimeBasedTriggeringPolicy interval="1" modulate="true" />
                    <SizeBasedTriggeringPolicy size="1 KB" />
                </Policies>
                <DefaultRolloverStrategy max="10" />
            </RollingFile>
        </Appenders>
        <Loggers>
            <Root level="INFO" additivity="false">
                <AppenderRef ref="csvFileAppender"/>
            </Root>
        </Loggers>
    </Configuration>
```

The test java class is as follows:

```
J Log4JExample24.java ☒
+import org.apache.logging.log4j.LogManager;

public class Log4JExample24 {

    // get the logger object from the LogManager
    private static final Logger LOG = LogManager.getLogger(Log4JExample24.class);

    public static void main(String args[]) throws InterruptedException {

        // add standard log statements in a loop
        for (int i = 0; i < 40; i++) {
            LOG.warn("Warning message", "message 1", +i);
        }

        for (int i = 0; i < 40; i++) {
            LOG.info("Information Message", "message 2", +i);
        }
    }
}
```

On executing the above test class, we can see that 2 files that have a csv format have been created in the project structure as shown below:

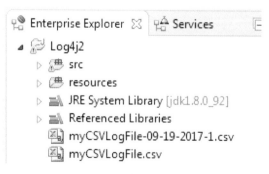

A snippet from the output file is as follows:

	A9

	A
1	column1,column2
2	message 2,35
3	message 2,36
4	message 2,37
5	message 2,38
6	message 2,39

Example 25: Failover Appender

The failover appender is a fail-safe appender. We have the possibility of adding several appenders to the failover appender. If the main appender crashes or fails, the next appender in the list is invoked and if this one fails, the next one is called and so on. This process is repeated until no appender is left in the list. This appender provides backups for the existing appenders.

The configuration for this appender is simple. We write a configuration file in the usual way. Here we have a rolling file appender and a console appender in our configuration. To provide a fail-safe, we use the element <FailOver>. Within this element, we provide the list of all the backup appenders.

In case of our configuration, we provide a single appender in this list.

But in real life applications, this list is longer.

The configuration file is as follows:

```
x log4j2.xml
<?xml version="1.0" encoding="UTF-8"?>
<Configuration status="fatal">
    <Appenders>
        <RollingFile name="rollingFileAppender" fileName="myLogFile.log"
            filePattern="myLogFile-%d{MM-dd-yyyy}.log.gz" ignoreExceptions="false">
            <PatternLayout>
                <Pattern>%-5p | %d{yyyy-MM-dd HH:mm:ss} | [%t] %C{2} (%F:%L) - %m%n</Pattern>
            </PatternLayout>
            <TimeBasedTriggeringPolicy />
        </RollingFile>
        <Console name="consoleAppender" target="SYSTEM_OUT">
            <PatternLayout pattern="%m%n" />
        </Console>
        <Failover name="FailoverAppender" primary="rollingFileAppender">
            <Failovers>
                <AppenderRef ref="consoleAppender" />
            </Failovers>
        </Failover>
    </Appenders>
    <Loggers>
        <Root level="info">
            <AppenderRef ref="FailoverAppender" />
        </Root>
    </Loggers>
</Configuration>
```

The test java class is as follows:

```
J Log4JExample25.java ⊠
  ⊕ import org.apache.logging.log4j.LogManager;

    public class Log4JExample25 {

        // get the logger object from the LogManager
        private static final Logger LOG = LogManager.getLogger(Log4JExample25.class);

        public static void main(String args[]) throws InterruptedException {

            // add standard log statements
            LOG.error("Error message");
            LOG.fatal("Fatal message");
            LOG.warn("Warning message ");
            LOG.info("Information message");
        }
    }
```

A file called as myLogFile.log with the following content is generated on executing the above java class:

```
myLogFile.log ⊠
ERROR | 2017-09-19 18:11:09 | [main] Log4JExample25 (Log4JExample25.java:12) - Error message
FATAL | 2017-09-19 18:11:09 | [main] Log4JExample25 (Log4JExample25.java:13) - Fatal message
WARN  | 2017-09-19 18:11:09 | [main] Log4JExample25 (Log4JExample25.java:14) - Warning message
INFO  | 2017-09-19 18:11:09 | [main] Log4JExample25 (Log4JExample25.java:15) - Information message
```

Example 26: Log4j configuration using VM parameters

Consider the following log4j configuration file.

```
X log4j2.xml ⊠
  <?xml version="1.0" encoding="UTF-8"?>
  <Configuration status="WARN">
      <Appenders>
          <Console name="consoleAppender" target="SYSTEM_OUT">
              <PatternLayout pattern="%d{HH:mm:ss.SSS} [%t] %-5level %logger{56} - %msg%n" />
          </Console>
      </Appenders>
      <Loggers>
          <Root level="debug">
              <AppenderRef ref="consoleAppender" />
          </Root>
      </Loggers>
  </Configuration>
```

It is placed in a location different from the resources folder. In this case, we place it in a temporary folder located in C drive (C:\TEMP) in this case.

We use the following java class to implement the logging functionality:

```
J Log4jExample26.java ⊠
  ⊕ import org.apache.logging.log4j.LogManager;

    public class Log4jExample26 {

        //get the logger
        private static final Logger logger = LogManager.getLogger(Log4jExample26.class);

        public static void main(String args[])
        {
            //log messages
            logger.debug("Debug Message");
            logger.error("Error Message");
            logger.info("Info Message");
            logger.warn("Warning Message");

        }
    }
```

To specify the location of the configuration file we provide its location in the vm arguments as follows:

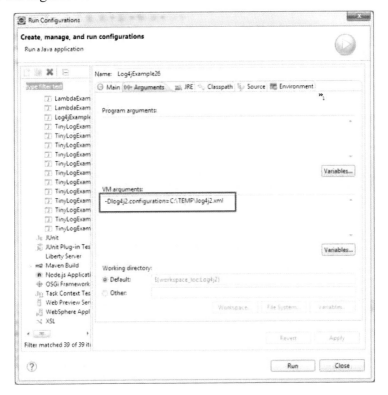

On execution, the output is as follows:

Example 27: Parameterized Logging

In this example, we demonstrate the use of parameterized logging using log4j.

Consider the following configuration file:

```xml
log4j2.xml
<?xml version="1.0" encoding="UTF-8"?>
<Configuration status="WARN">
    <Appenders>
        <Console name="consoleAppender" target="SYSTEM_OUT">
            <PatternLayout pattern="%d{HH:mm:ss} [%t] %-5level %logger{50} - %msg%n" />
        </Console>
    </Appenders>
    <Loggers>
        <Root level="debug">
            <AppenderRef ref="consoleAppender" />
        </Root>
    </Loggers>
</Configuration>
```

Consider the following Java class:

```
Log4jExample27.java
import org.apache.logging.log4j.LogManager;
import org.apache.logging.log4j.Logger;

public class Log4jExample27 {

    // get the logger
    private static final Logger logger = LogManager.getLogger(Log4jExample27.class);

    public static void main(String args[]) {
        // log messages
        logger.debug("Debug Message");
        logger.error("Error Message");
        logger.info("Info Message");
        logger.warn("Warning Message");

        // log parameterized messages
        logger.debug("Message is {}", getMessage());
        logger.warn("Warning! There are less than {} left on the system!", getStorageData());
        logger.error("The following error : '{}' was reported on the application.", getErrorMessage());
    }

    private static String getErrorMessage() {
        return "The configuration file was not found";
    }

    private static int getStorageData() {
        return 5;
    }

    private static String getMessage() {
        return "The application is stable.";
    }
}
```

In the above class, we make use of parametrized log messages that invoke static methods at runtime and replace the placeholders {} with the value returned from the static method.

The output generated on execution of the above class is as follows:

```
Console    Problems    Javadoc    Declaration    Annotations    Call Hierarchy

<terminated> Log4jExample27 [Java Application] C:\Program Files (x86)\Java\
18:33:00 [main] DEBUG Log4jExample27 - Debug Message
18:33:00 [main] ERROR Log4jExample27 - Error Message
18:33:00 [main] INFO  Log4jExample27 - Info Message
18:33:00 [main] WARN  Log4jExample27 - Warning Message
18:33:00 [main] DEBUG Log4jExample27 - Message is The application is stable.
18:33:00 [main] WARN  Log4jExample27 - Warning! There are less than 5 left on the system!
18:33:00 [main] ERROR Log4jExample27 - The following error : 'The configuration file was not found' was reported on the application.
```

Example 28: Logging using Lambda Expressions

In this example, we make use of lambda expressions to log messages.

This is shown by the java class below:

```
Log4jExample28.java
+ import org.apache.logging.log4j.LogManager;

public class Log4jExample28 {

    // get the logger
    private static final Logger logger = LogManager.getLogger(Log4jExample28.class);

    public static void main(String args[]) {

        // log messages
        logger.error("Error Message");
        logger.info("Info Message");
        logger.warn("Warning Message");

        // log parameterized messages
        logger.debug("The Debug Message is {}", () -> getMessage());
        logger.warn("Warning! There are less than {} left on the system!", () -> getStorageData());
        logger.error("The following error : '{}' was reported on the application.", () -> getErrorMessage());
    }

    // provide static methods invoked by the logger
    private static String getErrorMessage() {
        return "The configuration file was not found";
    }

    private static String getMessage() {
        return "The application is stable.";
    }

    private static int getStorageData() {
        return 6;
    }
}
```

The above class is similar to the previous example, but here we use lambda expressions in our log statements.

We make use of a simple console appender as shown below:

```xml
x| log4j2.xml

<?xml version="1.0" encoding="UTF-8"?>
<Configuration status="WARN">
    <Appenders>
        <Console name="consoleAppender" target="SYSTEM_OUT">
            <PatternLayout pattern="%d{HH:mm:ss} [%t] %-5level %logger{50} - %msg%n" />
        </Console>
    </Appenders>
    <Loggers>
        <Root level="debug">
            <AppenderRef ref="consoleAppender" />
        </Root>
    </Loggers>
</Configuration>
```

On execution of the java class, the following output is generated:

```
Console     Problems   Javadoc   Declaration   Annotation   Call Hierarchy
<terminated> Log4jExample28 [Java Application] C:\Program Files (x86)\java\
18:46:28 [main] ERROR Log4jExample28 - Error Message
18:46:28 [main] INFO  Log4jExample28 - Info Message
18:46:28 [main] WARN  Log4jExample28 - Warning Message
18:46:28 [main] DEBUG Log4jExample28 - The Debug Message is The application is stable.
18:46:28 [main] WARN  Log4jExample28 - Warning! There are less than 6 left on the system!
18:46:28 [main] ERROR Log4jExample28 - The following error : 'The configuration file was not found' was reported on the application.
```

Example 29: Lambda Expressions with Interfaces

In this example, we implement lambda expressions combined with the use of interfaces to perform logging.

First, we create two interfaces in the same package as follows:

```java
J Interface1.java

public interface Interface1 {

    public String infoMessage();
}
```

```java
J Interface2.java

public interface Interface2 {

    public String warningMessage();
}
```

Consider the following configuration file:

```
X log4j2.xml
    <?xml version="1.0" encoding="UTF-8"?>
  <Configuration status="WARN">
      <Appenders>
          <Console name="consoleAppender" target="SYSTEM_OUT">
              <PatternLayout pattern="%d{HH:mm:ss} [%t] %-5level %logger{50} - %msg%n" />
          </Console>
      </Appenders>
      <Loggers>
          <Root level="debug">
              <AppenderRef ref="consoleAppender" />
          </Root>
      </Loggers>
  </Configuration>
```

This file is present in the resources folder as shown below:

We implement a simple console appender that log to the console as shown above.

The Java class used to implement the logging functionality is as follows:

```java
J Log4jExample29.java
    import org.apache.logging.log4j.LogManager;
    import org.apache.logging.log4j.Logger;

    public class Log4jExample29 {

        // get the logger
        private static final Logger logger = LogManager.getLogger(Log4jExample29.class);

        public static void main(String args[]) {

            // log messages
            logger.error("Error Message");
            logger.info("Info Message");
            logger.warn("Warning Message");

            // Provide functional implementation of the interface method
            // infoMessage()
            Interface1 int1 = () -> {
                return "The Application is stable.";
            };
            // Provide functional implementation of the interface method
            // warningMessage()
            Interface2 int2 = () -> {
                return "Warning!! Some files are missing!";
            };

            // Provide another functional implementation of the interface method
            // warningMessage()
            Interface2 int3 = () -> {
                return "Warning: Configfuration not complete";
            };

            // log messages
            logger.warn("Warning Message:", int2.warningMessage());
            logger.warn("Second Warning Message:", int3.warningMessage());
            logger.info("Information Message:" + int1.infoMessage());
            logger.error("Error: '{}' was reported.", () -> getErrorMessage());
        }

        // provide static methods invoked by the logger
        private static String getErrorMessage() {
            return "WAR file missing";
        }
    }
```

The output generated on execution of the above java class is as follows:

```
Console 🛇  Problems  Javadoc  Declaration  Annotations  Call Hierarchy
<terminated> Log4jExample29 [Java Application] C:\Program Files (x86)\java
19:09:37 [main] ERROR Log4jExample29 - Error Message
19:09:37 [main] INFO  Log4jExample29 - Info Message
19:09:37 [main] WARN  Log4jExample29 - Warning Message
19:09:37 [main] WARN  Log4jExample29 - Warning Message:
19:09:37 [main] WARN  Log4jExample29 - Second Warning Message:
19:09:37 [main] INFO  Log4jExample29 - Information Message:The Application is stable.
19:09:37 [main] ERROR Log4jExample29 - Error: 'WAR file missing' was reported.
```

Example 30: Lambda Expressions with Interfaces and Parameters

In this example, we go one step further and implement lambda expressions that take in parameters.

We define two interfaces: Interface3 that takes in an int parameter and Interface4 that takes in a String parameter. This is shown below:

```
J Interface3.java 🛇

public interface Interface3 {

    public int warningMessage(int count);
}
```

```
J Interface4.java 🛇

public interface Interface4 {

    public String errorMessage(String message);
}
```

We use the following log4j2 configuration:

```
x log4j2.xml 🛇

<?xml version="1.0" encoding="UTF-8"?>
<Configuration status="WARN">
    <Appenders>
        <Console name="consoleAppender" target="SYSTEM_OUT">
            <PatternLayout pattern="%d{HH:mm:ss} [%t] %-5level %logger{50} - %msg%n" />
        </Console>
    </Appenders>
    <Loggers>
        <Root level="debug">
            <AppenderRef ref="consoleAppender" />
        </Root>
    </Loggers>
</Configuration>
```

We then proceed to implement the logging functionality using parameterized lambda expressions using the following java class:

```java
Log4jExample30.java ⬚

import org.apache.logging.log4j.LogManager;
import org.apache.logging.log4j.Logger;

public class Log4jExample30 {

    // get the logger
    private static final Logger logger = LogManager.getLogger(Log4jExample30.class);

    public static void main(String args[]) {

        // log messages
        logger.error("Error Message");
        logger.info("Info Message");
        logger.warn("Warning Message");

        // Provide functional implementation of the interface method
        // warningMessage(count)
        Interface3 int3 = (count) -> count + 1;
        // Provide functional implementation of the interface method
        // errorMessage(message)
        Interface4 int4 = (message) -> message + "Parameter Missing";

        // log messages with parameters
        logger.warn("Warning Message: Count of files is: " + int3.warningMessage(4));
        logger.error("Error Message:" + int4.errorMessage("Attention!"));
    }

}
```

On executing the above class, we get the following output:

```
Console ⬚   Problems  Javadoc  Declaration  Annotations  Call Hierarchy
<terminated> Log4jExample30 [Java Application] C:\Program Files (x86)\java
19:40:44 [main] ERROR Log4jExample30 - Error Message
19:40:44 [main] INFO  Log4jExample30 - Info Message
19:40:44 [main] WARN  Log4jExample30 - Warning Message
19:40:44 [main] WARN  Log4jExample30 - Warning Message: Count of files is: 5
19:40:44 [main] ERROR Log4jExample30 - Error Message:Attention! Parameter Missing
```

CHAPTER
4

LOGBACK

CONTENTS

4.1. INTRODUCTION

Log back is logging framework that was released in 2006. Designed by Ceki Gülcü, the creator of log4j, this framework was preconceived as a successor to log4j (Logback Home, 2017).

Log back is based upon experience gained from the study and design of logging systems in the industry. Log back is faster and has a smaller footprint as compared to the other logging systems.

Log back provides an array of features big and small that make it an easy logging system to understand and use. It is very similar in concept to log4j but has several improvements. The latest version of log ack is 1.2.3.

Some of the features of Log back are as follows:

Log back is faster as compared to log4j as the internal source code has been written to perform operations faster. The executions of certain paths that are critical have been made faster by the rewriting of the code. The Log back components are faster and occupy less memory as well. In other words, its memory footprint is small (Log back Home, 2017).

Log back is a framework that comes with a long list of tests that ensure the strength, durability, and dependability of this framework even under stress conditions.

Log back provides detailed documentation which is updated regularly. Additionally, it has a large community support which makes it easy for users to use and implement this framework.

Logback is compatible with SL4j. Logback implementation is built upon sl4j api natively and hence an sl4j logger can be used easily with logback being the underlying logging framework used for logging. As logback integrates seamlessly with SL4J, it is easy to switch between logging frameworks without having to change your code. SL4J is discussed in detail in Chapter 5.

Logback framework supports either XML or Groovy file types for the configuration file. The groovy file types us widely used by developers as its syntax is shorter, consistent and easy to understand and configure.

Additionally, logback provides an automatic tool that helps migrate configuration files written in XML to the Groovy format. The groovy style configuration has been made available since logback version 0.9.22.

The Logback framework provides automated reload of the configuration files. Once a change has been made to the file, it is reloaded on its own. It uses a scanning process to scan the configuration files. This mechanism is extremely rapid, dynamic and scalable in terms of a large amount of parallelly executing threads and is free of contention. Additionally, it doesn't make use of another separate thread for the purpose of scanning which saves memory.

Logback has a strong failure recovery system in terms of I/O. The File Appender and all its subclasses have the capability of handling I/O failures without additional overhead. In case a file server stops working for some time, a reboot of the system is no longer needed in order to have continued logging. Once the server starts functioning, the appender will recover from the error quickly and continue its work.

Another interesting feature provided by the logback framework is that now provides API to handle the removal/deletion of archived log records automatically. A property called <<max History>> for rolling appenders is provided which stands for the maximum number of archived log records that can be kept. For example, if we set a monthly rolling policy and wish to delete logs that are older than a year, this property can be set to 12. This will automatically delete log records that are older than 12 months. This property is explained with the use of in Section 4.6

Logback also has the capability of being able to compress log files that are archived at the time of a file rollover in the rolling file appender. This event is an asynchronous event and hence is a non-blocking event and doesn't put your application on hold during the time it compresses the files.

The logback framework supports the writing of a single file by several File Appenders that run on multiple JVM machines. This is done via the prudent mode.

Logback supports Lilith which is a logging and access event viewer for logback. It is capable of handling large amounts of log records.

Another attractive feature provided by logback is that it provides us the possibility to execute only parts of the configuration based on certain conditions. For example, in a software development life cycle, the developers make use of different environments such as development, testing, pre-production, and production. Although these files have many properties in common, we generally have to create separate configuration files for each environment. But this is not the case with logback. Logback prevents duplication of code by supporting conditional operators such as

<if>, <then> and else. These elements reduce redundancy and allow the use of a single configuration file for several development environments.

Logback has an advanced Filtering mechanism as compared to other logging frameworks. It allows filtering on a user basis. Imagine an application that has been deployed on a server. To avoid a large volume of log records the logging level is set to either 'WARN' or 'ERROR.' But, if an issue arises someday that is visible only in the production environment or if the server is at a remote location, we need to set the level to DEBUG to analyze the issue which will generate a large quantity of logs.

But, in logback, all this can be avoided by means of user level filtering. Logback gives us an option of maintaining the original log level for all users except for a particular user (the user who is analyzing the issue) who can see the logs at a more detailed level than everyone else. So, when this particular user logs in, he/she will be generating logs at a debug level and all the other at the ERROR or WARN level. This can be done with the help of an MDC Filter which is not discussed in the scope of this book.

Logback comes with an excellent appender namely the sifting appender. This appender can be used to filter/sift the log information based on any attribute at runtime. For instance, this appender can separate logs based on user login/session and generate log files per user. This can be done with environment and many other runtime parameters which makes logback very powerful.

Another useful feature of logback is that when an exception occurs, not only is the stack trace printed in the logs, but also the packaging data is printed along with it.

This means that logback will print the packages used by the application such as hibernate, spring, etc. This lets the user know which class generated the exception and also which package and which version of this package the class uses. For instance, if you are using spring boot version 3.2.2 this information will be present in the stack trace. So, the work of a developer is made incredibly easier as now he doesn't need to go back to the customer for additional information.

The logback family provides us with another smart module called as the logback-access. This module is part of the logback package and it integrates containers for servlets such as Tomcat, Jetty thereby providing http-access with logging functionalities. This module is yet another powerful feature of logback and it has all of the components of the logback classic module.

4. 2. LOG BACK'S ARCHITECTURE

The architecture of Logback is similar to that of Log4j. It is made up of three modules:

    a.   logback-core

The core module is the base module for the logback-classic and logback-access module. This module consists of the basic api and components that are used by the other two modules.

    b.   logback-classic

This module extends the core module. It is a subclass of the logback-core module and internally it implements SL4J. SL4J API implemented by this module enables switching between various logging frameworks

    c.   logback-access

This module extends the core module as well. It implements sl4j as well. It provides logging in an HTTP environment. It integrates Servlet containers that help provide HTTP access logging functionality (Gülcü & Pennec, 2011).

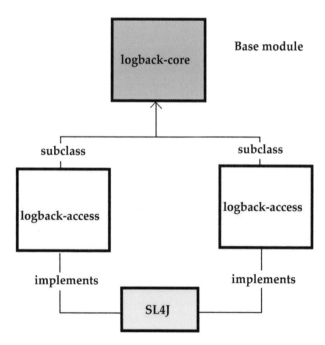

The working of logback is as follows:

Initially, the Java application calls the logging API. The control is then passed on to the SLF4J API which then passes the control it on to the logback-core and logback-classic modules to compete the logging process. As SLF4J is implemented by logback internally, any logging framework can be plugged in at runtime which offers logback an edge over other logging frameworks.

The high-level control flow is as follows:

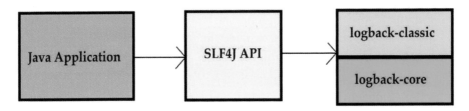

4.3. COMPONENTS OF LOGBACK

Similar to log4j and java util logging, the main components of logback are as follows:

1.   Logger
2.   Appender
3.   Level
4.   Layout

We shall take a look at these components in detail now.

1.   Loggers

As described earlier, a logger is one of the core components of a logging framework. They store and capture the logging data. Logback has a Logger class that performs this functionality. This class is present in the logback-classic module. Similar to log4j, loggers in logback are named entities. They follow the same named hierarchy rule as that described for the log4j framework (Gülcü and Pennec, 2011). Each logger has a Logger Context that provides the loggers and arranges them as per the naming hierarchy. The root logger is located at the top part of the tree.

2.   Appenders

This component helps publish the logging messages to the desired destination. In logback, an Appender class performs this functionality. The appender class is part of the logback-care module.

The logger delegates the work of printing the log information to the appender. The logger does it by invoking the doAppend() method on a log event. This method publishes the logs to the requested destination.

The working of the Appender is as shown below:

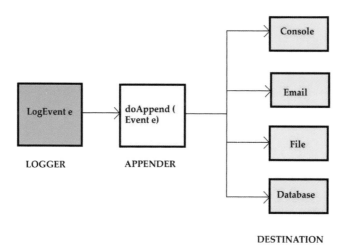

Appenders are present in the logback-core and logback-classic modules. The logback core module provides an Output Stream Appender which serves as the base class for other appenders such Console and File. The logback-classic module provides network appenders such as Socket Appender, SMTP Appender, SSL Socket Appender, etc.

The Output Stream Appender basically writes events to the output stream and provides the basic api which is used by the appenders that subclass this class. This class is subclassed by the Console Appender and the File Appender. The Rolling File Appender class inherits from the File Appender class (Logback-Parent 1.2.3 API, 2017).

The class hierarchy for this appender is as follows:(Figure 4.1)

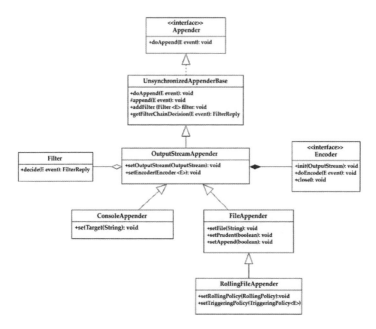

Figure 4.1: OutputStream Appender (Gülcü and Pennec, 2011).

Let us take a brief look at the Console, File and Rolling File Appenders.

1. Console Appender: This is one of the most common appenders which is used to print/display the log messages on the console. They output the log information on to system. out or system.err.

2. File Appender: This appender is also a well-known appender which is used to write logging information to files. Various ways to name, format and control the way one logs to a file are provided by logback.

3. Rolling File Appender: This appender is a subclass of the File Appender class that has the added functionality of rolling over files. This appender has 2 sub-components namely Rolling Policy and Triggering Policy. The rolling policy decides the way in which the file will be rolled over such as the name pattern, size etc. The triggering policy defines when exactly the rollover will take place such as daily, weekly, etc. This appender must implement both policies. But, some rolling policies also implement the triggering policy internally then the triggering policy component doesn't need to be specified. Some of the rolling and triggering policies are as follows:

a.   Time-Based Rolling Policy: This policy defines the rollover of log files based on time and internally implements the Time Based Triggering Policy as well. In addition to several filename patterns, this policy has the capability to perform compression of files as well.

b.   Fixes Window Based Rolling Policy: This policy rolls over files based on a fixed window size that takes in the maximum and minimum window size. This means that if the maximum value if a window is 10, the file will be rolled over 10 times and once this limit is reached, the oldest files will be deleted one by one. This policy doesn't implement a triggering policy, but it is generally used with a SizeBasedTriggeringPolicy which is discussed next.

c.   Size Based Triggering Policy: This policy triggers file rollover based on the size of the file.

d.   Size and Time-Based Rolling Policy: This policy provides the functionality of rolling over files on the basis of size and time. This policy internally implements a Triggering Policy.

A few file name patterns along with their descriptions are provided below:

File Name Pattern	Rollover Schedule	Example
/logFile.%d.log	Daily	No timestamp added logFile.2017-08-10.log
/logFile.%d{yyyy-MM}.log	Monthly	logFile.2017-08.log
/logFile.%d{ yyyy-MM-dd_HH }.log	Hourly	logFile.2017-08-10_8.log
/logFile.%d{ yyyy-MM-dd_HH-mm}.log	Minute	logFile.2017-08-10_09-12.log
/logFile.%d{ yyyy-ww }.zip	Weekly	logFile.2017-08.zip

Now we proceed to see the appenders provided by the logback-classic module.

1.   Async Appender: This appender is used to perform logging in an asynchronous manner. A blocking queue is used to pool/save the logging events. This increased the time of processing. By default, if the queue is filled up to 80%, this appender drops the logs of level trace, info and debug.

2.   Socket Appender: This appender is used to log events to a remote location by means of a serialized access event.

3. SSL Socket Appender: This appender is an subclass of the Socket Appender which permits logging over a Secure Socket Layer (SSL) connection

4. SSL Server Socket Appender: This appender is exactly like the Socket Appender except that in this appender, the appender acts like a real server and listens on a socket (TCP) and waits for open connections.

5. SMTP Appender: This appender places/holds the logging events in a buffer and then sends the log information in an email after the occurrence of the events. This sending occurs asynchronously. This appender can also be configured to send emails to your Gmail account.

6. Sifting Appender: This appender is used to separate or sift logging events on the basis of certain properties (Gülcü and Pennec, 2011). A simple example is the separation of log files on the basis of user sessions. This appender can be employed to check the user id and then based on the id, a log file is generated on a per-user basis. Another example is to generate different files based on the current thread. This may be useful in case of large multithreaded applications that generate large volumes of logs. Separation on the basis of the thread name is an efficient way to simplify the monitoring process.

7. DB Appender: This appender is used to insert logging events into a database table. This appender enables to store log data in a manner that is independent of the Java language.

3. Levels

As we have already seen in the previous chapters, loggers and appenders can be assigned levels based on their priorities. Logback supports the following levels (in increasing order of importance): TRACE, DEBUG, INFO, WARN and ERROR. Logback has a class called as Level (a final class) that handles levels. In logback, the Level class is present is in the logback classic module.

If no level is specified for a logger, it inherits the Level of the first logger in the hierarchy that has a Level that is not null. If the value for the level for all the loggers up in the hierarchy is null, then the logger inherits the log level from the root logger. The default log level of the root logger is debug.

4.   Layouts

In logback layouts are akin to formatter in log4j and java util logging. They are the components that are used to convert an incoming logging event/ message into a representable string format. The core base layout component is present in the logback-core module. But, the specific layout classes such as Pattern Layout etc. are present in the logback-classic package and they inherit from the base layout component. Several possible layout classes are provided by logback. A layout is applied to an event by calling the doLayout() method on a logging event.

The working of a layout is as follows:

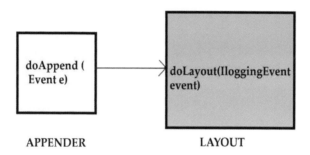

APPENDER   LAYOUT

The above-mentioned components work collectively to enable logging of messages based on their level, type, and their respective destinations.

5. Filters

Filters are used to filter out log messages. They decide which log messages to pass on to the appender or the logger in itself. The filters are present in the logback-classic module but the base class is present in the core module. Logback has two different types of filters based on ternary logic:

a.   Regular Filters

These filters are the standard filters provided by logback. All the filters in logback are subclassed from the base class named **Filter** consisting of a decide() method that decides whether the log message will be accepted or rejected. They are based on ternary logic and are stored in an ordered list. Based on the result received from the decide() method, the filter accepts or rejects the log message.

The working of a filter is described in the following figure:

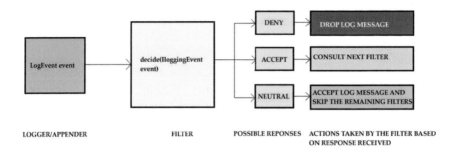

The filter has a decide() method that accepts a parameter of type I Logging

Event. This method returns 3 possible enumeration values: ACCEPT, DENY or NEUTRAL. If the response is ACCEPT, the log message is accepted. If the message is DENY, the log message is rejected and none of the remaining filters are consulted. If the message is NEUTRAL, then the control is passed on to the next filter and its response is checked and so on. If the list of filters is exhausted and has reached its end, the logging event is handled normally.

Some of the available filters in logback are as follows:

- Threshold Filter: This filter filters log events below a specified threshold level. All events of this particular threshold level and above this level.

- Level Filter: This filter filters log events based on exact matching of Levels.

- Evaluator Filter: This is an abstract filter class that has an event evaluator. The event evaluator evaluates a given criteria and checks if it is met or not. Based on the result (match/ mismatch) it returns the value specified by on Match/on Mismatch property.

- Counting Filter: This filter is used to obtain statistical data about the access of a remote web server by your application. Details such as average time spent daily, weekly, monthly, yearly and so on.

- Duplicate Message Filter: This filter separates duplicate log messages. It detects duplicate log messages and if they are repeated more than a fixed number of times, the log messages are discarded.

- GE Event Evaluator Filter: This is a concrete class and it takes Boolean expressions written in Groovy language as the criteria for evaluation.

- Janino Event Evaluator Filter: This is a concrete class filter and it takes a Java language block that returns a Boolean value as the criteria for evaluation.

b.   Turbo Filters

Turbo Filters are slightly different from the regular filters. All the objects from this filter inherit from the TurboFilter class which is an abstract base class. Turbo Filters work in a manner similar to regular filters and also use ternary logic to perform evaluation of the criteria.

They differ from the regular filters in terms of context. In addition to being called when invoked by an appender or a logger, these filters are called each time a logging event is initiated which gives them a wider scope than the regular filters. Another major difference between the regular and the turbo filters is that these objects do not need the creation or instantiation of a logging event to perform filtering. Hence, these filters are generally used for fast, speedy filtering of logs before the logging events have been created (Gülcü and Pennec, 2011).

6.   Encoders

Encoders were introduced in the version 0.9.19 of logback. Encoders are used to change or format the log event into a byte array format. With the use of an encoder, once the log information is converted into a byte array, it can be further written to an output stream.

Previous to the introduction of encoders appenders would use layouts to format the log information. But starting from this version, the File Appender and all its subclasses use an encoder instead of a layout. This change was introduced as encoders have better control over the formatting of the logging events which makes them quite useful. The encoder functionality is provided by the Encoder interface in logback whose base class is present in the logback core and its implementations are present in logback-classic module.

Appenders are configured to use an encoder just as they are configured to use layouts and filters. The Encoder Interface has a doEncode() method which is called each time the appender is called.

Logback had the following two encoders:

- Layout Wrapping Encoder: This encoder is basically an adapter to connect the encoders and layouts so that they can work together. This class implements the Encoder interface and additionally wraps a layout which converts the input event into a string format.

- Pattern Layout Encoder: This is an implementation of the Layout Wrapping Encoder for the layout Pattern Layout which is one of the most frequently used layouts. It wrap instances of the Pattern Layout class (Logback-Parent 1.2.3 API,2017)

Now that we have the basic components of logback, we shall proceed to take a closer look at a few of the important API provided by the logback packages.

4.4. LOGBACK API

Logger Class: Present in logback classic package.

Table 4.1: Logger class methods (Logback-Parent 1.2.3. API, 2017)

Method	Description
void addAppender(Appender<ILoggingE vent appender)	This method adds an appender to the logger.
void detach Appender(Apender<ILoggingEvent appender)	This method detaches the appender provided as a parameter from the list of appenders of the logger.
void call Appenders(ILoggingEvent event)	This method invokes all the declared appenders of this logger.
void detachAppender(String name)	This method detaches the appender with the given name parameter from the logger.
void detachAndStopAllAppenders()	This method detaches all appenders for the logger.
Appender<IloggingEvent> getAppender(String name)	This method returns the appender with the given name.
void debug(String message)	This method logs a message of level debug.
void error(String message)	This method logs a message of level error.
void info(String message)	This method logs a message of level info.
void warn(String message)	This method logs a message of level warning.
void trace(String message)	This method logs a message of level trace.
void debug(String message, Throwable t)	This method logs a message of level debug and prints stack trace of the throwable argument t.
void info(String message, Throwable t)	This method logs a message of level info and prints stack trace of the throwable argument t.

void warn(String message, Throwable t)	This method logs a message of level warn and prints stack trace of the throwable argument t.
void error(String message, Throwable t)	This method logs a message of level error and prints stack trace of the throwable argument t.
void trace(String message, Throwable t)	This method logs a message of level trace and prints stack trace of the throwable argument t.
Level getLevel()	This method returns the effective logger level.
void setLevel(Level level)	This method sets the logger level to the level specified as the parameter.
Logger Context get Logger Context ()	This method returns the logger context of the logger.

Appender

1. Appender Interface

This interface provides abstract methods that are implemented by all the appender classes in the logback package.

Table 4.2: Appender Interface methods (Logback-Parent 1.2.3 API, 2017)

Method	Description
void doAppend(E event)	This abstract method performs the task of the appender of writing logs to the specified destination.
String getName()	This method is returns the name of the appender.
void setName(String name)	This method sets the name of the appender.

2. Appender Base class

This class implements the Appender Interface and provides a skeleton for the appender classes provided by the logback package. Appender Base class provides synchronization for all its derived appender classes. Appender Base provides a skeleton for all the Appender classes that require synchronization such as the Abstract Socket Server Appender, Syslog Appender Base and so on.

Table 4.3: Appender Base class methods (Logback-Parent 1.2.3 API, 2017)

Method	Description
void do Append ()	This method writes the log message to the specified destination.

void add Filter(Filter<E> filter)	This method adds the specified filter to the appender.
String get Name ()	This method returns the name of the appender.
abstract void append (E event)	This is an abstract method which can be overridden by its subclasses to provide class-specific behavior.
void clear All Filters ()	This method clears all the filters declared for the appender.

3. Unsynchronized Appender Base class

This class is similar to the Appender Base class. It differs from the Appender Base class in terms of synchronization. Any class that is derived from the Unsynchronized Appender Base class needs to handle synchronization on its own.

Some of the important methods provided by this class are as follows:

Table 4.4: Unsynchronized Appender Base class methods (Logback-Parent 1.2.3 API, 2017)

Method	Description
void append()	This method writes the log message to the specified destination.
void addFilter(Filter<E> filter)	This method adds the specified filter to the appender.
String getName()	This method returns the name of the appender.
abstract void append(E event)	This is an abstract method which can be overridden by its subclasses to provide class-specific behavior.
void clearAllFilters()	This method clears all the filters declared for the appender.
List<Filter<E>> getCopyOfAttached-FiltersList()	The method returns a copy of all the filters held within the specified object.
FilterReply getFilterChainDecision(E event)	This method loops/iterates over all the filters present in the current filter chain.

4. Layout

The layout interface, present in the logback-core package consists of methods that are implemented by all the concrete layout classes in the logback package.

Some of the important methods of this class are as follows:

Table 4.5: Layout interface methods (Logback-Parent 1.2.3 API, 2017)

Method	Description
String doLayout(E event)	This method takes an event as an input and converts/formats it into a representable string format.
String getContentType()	This method returns the content type of the logging information
String getFileFooter()	This method returns the footer of the file for the current layout.
String getFileHeader()	This method returns the header of the file for the current layout.
String getPresentationFooter()	This method returns the footer of the formatted logging event.
String getPresentationHeader()	This method returns the header of the formatted logging event.

5. Layout Base class

This class implements the Layout interface and provides a skeleton for the derived Layout classes such Pattern Layout, HTML Layout, etc. In addition to implementing all the methods of the Layout interface, it provides the following useful methods:

Table 4.6: Layout Base class methods (Logback-Parent 1.2.3 API, 2017)

Method	Description
void set File Footer (String footer)	This method sets the file footer for the current layout.
void set File Header (String header)	This method sets the file footer for the current layout.
void set Presentation Footer (String footer)	This method sets the footer for the current logging event.

void set Presentation Header (String header)	This method sets the header for the current logging event.

6. Encoders

The encoder interface provides methods that are implemented by the all the derived encoder classes such as Pattern Layout Encoder and Layout Wrapping Encoder.

Table 4.7: Encoder interface methods (Logback-Parent 1.2.3 API, 2017)

Method	Description
byte [] encode (E event)	This method encodes the logging events in a byte array.
Byte [] footer Bytes ()	This method returns the bytes held by the footer of the encoded event.
Byte [] header Bytes ()	This method returns the bytes held by the header of the encoded event.

4.5. CONFIGURATION

Logback is distributed under a dual license under the LPGL and EPL.

Similar to log4j and java util logging, the configuration in logback is done with a configuration file. This file is named as logback-test.xml or logback.xml.

But, if a file is not provided it looks for the following three files in order.

– logback-test.xml
– logback. groovy
- logback.xml

If no file is found, it still lets you add logging to your application. It defaults to the Basic Configurator configuration. This configuration logs to the console.

In order to use logback in your eclipse project, slf4j, the logback-core and logback-classic packages (jar files) must be present on the classpath of your project. The logback-core and logback-classic jar can be downloaded at the following location:

https://logback.qos.ch/download.html

Download the zip file and extract the contents of the file. To download the sjf4j file, it needs to be downloaded from another location as follows:

https://www.slf4j.org/download.html

We now add these files to our java project.

These can be added to your project as follows:

In your project right click and click on configure build path. The following window is displayed:

Click on "Add External JARs." Select the path containing the jars and click on Ok.

We shall now see a simple example demonstrating the use of logback without the configuration file.

Once we add the jar files, we create the following Java class:

```java
LogbackExample.java ⋈

package com.java.logback.examples;

//import the slf4j Logger and LoggrFactory
import org.slf4j.Logger;

public class LogbackExample {

    public static void main(String[] args) {

        //get logger object
        Logger logger = LoggerFactory.getLogger(LogbackExample.class);

        //log messages
        logger.info("An Information Message");
        logger.debug("A Debug Message");
        logger.warn("A Warning Message");

    }
}
```

The output generated is as follows:

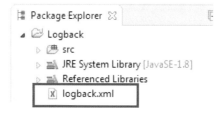

```
Console 🖵    Problems  Javadoc  Declaration  Annotations
<terminated> MyApp2 [Java Application] C:\Program Files\java\jdk1.8.0_92\bin\javaw.exe
18:12:49,651 |-INFO in ch.qos.logback.classic.LoggerContext[default] - Could NOT find resource [logback-test.xml]
18:12:49,651 |-INFO in ch.qos.logback.classic.LoggerContext[default] - Could NOT find resource [logback.groovy]
18:12:49,651 |-INFO in ch.qos.logback.classic.LoggerContext[default] - Could NOT find resource [logback.xml]
18:12:49,651 |-INFO in ch.qos.logback.classic.BasicConfigurator@c4437c4 - Setting up default configuration.

18:12:49,651 [main] INFO com.java.logback.examples.LogbackExample - An Information Message
18:12:49,651 [main] DEBUG com.java.logback.examples.LogbackExample - A Debug Message
18:12:49,651 [main] WARN com.java.logback.examples.LogbackExample - A Warning Message
```

The configuration with a logback.xml file is as follows:

```
🖿 Package Explorer 🖾                    ⬚

   ▲ 🗁 Logback
        ▷ 🏛 src
        ▷ ⚌ JRE System Library [JavaSE-1.8]
        ▷ ⚌ Referenced Libraries
          x logback.xml
```

The contents of this configuration file are as follows:

```xml
x logback.xml 🖾
    <?xml version="1.0" encoding="UTF-8"?>
    <configuration>
        <appender name="consoleAppender" class="ch.qos.logback.core.ConsoleAppender">
            <encoder>
                <pattern>%d{yyyy-MM-dd HH:mm:ss} [%thread] %-5level %logger{36} - %msg%n</pattern>
            </encoder>
        </appender>
        <root level="trace">
            <appender-ref ref="consoleAppender" />
        </root>
    </configuration>
```

We write a simple java class that implements logging functionality using logback.

```java
SimpleLogbackExample.java 🖾

    package com.java.logback.examples;

    //import the slf4j Logger and LoggrFactory
    import org.slf4j.Logger;
    import org.slf4j.LoggerFactory;

    public class SimpleLogbackExample {

        public static void main(String[] args) {

            //get logger object
            Logger logger = LoggerFactory.getLogger(SimpleLogbackExample.class);

            //log messages
            logger.info("An Information Message");
            logger.debug("A Debug Message");

        }
    }
```

The output is:

```
Console ⟫  Problems  @ Javadoc  Declaration  Annotations
<terminated> SimpleLogbackExample [Java Application] C:\Program Files\java\jre1.8.0_101\bin\javaw.exe
18:01:38.527 [main] INFO com.java.logback.examples.SimpleLogbackExample - An Information Message
18:01:38.527 [main] DEBUG com.java.logback.examples.SimpleLogbackExample - A Debug Message
```

We shall now look at examples that demonstrate the use of logback API.

4.6. EXAMPLES

Example 1: Simple Console Appender with Date and Time

In this example, we implement a simple console appender that outputs the logs with a date and time.

```xml
X logback.xml ⟫

  <?xml version="1.0" encoding="UTF-8"?>
  <configuration>
    <appender name="consoleAppender" class="ch.qos.logback.core.ConsoleAppender">
      <encoder>
        <pattern>%d{yyyy-MM-dd HH:mm:ss} [%thread] %-5level %logger{36} - %msg%n</pattern>
      </encoder>
    </appender>
    <root level="trace">
      <appender-ref ref="consoleAppender" />
    </root>
  </configuration>
```

The java class is as follows:

```java
J LogbackExample1.java ⟫

    package com.java.logback.examples;

  + import org.slf4j.Logger;

    public class LogbackExample1 {

        public static void main(String[] args) {

            // get logger object
            Logger logger = LoggerFactory.getLogger(LogbackExample1.class);

            // log messages
            logger.info("An Information Message");
            logger.debug("A Debug Message");
            logger.warn("A Warning Message");
            logger.error("An Error Message");
            logger.trace("A Trace Message");
        }
    }
```

The output is as follows:

```
Console ⟫  Problems  Javadoc  Declaration  Annotations
<terminated> LogbackExample1 [Java Application] C:\Program Files\java\jre1.8.0_101\bin\javaw.exe
2017-09-12 18:42:17 [main] INFO  c.j.logback.examples.LogbackExample - An Information Message
2017-09-12 18:42:17 [main] DEBUG c.j.logback.examples.LogbackExample - A Debug Message
2017-09-12 18:42:17 [main] WARN  c.j.logback.examples.LogbackExample - A Warning Message
2017-09-12 18:42:17 [main] ERROR c.j.logback.examples.LogbackExample - An Error Message
2017-09-12 18:42:17 [main] TRACE c.j.logback.examples.LogbackExample - A Trace Message
```

Example 2: Simple File Appender

In this example, we implement a simple file appender.

```xml
logback.xml
<configuration>
    <appender name="fileAppender" class="ch.qos.logback.core.FileAppender">
        <file> myLogFile.log </file>
        <append>true</append>
        <encoder>
            <pattern>%d{yyyy-MM-dd HH:mm:ss} [%thread] %-5level %logger{55} - %msg%n</pattern>
        </encoder>
    </appender>
    <root level="trace">
        <appender-ref ref="fileAppender" />
    </root>
</configuration>
```

The java class:

```java
LogbackExample2.java
package com.java.logback.examples;

import org.slf4j.Logger;

public class LogbackExample2 {

    public static void main(String[] args) {

        // get logger object
        Logger logger = LoggerFactory.getLogger(LogbackExample2.class);

        // log messages
        logger.info("An Information Message");
        logger.debug("A Debug Message");
        logger.warn("A Warning Message");
        logger.error("An Error Message");
        logger.trace("A Trace Message");

        //create an exception
        Integer x =null;

        try
        {
            x.doubleValue();
        }
        //log the exception
        catch(NullPointerException e)
        {
            logger.error("The object is null! " + e);
        }

    }
}
```

An output log file is generated in the project structure/tree as follows:

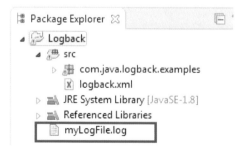

The contents of this file are as follows:

```
myLogFile.log ⊠
2017-09-26 19:01:56 [main] INFO  com.java.logback.examples.LogbackExample - An Information Message
2017-09-26 19:01:56 [main] DEBUG com.java.logback.examples.LogbackExample - A Debug Message
2017-09-26 19:01:56 [main] WARN  com.java.logback.examples.LogbackExample - A Warning Message
2017-09-26 19:01:56 [main] ERROR com.java.logback.examples.LogbackExample - An Error Message
2017-09-26 19:01:56 [main] TRACE com.java.logback.examples.LogbackExample - A Trace Message
2017-09-26 19:01:56 [main] ERROR com.java.logback.examples.LogbackExample - The object is null! java.lang.NullPointerException
```

Example 3: Multiple Appenders – Console and File

In this example, we configure our application to use multiple appenders. We define 2 appenders: console and file.

```xml
logback.xml ⊠
<configuration>
    <appender name="consoleAppender" class="ch.qos.logback.core.ConsoleAppender">
        <encoder>
            <pattern>%d{yyyy-MM-dd HH:mm:ss} [%thread] %-5level %logger{36} - %msg%n</pattern>
        </encoder>
    </appender>
    <appender name="fileAppender" class="ch.qos.logback.core.FileAppender">
        <file> myLogFile.log </file>
        <append>true</append>
        <encoder>
            <pattern>%d{yyyy-MM-dd HH:mm:ss} [%thread] %-5level %logger{55} - %msg%n</pattern>
        </encoder>
    </appender>
    <root level="trace">
        <appender-ref ref="fileAppender" />
    </root>
</configuration>
```

The java class is as follows:

```java
LogbackExample3.java ⊠
package com.java.logback.examples;

import org.slf4j.Logger;

public class LogbackExample3 {

    public static void main(String[] args) {

        // get logger object
        Logger logger = LoggerFactory.getLogger(LogbackExample3.class);

        // log messages
        logger.info("An Information Message");
        logger.debug("A Debug Message");
        logger.warn("A Warning Message");
        logger.error("An Error Message");

        //induce an exception and log it

        int a = 0, b = 0;
        try {
            a = a / b;
        } catch (Exception e) {
            logger.error("You cannot divide by zero! ");
        }

    }
}
```

The console output is as follows:

```
Console ⊠    Problems    Javadoc    Declaration    Annotations
<terminated> LogbackExample3 [Java Application] C:\Program Files\java\jre1.8.0_101\bin\javaw.exe
2017-09-12 19:16:51 [main] INFO  com.java.logback.examples.LogbackExample - An Information Message
2017-09-12 19:16:51 [main] DEBUG com.java.logback.examples.LogbackExample - A Debug Message
2017-09-12 19:16:51 [main] WARN  com.java.logback.examples.LogbackExample - A Warning Message
2017-09-12 19:16:51 [main] ERROR com.java.logback.examples.LogbackExample - An Error Message
2017-09-12 19:16:51 [main] ERROR com.java.logback.examples.LogbackExample - You cannot divide by zero!
```

The file output is as follows:

```
myLogFile.log
2017-09-26 19:16:51 [main] INFO  com.java.logback.examples.LogbackExample - An Information Message
2017-09-26 19:16:51 [main] DEBUG com.java.logback.examples.LogbackExample - A Debug Message
2017-09-26 19:16:51 [main] WARN  com.java.logback.examples.LogbackExample - A Warning Message
2017-09-26 19:16:51 [main] ERROR com.java.logback.examples.LogbackExample - An Error Message
2017-09-26 19:16:51 [main] ERROR com.java.logback.examples.LogbackExample - You cannot divide by zero!
```

Example 4: Rolling File Appender based on time

In this example, we implement a rolling file appender that rolls out files based on time.

```xml
logback.xml
<?xml version="1.0" encoding="UTF-8"?>
<configuration>
    <appender name="rollingFileAppender"
        class="ch.qos.logback.core.rolling.RollingFileAppender">
        <file>myLogFile.log</file>
        <rollingPolicy class="ch.qos.logback.core.rolling.TimeBasedRollingPolicy">
            <!-- roll-over on a daily basis -->
            <fileNamePattern>myLogFile.%d{yyyy-MM-dd-HH-mm}.log
            </fileNamePattern>
            <maxHistory>30</maxHistory>
        </rollingPolicy>
        <encoder>
            <pattern>%d{yyyy-MM-dd HH:mm:ss} [%thread] %-5level %logger{55} - %msg%n</pattern>
        </encoder>
    </appender>
    <root level="trace">
        <appender-ref ref="rollingFileAppender" />
    </root>
</configuration>
```

The Java class used to test the above configuration is as follows:

```java
LogbackExample4.java
package com.java.logback.examples;

+ import org.slf4j.Logger;

public class LogbackExample4 {

    public static void main(String[] args) {

        // get logger object
        Logger logger = LoggerFactory.getLogger(LogbackExample4.class);

        // log messages
        logger.info("An Information Message");
        logger.debug("A Debug Message");
        logger.warn("A Warning Message");
        logger.error("An Error Message");

        for(int i=0; i< 25; i ++)
        {
            logger.info("Information Log Message: " + i);
            //add sleep statements to add delay
            //this will generate several output log files
            try {
                Thread.sleep( 5000L );
            } catch ( final InterruptedException e ) {
                logger.error( "An exception occured during processing", e );
            }
        }
    }
}
```

On execution of the above class, the following log files are generated in the project tree:

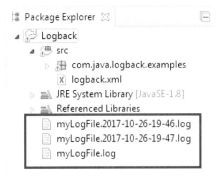

The contents of this file are as follows:

```
myLogFile.2017-09-26-13-46.log

2017-09-27 13:50:18 [main] INFO  com.java.logback.examples.LogbackExample - An Information Message
2017-09-27 13:50:18 [main] DEBUG com.java.logback.examples.LogbackExample - A Debug Message
2017-09-27 13:50:18 [main] WARN  com.java.logback.examples.LogbackExample - A Warning Message
2017-09-27 13:50:18 [main] ERROR com.java.logback.examples.LogbackExample - An Error Message
2017-09-27 13:50:18 [main] INFO  com.java.logback.examples.LogbackExample - Information Log Message: 0
2017-09-27 13:50:23 [main] INFO  com.java.logback.examples.LogbackExample - Information Log Message: 1
2017-09-27 13:50:28 [main] INFO  com.java.logback.examples.LogbackExample - Information Log Message: 2
2017-09-27 13:50:33 [main] INFO  com.java.logback.examples.LogbackExample - Information Log Message: 3
2017-09-27 13:50:38 [main] INFO  com.java.logback.examples.LogbackExample - Information Log Message: 4
2017-09-27 13:50:43 [main] INFO  com.java.logback.examples.LogbackExample - Information Log Message: 5
2017-09-27 13:50:48 [main] INFO  com.java.logback.examples.LogbackExample - Information Log Message: 6
2017-09-27 13:50:53 [main] INFO  com.java.logback.examples.LogbackExample - Information Log Message: 7
2017-09-27 13:50:58 [main] INFO  com.java.logback.examples.LogbackExample - Information Log Message: 8


myLogFile.2017-09-26-13-47.log

2017-09-27 13:51:03 [main] INFO  com.java.logback.examples.LogbackExample - Information Log Message: 9
2017-09-27 13:51:08 [main] INFO  com.java.logback.examples.LogbackExample - Information Log Message: 10
2017-09-27 13:51:13 [main] INFO  com.java.logback.examples.LogbackExample - Information Log Message: 11
2017-09-27 13:51:18 [main] INFO  com.java.logback.examples.LogbackExample - Information Log Message: 12
2017-09-27 13:51:23 [main] INFO  com.java.logback.examples.LogbackExample - Information Log Message: 13
2017-09-27 13:51:28 [main] INFO  com.java.logback.examples.LogbackExample - Information Log Message: 14
2017-09-27 13:51:33 [main] INFO  com.java.logback.examples.LogbackExample - Information Log Message: 15
2017-09-27 13:51:38 [main] INFO  com.java.logback.examples.LogbackExample - Information Log Message: 16
2017-09-27 13:51:43 [main] INFO  com.java.logback.examples.LogbackExample - Information Log Message: 17
2017-09-27 13:51:48 [main] INFO  com.java.logback.examples.LogbackExample - Information Log Message: 18
2017-09-27 13:51:53 [main] INFO  com.java.logback.examples.LogbackExample - Information Log Message: 19
2017-09-27 13:51:58 [main] INFO  com.java.logback.examples.LogbackExample - Information Log Message: 20


myLogFile.log

2017-09-27 13:52:03 [main] INFO  com.java.logback.examples.LogbackExample - Information Log Message: 21
2017-09-27 13:52:08 [main] INFO  com.java.logback.examples.LogbackExample - Information Log Message: 22
2017-09-27 13:52:13 [main] INFO  com.java.logback.examples.LogbackExample - Information Log Message: 23
2017-09-27 13:52:18 [main] INFO  com.java.logback.examples.LogbackExample - Information Log Message: 24
```

Example 5: Rolling File Appender based on window size

In this example, we implement a rolling file appender that rolls files based a fixed window size as follows:

```
X logback.xml
    <?xml version="1.0" encoding="UTF-8"?>
    <configuration>
        <appender name="windowRollingFileAppender" class="ch.qos.logback.core.rolling.RollingFileAppender">
            <file>myLogFile.log</file>
        <rollingPolicy class="ch.qos.logback.core.rolling.FixedWindowRollingPolicy">
                <fileNamePattern>myLogFile%i.log</fileNamePattern>
                <minIndex>1</minIndex>
                <maxIndex>10</maxIndex>
        </rollingPolicy>

            <triggeringPolicy class="ch.qos.logback.core.rolling.SizeBasedTriggeringPolicy">
                <maxFileSize>1KB</maxFileSize>
        </triggeringPolicy>

        <encoder>
                <pattern>%d{yyyy-MM-dd HH:mm:ss} [%thread] %-5level %logger{55} - %msg%n</pattern>
        </encoder>
        </appender>
        <root level="debug">
            <appender-ref ref="windowRollingFileAppender" />
        </root>
    </configuration>
```

The java class is as follows:

```
J LogbackExample5.java
    package com.java.logback.examples;

  ⊕ import org.slf4j.Logger;

    public class LogbackExample5 {

        public static void main(String[] args) {

            // get logger object
            Logger logger = LoggerFactory.getLogger(LogbackExample5.class);

            // log messages
            for (int i = 0; i < 25; i++) {
                logger.info("Information Log Message: " + i);
                // add sleep statements to add delay this will generate several
                // output log files based on the size of the output file
                try {
                    Thread.sleep(1000L);
                } catch (final InterruptedException e) {
                    logger.error("An exception occured during processing", e);
                }
            }
        }
    }
```

Three files have been generated as shown below:

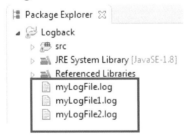

The contents of these files are as follows:

```
myLogFile2.log
   2017-09-27 13:42:04 [main] INFO  com.java.logback.examples.LogbackExample - Information Log Message: 0
   2017-09-27 13:42:05 [main] INFO  com.java.logback.examples.LogbackExample - Information Log Message: 1
   2017-09-27 13:42:06 [main] INFO  com.java.logback.examples.LogbackExample - Information Log Message: 2
   2017-09-27 13:42:07 [main] INFO  com.java.logback.examples.LogbackExample - Information Log Message: 3
   2017-09-27 13:42:08 [main] INFO  com.java.logback.examples.LogbackExample - Information Log Message: 4
   2017-09-27 13:42:09 [main] INFO  com.java.logback.examples.LogbackExample - Information Log Message: 5
   2017-09-27 13:42:10 [main] INFO  com.java.logback.examples.LogbackExample - Information Log Message: 6
   2017-09-27 13:42:11 [main] INFO  com.java.logback.examples.LogbackExample - Information Log Message: 7
   2017-09-27 13:42:12 [main] INFO  com.java.logback.examples.LogbackExample - Information Log Message: 8
   2017-09-27 13:42:13 [main] INFO  com.java.logback.examples.LogbackExample - Information Log Message: 9

myLogFile1.log
   2017-09-27 13:42:14 [main] INFO  com.java.logback.examples.LogbackExample - Information Log Message: 10
   2017-09-27 13:42:15 [main] INFO  com.java.logback.examples.LogbackExample - Information Log Message: 11
   2017-09-27 13:42:16 [main] INFO  com.java.logback.examples.LogbackExample - Information Log Message: 12
   2017-09-27 13:42:17 [main] INFO  com.java.logback.examples.LogbackExample - Information Log Message: 13
   2017-09-27 13:42:18 [main] INFO  com.java.logback.examples.LogbackExample - Information Log Message: 14
   2017-09-27 13:42:19 [main] INFO  com.java.logback.examples.LogbackExample - Information Log Message: 15
   2017-09-27 13:42:20 [main] INFO  com.java.logback.examples.LogbackExample - Information Log Message: 16
   2017-09-27 13:42:21 [main] INFO  com.java.logback.examples.LogbackExample - Information Log Message: 17
   2017-09-27 13:42:22 [main] INFO  com.java.logback.examples.LogbackExample - Information Log Message: 18
   2017-09-27 13:42:23 [main] INFO  com.java.logback.examples.LogbackExample - Information Log Message: 19

myLogFile.log
   2017-09-27 13:42:24 [main] INFO  com.java.logback.examples.LogbackExample - Information Log Message: 20
   2017-09-27 13:42:25 [main] INFO  com.java.logback.examples.LogbackExample - Information Log Message: 21
   2017-09-27 13:42:26 [main] INFO  com.java.logback.examples.LogbackExample - Information Log Message: 22
   2017-09-27 13:42:27 [main] INFO  com.java.logback.examples.LogbackExample - Information Log Message: 23
   2017-09-27 13:42:28 [main] INFO  com.java.logback.examples.LogbackExample - Information Log Message: 24
```

Example 6: Rolling File Appender based on size and window

In this example, we implement a rolling file appender that rolls log files based on both time and size.

```xml
logback.xml

<?xml version="1.0" encoding="UTF-8"?>
<configuration>
    <appender name="siezAndTimeRollingFileAppender" class="ch.qos.logback.core.rolling.RollingFileAppender">
        <file>myLogFile.log</file>
        <rollingPolicy class="ch.qos.logback.core.rolling.SizeAndTimeBasedRollingPolicy">
            <!-- rollover daily -->
            <fileNamePattern>myLogFile-%d{yyyy-MM-dd}.%i.log</fileNamePattern>
            <!-- The size of each file should be at most 1KB, and the log files must be kept for at most 30 days at a
                 capacity limit of 15 GB -->
            <maxFileSize>1KB</maxFileSize>
            <maxHistory>30</maxHistory>
            <totalSizeCap>15GB</totalSizeCap>
        </rollingPolicy>
        <encoder>
            <pattern>%d{yyyy-MM-dd HH:mm:ss} [%thread] %-5level %logger{55} - %msg%n</pattern>
        </encoder>
    </appender>

    <root level="DEBUG">
        <appender-ref ref="siezAndTimeRollingFileAppender" />
    </root>
</configuration>
```

The Java class is:

```java
LogbackExample6.java

package com.java.logback.examples;

import org.slf4j.Logger;

public class LogbackExample6 {

    public static void main(String[] args) {

        // get logger object
        Logger logger = LoggerFactory.getLogger(LogbackExample6.class);

        // log messages
        for (int i = 0; i < 50; i++) {
            logger.debug(" Debug Message: " + i);
            // add sleep statements to add delay this will generate several
            // output log files based on the size and time of the output file
            try {
                Thread.sleep(500L);
            } catch (final InterruptedException e) {
                logger.error("An exception occured during processing", e);
            }
        }

    }
}
```

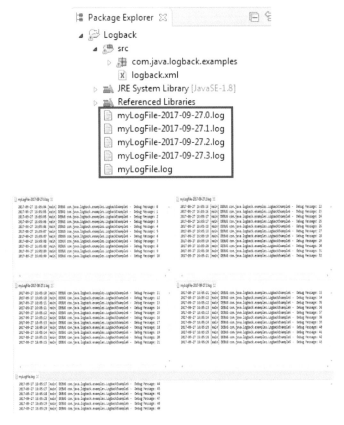

Example 7: Simple Level Filter Example

In this example, we implement a simple filter that filters log events based on their level.

```xml
<?xml version="1.0" encoding="UTF-8"?>
<configuration>
<appender name="sizeAndTimeBasedRollingFileAppender" class="ch.qos.logback.core.rolling.RollingFileAppender">
    <file>myLogFile.log</file>
    <rollingPolicy class="ch.qos.logback.core.rolling.SizeAndTimeBasedRollingPolicy">
        <!-- rollover daily -->
        <fileNamePattern>myLogFile-%d{yyyy-MM-dd}.%i.log</fileNamePattern>
        <!-- The size of each file should be at most 1KB, and the log file
            must be kept at most for 30 days at a capacity of 15GB -->
        <maxFileSize>1KB</maxFileSize>
        <maxHistory>30</maxHistory>
        <totalSizeCap>15GB</totalSizeCap>
    </rollingPolicy>
    <encoder>
        <pattern>%d{yyyy-MM-dd HH:mm:ss} [%thread] %-5level %logger{55} - %msg%n</pattern>
    </encoder>
</appender>
    <appender name="consoleAppender" class="ch.qos.logback.core.ConsoleAppender">
    <filter class="ch.qos.logback.classic.filter.LevelFilter">
        <level>INFO</level>
        <onMatch>ACCEPT</onMatch>
        <onMismatch>DENY</onMismatch>
    </filter>
    <encoder>
        <pattern>%d{yyyy-MM-dd HH:mm:ss} [%thread] %-5level %logger{55} - %msg%n</pattern>
    </encoder>
    </appender>
    <root level="DEBUG">
    <appender-ref ref="sizeAndTimeBasedRollingFileAppender" />
        <appender-ref ref="consoleAppender" />
    </root>
</configuration>
```

The java class is as follows:

```
LogbackExample7.java

    package com.java.logback.examples;

 * import org.slf4j.Logger;

    public class LogbackExample7 {

        public static void main(String[] args) {
            // get logger object
            Logger logger = LoggerFactory.getLogger(LogbackExample7.class);
            // log messages
            // all the messages will be printed to the output log file
            logger.debug(" Debug Message");
            logger.warn(" Warning Message");
            logger.error("Error Message");
            logger.error("Another Error Message");
            // only the following 'INFO' level messages will be printed on the console
            logger.info("Information Message");
            logger.info("Information Message 2");
            logger.info("Information Message 3");
        }
    }
```

The output generated on the console is as follows:

```
Console    @ Javadoc    Declaration    Problems
<terminated> LogbackExample7 [Java Application] C:\Program Files\Java\jdk1.7.0_71\bin\javaw.exe
2017-09-28 11:28:11 [main] INFO  com.java.logback.examples.LogbackExample7 - Information Message
2017-09-28 11:28:11 [main] INFO  com.java.logback.examples.LogbackExample7 - Information Message 2
2017-09-28 11:28:11 [main] INFO  com.java.logback.examples.LogbackExample7 - Information Message 3
```

The contents of the log file are as follows:

```
myLogFile.log
2017-09-28 11:03:33 [main] DEBUG com.java.logback.examples.LogbackExample7 -  Debug Message
2017-09-28 11:03:33 [main] WARN  com.java.logback.examples.LogbackExample7 -  Warning Message
2017-09-28 11:03:33 [main] ERROR com.java.logback.examples.LogbackExample7 - Error Message
2017-09-28 11:03:33 [main] ERROR com.java.logback.examples.LogbackExample7 - Another Error Message
2017-09-28 11:03:33 [main] INFO  com.java.logback.examples.LogbackExample7 - Information Message
2017-09-28 11:03:33 [main] INFO  com.java.logback.examples.LogbackExample7 - Information Message 2
2017-09-28 11:03:33 [main] INFO  com.java.logback.examples.LogbackExample7 - Information Message 3
```

Example 8: TimeStamped File Appender

With a timestamp, each time the application is launched, a new file is created. This is useful in case of small short-lived applications such as batch applications for example.

```
X logback.xml
    <?xml version="1.0" encoding="UTF-8"?>
    <configuration>
        <!-- Declare a timestamp key with the time format "yyyyMMdd'T'HHmmss".
        This key can be used by all appenders -->
        <timestamp key="stampPerSecond" datePattern="yyyyMMdd'T'HHmmss"/>
        <appender name="fileAppender" class="ch.qos.logback.core.FileAppender">
            <!-- use the timestamp to name the log file uniquely -->
            <file>myLogFile-${stampPerSecond}.txt</file>
            <encoder>
                <pattern>%d{yyyy-MM-dd HH:mm:ss} [%thread] %-5level %logger{55} - %msg%n</pattern>
            </encoder>
        </appender>
        <root level="INFO">
            <appender-ref ref="fileAppender" />
        </root>
    </configuration>
```

The Java class is as follows:

```
LogbackExample8.java
    package com.java.logback.examples;

    import org.slf4j.Logger;

    public class LogbackExample8 {

        public static void main(String[] args) throws InterruptedException {
            // get logger object
            Logger logger = LoggerFactory.getLogger(LogbackExample8.class);
            // log messages
            // all the messages will be printed to the output log file which will be
            // timestamped
            for (int i = 0; i < 5; i++) {
                logger.debug(" Debug Message");
                logger.warn(" Warning Message");
                logger.error("Error Message");
                logger.trace("Trace Message");
                logger.info("Information Message");
            }
        }
    }
```

A log file with the timestamp is generated in the project structure as shown below:

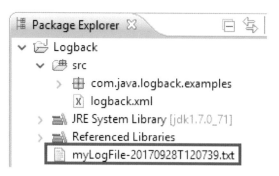

The contents of this file are as follows:

```
myLogFile-20170928T120739.txt
2017-09-28 12:07:39 [main] WARN  com.java.logback.examples.LogbackExample9  -  Warning Message
2017-09-28 12:07:39 [main] ERROR com.java.logback.examples.LogbackExample9  -  Error Message
2017-09-28 12:07:39 [main] INFO  com.java.logback.examples.LogbackExample9  -  Information Message
2017-09-28 12:07:39 [main] WARN  com.java.logback.examples.LogbackExample9  -  Warning Message
2017-09-28 12:07:39 [main] ERROR com.java.logback.examples.LogbackExample9  -  Error Message
2017-09-28 12:07:39 [main] INFO  com.java.logback.examples.LogbackExample9  -  Information Message
2017-09-28 12:07:39 [main] WARN  com.java.logback.examples.LogbackExample9  -  Warning Message
2017-09-28 12:07:39 [main] ERROR com.java.logback.examples.LogbackExample9  -  Error Message
2017-09-28 12:07:39 [main] INFO  com.java.logback.examples.LogbackExample9  -  Information Message
2017-09-28 12:07:39 [main] WARN  com.java.logback.examples.LogbackExample9  -  Warning Message
2017-09-28 12:07:39 [main] ERROR com.java.logback.examples.LogbackExample9  -  Error Message
2017-09-28 12:07:39 [main] INFO  com.java.logback.examples.LogbackExample9  -  Information Message
2017-09-28 12:07:39 [main] WARN  com.java.logback.examples.LogbackExample9  -  Warning Message
2017-09-28 12:07:39 [main] ERROR com.java.logback.examples.LogbackExample9  -  Error Message
2017-09-28 12:07:39 [main] INFO  com.java.logback.examples.LogbackExample9  -  Information Message
```

Example 9: Aysnc Appender Example

In this example, we implement an async file appender. This appender used a buffer queue and discards log events if the queue fills up to 80%.

```xml
logback.xml
<?xml version="1.0" encoding="UTF-8"?>
<configuration>
  <appender name="fileAppender" class="ch.qos.logback.core.FileAppender">
    <file>myLogFile.log</file>
    <encoder>
      <pattern>%logger{55} - %msg%n</pattern>
    </encoder>
  </appender>

  <appender name="ASYNC" class="ch.qos.logback.classic.AsyncAppender">
    <appender-ref ref="fileAppender" />
  </appender>

  <root level="INFO">
    <appender-ref ref="ASYNC" />
  </root>
</configuration>
```

The Java class used to test the above configuration is:

```java
LogbackExample9.java
package com.java.logback.examples;

import org.slf4j.Logger;

public class LogbackExample9 {

    public static void main(String[] args) throws InterruptedException {

        // get logger object
        Logger logger = LoggerFactory.getLogger(LogbackExample9.class);

        // log messages
        logger.error(" Error Message 1");
        logger.warn(" Warning Message 1");
        logger.error("Error Message 2");
        logger.warn("Warning Message 2");
        logger.warn("Warning Message 3");
    }
}
```

A new file is created in the project structure as follows:

The contents of this file are as follows:

```
myLogFile.log ☒
    com.java.logback.examples.LogbackExample9 -   Error Message 1
    com.java.logback.examples.LogbackExample9 -   Warning Message 1
    com.java.logback.examples.LogbackExample9 - Error Message 2
    com.java.logback.examples.LogbackExample9 - Warning Message 2
```

As we can see, only error and warning messages have been displayed. A warning message has been dropped as well. If we don't want loss of logging information, then the discarding threshold property can be set to zero as follows:

```
logback.xml ☒
    <?xml version="1.0" encoding="UTF-8"?>
    <configuration>
      <appender name="fileAppender" class="ch.qos.logback.core.FileAppender">
        <file>myLogFile.log</file>
        <encoder>
          <pattern>%logger{55} - %msg%n</pattern>
        </encoder>
      </appender>

      <appender name="ASYNC" class="ch.qos.logback.classic.AsyncAppender">
        <discardingThreshold>0</discardingThreshold>
        <appender-ref ref="fileAppender" />
      </appender>

      <root level="INFO">
        <appender-ref ref="ASYNC" />
      </root>
    </configuration>
```

After making this change, we now execute our java program again and check the contents of the output log file. They are as follows:

```
myLogFile.log ☒
    com.java.logback.examples.LogbackExample9 -   Error Message 1
    com.java.logback.examples.LogbackExample9 -   Warning Message 1
    com.java.logback.examples.LogbackExample9 - Error Message 2
    com.java.logback.examples.LogbackExample9 - Warning Message 2
    com.java.logback.examples.LogbackExample9 - Warning Message 3
```

As we can see, all the log messages have been logged to the file.

Example 10: Async Appender queue size parameter

In the previous example, we saw the use of an asynchronous appender. We set the discarding threshold to zero, but sometimes it isn't enough. Even though we set the discarding threshold value to 0, we sometimes loose some log messages as the queue size and number of queues is limited.

Consider the previous configuration file:

```xml
<?xml version="1.0" encoding="UTF-8"?>
<configuration>
  <appender name="fileAppender" class="ch.qos.logback.core.FileAppender">
    <file>myLogFile.log</file>
    <encoder>
      <pattern>%logger{55} - %msg%n</pattern>
    </encoder>
  </appender>

  <appender name="ASYNC" class="ch.qos.logback.classic.AsyncAppender">
    <discardingThreshold>0</discardingThreshold>
    <appender-ref ref="fileAppender" />
  </appender>

  <root level="INFO">
    <appender-ref ref="ASYNC" />
  </root>
</configuration>
```

We modify the java class by adding a loop as follows:

```java
package com.java.logback.examples;

import org.slf4j.Logger;

public class LogbackExample10 {

    public static void main(String[] args) throws InterruptedException {

        // get logger object
        Logger logger = LoggerFactory.getLogger(LogbackExample10.class);
        for (int i = 0; i < 5; i++) {
            // log messages
            logger.error(" Error Message 1");
            logger.warn(" Warning Message 1");
            logger.error("Error Message 2");
            logger.warn("Warning Message 2");
            logger.warn("Warning Message 3");
        }
    }
}
```

On running this program, a log file is generated. But it doesn't log all of the log messages. This is shown in the figure below:

```
com.java.logback.examples.LogbackExample9 -  Error Message 1
com.java.logback.examples.LogbackExample9 -  Warning Message 1
com.java.logback.examples.LogbackExample9 - Error Message 2
com.java.logback.examples.LogbackExample9 - Warning Message 2
com.java.logback.examples.LogbackExample9 - Warning Message 3
com.java.logback.examples.LogbackExample9 -  Error Message 1
com.java.logback.examples.LogbackExample9 -  Warning Message 1
com.java.logback.examples.LogbackExample9 - Error Message 2
com.java.logback.examples.LogbackExample9 - Warning Message 2
```

This is due to the limited queue size. We can set this size to a value of our choice as follows:

```xml
<?xml version="1.0" encoding="UTF-8"?>
<configuration>
  <appender name="fileAppender" class="ch.qos.logback.core.FileAppender">
    <file>myLogFile.log</file>
    <encoder>
      <pattern>%logger{55} - %msg%n</pattern>
    </encoder>
  </appender>

  <appender name="ASYNC" class="ch.qos.logback.classic.AsyncAppender">
    <discardingThreshold>0</discardingThreshold>
    <queueSize>10</queueSize>
    <appender-ref ref="fileAppender" />
  </appender>

  <root level="INFO">
    <appender-ref ref="ASYNC" />
  </root>
</configuration>
```

After modifying the configuration file, we now execute the program again and check the contents of the log file. They are as follows:

```
myLogFile.log
com.java.logback.examples.LogbackExample10 -  Error Message 1
com.java.logback.examples.LogbackExample10 -  Warning Message 1
com.java.logback.examples.LogbackExample10 -  Error Message 2
com.java.logback.examples.LogbackExample10 -  Warning Message 2
com.java.logback.examples.LogbackExample10 -  Warning Message 3
com.java.logback.examples.LogbackExample10 -  Error Message 1
com.java.logback.examples.LogbackExample10 -  Warning Message 1
com.java.logback.examples.LogbackExample10 -  Error Message 2
com.java.logback.examples.LogbackExample10 -  Warning Message 2
com.java.logback.examples.LogbackExample10 -  Warning Message 3
com.java.logback.examples.LogbackExample10 -  Error Message 1
com.java.logback.examples.LogbackExample10 -  Warning Message 1
com.java.logback.examples.LogbackExample10 -  Error Message 2
com.java.logback.examples.LogbackExample10 -  Warning Message 2
com.java.logback.examples.LogbackExample10 -  Warning Message 3
com.java.logback.examples.LogbackExample10 -  Error Message 1
com.java.logback.examples.LogbackExample10 -  Warning Message 1
com.java.logback.examples.LogbackExample10 -  Error Message 2
com.java.logback.examples.LogbackExample10 -  Warning Message 2
com.java.logback.examples.LogbackExample10 -  Warning Message 3
com.java.logback.examples.LogbackExample10 -  Error Message 1
com.java.logback.examples.LogbackExample10 -  Warning Message 1
com.java.logback.examples.LogbackExample10 -  Error Message 2
com.java.logback.examples.LogbackExample10 -  Warning Message 2
com.java.logback.examples.LogbackExample10 -  Warning Message 3
```

As we can see from the output, all the log messages have been logged 5 times as per our looping construct specified in the java class LogbackExample10.

Example 11: Threshold Filter

In this example, we implement s threshold filter that filters log messages based on a threshold log level and rejects messages below this log level.

```
logback.xml
<?xml version="1.0" encoding="UTF-8"?>
<configuration>
    <appender name="consoleAppender" class="ch.qos.logback.core.ConsoleAppender">
    <filter class = "ch.qos.logback.classic.filter.ThresholdFilter">
    <level>INFO</level>
    </filter>
        <encoder>
            <pattern>%d{yyyy-MM-dd HH:mm:ss} [%thread] %-5level %logger{55} - %msg%n</pattern>
        </encoder>
    </appender>

    <root level="DEBUG">
        <appender-ref ref="consoleAppender" />
    </root>
</configuration>
```

The java class:

```
[J] LogbackExample11.java
    package com.java.logback.examples;

  + import org.slf4j.Logger;

    public class LogbackExample11 {

        public static void main(String[] args) throws InterruptedException {

            // get logger object
            Logger logger = LoggerFactory.getLogger(LogbackExample11.class);

            // log messages
            // Messages of levels INFO or higher will be logged
            logger.error(" Error Message");
            logger.warn(" Warning Message");
            logger.info("Information Message");
            logger.error("Another Information Message");

            // the following messages will not be printed on the console
            logger.debug("Debug Message");
            logger.trace("Trace Message");
        }
    }
```

The console output is as follows:

```
Console    Javadoc   Declaration   Problems
<terminated> LogbackExample11 [Java Application] C:\Program Files\Java\jdk1.7.0_71\bin\javaw.exe
2017-09-28 14:51:27 [main] ERROR com.java.logback.examples.LogbackExample11 -  Error Message
2017-09-28 14:51:27 [main] WARN  com.java.logback.examples.LogbackExample11 -  Warning Message
2017-09-28 14:51:27 [main] INFO  com.java.logback.examples.LogbackExample11 - Information Message
2017-09-28 14:51:27 [main] ERROR com.java.logback.examples.LogbackExample11 - Another Information Message
```

Example 12: Custom Logger

In this example, we implement a custom logger. The configuration for a custom logger can be done as follows:

```
[x] logback.xml
    <?xml version="1.0" encoding="UTF-8"?>
    <configuration>
        <appender name="consoleAppender" class="ch.qos.logback.core.ConsoleAppender">
            <encoder>
                <pattern>%d{yyyy-MM-dd HH:mm:ss} [%thread] %-5level %logger{55} - %msg%n</pattern>
            </encoder>
        </appender>

        <logger name="myLogger" level="debug" >
            <appender-ref ref="consoleAppender" />
        </logger>

        <root level="debug">
            <appender-ref ref="consoleAppender" />
        </root>
    </configuration>
```

The java class is as follows:

```
[J] LogbackExample12.java
    package com.java.logback.examples;

  + import org.slf4j.Logger;

    public class LogbackExample12 {

        public static void main(String[] args) throws InterruptedException {

            // get logger object
            Logger logger = LoggerFactory.getLogger("myLogger");

            // log messages
            logger.error(" Error Message");
            logger.warn(" Warning Message");
            logger.info("Information Message");
            logger.debug("Debug Message");
        }
    }
```

The output generated is as follows:

```
Console ⊠    @ Javadoc  Declaration  Problems
<terminated> LogbackExample12 [Java Application] C:\Program Files\Java\jdk
2017-09-28 15:11:10 [main] ERROR myLogger -  Error Message
2017-09-28 15:11:10 [main] ERROR myLogger -  Error Message
2017-09-28 15:11:10 [main] WARN  myLogger -  Warning Message
2017-09-28 15:11:10 [main] WARN  myLogger -  Warning Message
2017-09-28 15:11:10 [main] INFO  myLogger - Information Message
2017-09-28 15:11:10 [main] INFO  myLogger - Information Message
2017-09-28 15:11:10 [main] DEBUG myLogger - Debug Message
2017-09-28 15:11:10 [main] DEBUG myLogger - Debug Message
```

As noted from the output, each log message has been printed twice on the console. This is because appenders are cumulative in logback. A logger will attach the appender that is defined for itself and any other appenders defined for its ancestors as well. Hence, the custom logger will attach the appender for the root logger as well. This causes duplicate log messages. If we want to avoid this, we have a few possible solutions. Removing the root appender from the configuration is one of the possible solutions. This is shown below:

```
logback.xml ⊠
    <?xml version="1.0" encoding="UTF-8"?>
    <configuration>
        <appender name="consoleAppender" class="ch.qos.logback.core.ConsoleAppender">
            <encoder>
                <pattern>%d{yyyy-MM-dd HH:mm:ss} [%thread] %-5level %logger{55} - %msg%n</pattern>
            </encoder>
        </appender>

        <logger name="myLogger" level="debug" >
            <appender-ref ref="consoleAppender" />
        </logger>
    </configuration>
```

The output is:

```
Console ⊠    @ Javadoc  Declaration  Problems
<terminated> LogbackExample12 [Java Application] C:\Program Files\Java\jdk
2017-09-28 15:11:42 [main] ERROR myLogger -  Error Message
2017-09-28 15:11:42 [main] WARN  myLogger -  Warning Message
2017-09-28 15:11:42 [main] INFO  myLogger - Information Message
2017-09-28 15:11:42 [main] DEBUG myLogger - Debug Message
```

Another solution is to use the <additivity> parameter for the custom logger as follows:

```xml
<?xml version="1.0" encoding="UTF-8"?>
<configuration>
    <appender name="consoleAppender" class="ch.qos.logback.core.ConsoleAppender">
        <encoder>
            <pattern>%d{yyyy-MM-dd HH:mm:ss} [%thread] %-5level %logger{55} - %msg%n</pattern>
        </encoder>
    </appender>

    <logger name="myLogger" level="debug" additivity="false">
        <appender-ref ref="consoleAppender" />
    </logger>

    <root level="debug">
        <appender-ref ref="consoleAppender" />
    </root>
</configuration>
```

The log messages are displayed just once as shown below:

```
Console    @ Javadoc    Declaration    Problems
<terminated> LogbackExample12 [Java Application] C:\Program Files\Java\jdk
2017-09-28 15:12:59 [main] ERROR myLogger -  Error Message
2017-09-28 15:12:59 [main] WARN  myLogger -  Warning Message
2017-09-28 15:12:59 [main] INFO  myLogger - Information Message
2017-09-28 15:12:59 [main] DEBUG myLogger - Debug Message
```

Example 13: Duplicate Message Filter

In this example, we implement a turbo filter: the duplicate Message Filter. This filter filters out duplicates in the log messages.

```xml
<?xml version="1.0" encoding="UTF-8"?>
<configuration>
<turboFilter class="ch.qos.logback.classic.turbo.DuplicateMessageFilter"/>
    <appender name="consoleAppender" class="ch.qos.logback.core.ConsoleAppender">
        <encoder>
            <pattern>%d{yyyy-MM-dd HH:mm:ss} [%thread] %-5level %logger{55} - %msg%n</pattern>
        </encoder>
    </appender>

    <logger name="myLogger" level="debug" additivity="false">
        <appender-ref ref="consoleAppender" />
    </logger>

    <root level="debug">
        <appender-ref ref="consoleAppender" />
    </root>
</configuration>
```

The java class is as follows:

```java
LogbackExample13.java

package com.java.logback.examples;

+ import org.slf4j.Logger;

public class LogbackExample13 {

    public static void main(String[] args) throws InterruptedException {

        // get logger object
        Logger logger = LoggerFactory.getLogger("myLogger");

        for (int i = 0; i < 10; i++) {
            // log the same log message multiple times
            logger.debug("Debug Message");
        }
    }
}
```

The output is as follows:

```
Console ⌧    @ Javadoc  Declaration  Problems
<terminated> LogbackExample13 [Java Application] C:\Program Files\Java\jdk
2017-09-28 15:48:41 [main] DEBUG myLogger - Debug Message
2017-09-28 15:48:41 [main] DEBUG myLogger - Debug Message
2017-09-28 15:48:41 [main] DEBUG myLogger - Debug Message
2017-09-28 15:48:41 [main] DEBUG myLogger - Debug Message
2017-09-28 15:48:41 [main] DEBUG myLogger - Debug Message
2017-09-28 15:48:41 [main] DEBUG myLogger - Debug Message
```

The console output shows that although we have programmed the logger to log the message 10 times via a loop, it is printed only 6 times. This is because the default value of the <AllowedRepetitions> parameter is set to 5 which means that it iterates from 0 to 5, thus printing the message 6 times.

String equality is used by the filter in order to check for duplication.

But if we want to reduce or increase its value, it can be configured via the <AllowedRepetitions> element as follows:

```
logback.xml ⌧
<?xml version="1.0" encoding="UTF-8"?>
<configuration>
<turboFilter class="ch.qos.logback.classic.turbo.DuplicateMessageFilter">
<AllowedRepetitions>2</AllowedRepetitions>
</turboFilter>
    <appender name="consoleAppender" class="ch.qos.logback.core.ConsoleAppender">
        <encoder>
            <pattern>%d{yyyy-MM-dd HH:mm:ss} [%thread] %-5level %logger{55} - %msg%n</pattern>
        </encoder>
    </appender>

    <logger name="myLogger" level="debug" additivity="false">
        <appender-ref ref="consoleAppender" />
    </logger>

    <root level="debug">
        <appender-ref ref="consoleAppender" />
    </root>
</configuration>
```

The output produced on execution of the java class is as follows:

```
Console ⌧    @ Javadoc  Declaration  Problems
<terminated> LogbackExample13 [Java Application] C:\Program Files\Java\jdk
2017-09-28 15:55:41 [main] DEBUG myLogger - Debug Message
2017-09-28 15:55:41 [main] DEBUG myLogger - Debug Message
2017-09-28 15:55:41 [main] DEBUG myLogger - Debug Message
```

As clearly visible from the console output, the message has been printed on the console a total of 3 times.

Example 14: Duplicate Message Filter with parameterized logging

In the previous example, we saw the use of the duplicate message filter which is useful in eliminating duplicate log messages.

The behavior of this filter in case of parameterized logs is slightly different which will we shall see now.

The Configuration remains the same as in the previous example.

```
X logback.xml
    <?xml version="1.0" encoding="UTF-8"?>
    <configuration>
    <turboFilter class="ch.qos.logback.classic.turbo.DuplicateMessageFilter">
    <AllowedRepetitions>2</AllowedRepetitions>
    </turboFilter>
        <appender name="consoleAppender" class="ch.qos.logback.core.ConsoleAppender">
            <encoder>
                <pattern>%d{yyyy-MM-dd HH:mm:ss} [%thread] %-5level %logger{55} - %msg%n</pattern>
            </encoder>
        </appender>

        <logger name="myLogger" level="debug" additivity="false">
            <appender-ref ref="consoleAppender" />
        </logger>

        <root level="debug">
            <appender-ref ref="consoleAppender" />
        </root>
    </configuration>
```

Consider the following Java class:

```
i LogbackExample14.java
    package com.java.logback.examples;

    import org.slf4j.Logger;
    import org.slf4j.LoggerFactory;

    public class LogbackExample14 {

        public static void main(String[] args) throws InterruptedException {

            // get logger object
            Logger logger = LoggerFactory.getLogger("myLogger");
            String param1 = "1";
            String param2 = "2";
            // log messages multiple times
            // the maximum number of repetitions is set to 2
            for (int i = 0; i < 10; i++) {

                // this debug message is printed twice
                logger.debug("Debug Msg {}", param1);
                    // this message is printed only once as it is considered to be the
                // same message as the previous message
                logger.debug("Debug Msg {}", param2);
            }
        }
    }
```

In the class, we make use of a parameter to log the messages. Here, the turbo filter compares the raw log message which is the part of the message before the parameter. In this case, it is "Debug Message {}." Hence, although the log messages are slightly different they are considered to be the same.

This explains the following console output:

```
Console     @ Javadoc   Declaration   Problems
<terminated> LogbackExample14 [Java Application] C:\Program Files\Java\jdk
2017-09-28 16:18:35 [main] DEBUG myLogger - Debug Msg 1
2017-09-28 16:18:35 [main] DEBUG myLogger - Debug Msg 2
2017-09-28 16:18:35 [main] DEBUG myLogger - Debug Msg 1
```

We see that the log message has been printed just 3 times on the console as configured by our turbo filter.

Example 15: Conditional Processing (if-then) of the configuration file

In any software development life cycle, during the course of software development, a developer may work on different environments such as development, testing, and production. Each environment is assigned a specific configuration file. But, most of these files have several parts of the configuration that are common to all environments. As a result, log configuration is duplicated and the configuration becomes redundant. Nevertheless, logback provides the ability to perform conditional processing of the logback configuration files using if, then, else constructs which enable to do all the configuration using a single file.

Logback makes use of the Janino library to enable conditional processing. The Janino library consists of the conditional processing and evaluation API. To add this library, download the janino.jar from the Janino homepage or from GitHub. (https://github.com/janino-compiler/janino). From the version 2.6.0 and above, the Janino jar file requires the commons-complier. jar as well. Download the jar files and them to your classpath as follows:

The configuration file is as follows:

```xml
<?xml version="1.0" encoding="UTF-8"?>
<configuration>
<property scope="context" resource="app.properties" />

  <if condition='property("ENVIRONMENT").contains("DEV")'>
    <then>
      <appender name="consoleAppender" class="ch.qos.logback.core.ConsoleAppender">
        <encoder>
          <pattern>%d{yyyy-MM-dd HH:mm:ss} %-5level %logger{55} - %msg %n</pattern>
        </encoder>
      </appender>
      <root>
        <appender-ref ref="consoleAppender" />
      </root>
    </then>
  </if>
  <appender name="fileAppender" class="ch.qos.logback.core.FileAppender">
    <file>conditional.log</file>
    <encoder>
      <pattern>%d{yyyy-MM-dd HH:mm:ss} %-5level %logger{55} - %msg %n</pattern>
    </encoder>
  </appender>

  <root level="DEBUG">
    <appender-ref ref="fileAppender" />
  </root>
</configuration>
```

We define a resource file that contains the properties for our application and we set the scope as context. In logback, a property can be defined in three possible scopes namely **local, context** or **system**.

In the local scope, the property is said to exist from the minute it is defined in the configuration file until the execution of the configuration file (Gülcü and Pennec, 2011). The variables defined in this scope are created each time a configuration file is read.

In the context scope, a property lasts as long as the context lasts or until its value is erased. Once a property is defined to be in this scope, it becomes a part of the context and is available to all the logging events, remote events included.

If a property is defined in the system scope, it is inserted into the system's properties of the JVM and this value exists until the JVM is not terminated or until its value is erased.

This file is created at the same level in our directory tree as the configuration file.

We initialize this file with the 'ENVIRONMENT' property set to DEV as shown below:

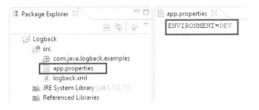

The java class is as follows:

```
package com.java.logback.examples;

import org.slf4j.Logger;
import org.slf4j.LoggerFactory;

public class LogbackExample15 {

    public static void main(String[] args) throws InterruptedException {

        // get logger object
        Logger logger = LoggerFactory.getLogger(LogbackExample15.class);

        // log messages
        logger.error("Error Message");
        logger.warn(" Warning Message");
        logger.info("Information Message");
        logger.debug("Debug Message");

        // induce an exception
        int a[] = { 1, 2, 0 };
        try {
            a[3] = 2;
        } catch (Exception e) {
            logger.error("Array Index is not within bounds");
        }
    }
}
```

The output is as follows:

```
Console 🔲    @ Javadoc  📄 Declaration  📄 Problems                                          ⬛ ✖ ✖
<terminated> LogbackExample15 [Java Application] C:\Program Files\Java\jdk
2017-09-28 18:09:19 ERROR com.java.logback.examples.LogbackExample15 - Error Message
2017-09-28 18:09:19 WARN  com.java.logback.examples.LogbackExample15 -  Warning Message
2017-09-28 18:09:19 INFO  com.java.logback.examples.LogbackExample15 - Information Message
2017-09-28 18:09:19 DEBUG com.java.logback.examples.LogbackExample15 - Debug Message
2017-09-28 18:09:19 ERROR com.java.logback.examples.LogbackExample15 - Array Index is not within bounds
```

As per our configuration, if the value of the property 'ENVIRONMENT' is set to 'DEV,' the logs should be printed on the console which is the result as shown above.

If we now set the value of the property 'ENVIRONMENT' to 'TEST,' the logs are sent to a file.

```
📄 app.properties 🔲
ENVIRONMENT=TEST
```

A file named conditional.log is generated in the project tree as shown below:

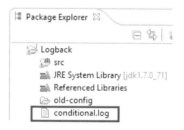

```
📇 Package Explorer 🔲
                                        ⊟ ⥮ |
  📂 Logback
    📁 src
    📚 JRE System Library [jdk1.7.0_71]
    📚 Referenced Libraries
    📂 old-config
    📄 conditional.log
```

The contents of this file are as follows:

```
📄 conditional.log 🔲
2017-09-28 18:14:24 ERROR com.java.logback.examples.LogbackExample15 - Error Message
2017-09-28 18:14:24 WARN  com.java.logback.examples.LogbackExample15 -  Warning Message
2017-09-28 18:14:24 INFO  com.java.logback.examples.LogbackExample15 - Information Message
2017-09-28 18:14:24 DEBUG com.java.logback.examples.LogbackExample15 - Debug Message
2017-09-28 18:14:24 ERROR com.java.logback.examples.LogbackExample15 - Array Index is not within bounds
```

Example 16: Conditional processing of configuration file: Using conditional processing in the appender configuration

In this example, we use conditional processing at a deeper level, namely the appender level. Here, based on a property, we decide the output file name of the FileAppender. The configuration file is as follows:

```
X logback.xml        X
    <?xml version="1.0" encoding="UTF-8"?>
  - <configuration>
    <property scope="context" resource="app.properties" />
        <appender name="fileAppender" class="ch.qos.logback.core.FileAppender">
        <if condition='property("ENVIRONMENT").contains("DEV")'>
            <then>
            <file>devLogFile.log</file>
            </then>
            <else>
                <file>uatLogFile.log</file>
            </else>
            </if>
            <encoder>
                <pattern>%d{yyyy-MM-dd HH:mm:ss} %-5level %logger{55} - %msg %n
                </pattern>
            </encoder>
        </appender>

        <root level="DEBUG">
            <appender-ref ref="fileAppender" />
        </root>
    </configuration>
```

The properties are stored in a file called ass app.properties. We set the value of the property 'ENVIRONMENT' to be 'DEV.'

The Java class file is as follows:

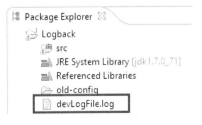

Based on the value of the property 'ENVIRONMENT,' a log file called devLogFile.log is generated.

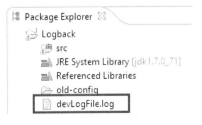

The contents of this file are as follows:

```
devLogFile.log ⊠

2017-09-28 22:05:17 ERROR com.java.logback.examples.LogbackExample16 - Error Message
2017-09-28 22:05:17 WARN  com.java.logback.examples.LogbackExample16 -  Warning Message
2017-09-28 22:05:17 INFO  com.java.logback.examples.LogbackExample16 - Information Message
2017-09-28 22:05:17 DEBUG com.java.logback.examples.LogbackExample16 - Debug Message
```

Example 17: Inclusion of files using the <include> parameter

In this example, we demonstrate the use of the <include> parameter provided by the Joran package which helps include/add configuration elements from another file.

Firstly, we declare our standard logback.xml configuration file as follows:

```
X logback.xml         ⊠

<?xml version="1.0" encoding="UTF-8"?>
<configuration>
<include file="F:\workspace\Logback\src\logback-prod.xml"/>
</configuration>
```

We use the include path to provide the path of the second configuration file that we wish to include.

Kindly note that the absolute path of the file must be provided.

We now create a file called logback-prod.xml. This file (also called as the TARGET file) must compulsorily have its elements declared/nested within an <included> element.

This is shown below:

```
X logback-prod.xml ⊠

<included>
<appender name="consoleAppender" class="ch.qos.logback.core.ConsoleAppender">
        <encoder>
                <pattern>%d{yyyy-MM-dd HH:mm:ss} [%thread] %-5level %logger(55) - %msg%n</pattern>
        </encoder>
</appender>
<appender name="fileAppender"
        class="ch.qos.logback.core.FileAppender">
        <file>productionLog.log</file>
        <encoder>
                <pattern>%d{yyyy-MM-dd HH:mm:ss} [%thread] %-5level %logger(55) - %msg%n</pattern>
        </encoder>
</appender>

<root level="debug">
        <appender-ref ref="consoleAppender" />
        <appender-ref ref="fileAppender" />
</root>
</included>
```

We define two appenders in this file: console and file.

These two appenders are defined just like we have seen so far.

The Java class file is as follows:

```
LogbackExample17.java
    package com.java.logback.examples;

    import org.slf4j.Logger;
    import org.slf4j.LoggerFactory;

    public class LogbackExample17 {

        public static void main(String[] args) throws InterruptedException {

            // get logger object
            Logger logger = LoggerFactory.getLogger(LogbackExample17.class);

            // log messages
            logger.error("Error Message");
            logger.warn(" Warning Message");
            logger.info("Information Message");
            logger.info("Another Information Message");
            logger.debug("Debug Message");

            Object o = null;
            try {
                o.hashCode();
            } catch (NullPointerException e) {
                logger.error("The object is null!!");
            }
        }
    }
```

The console and file outputs are as follows:

```
Console    Javadoc    Declaration    Problems
<terminated> LogbackExample17 [Java Application] C:\Program Files\Java\jdk
2017-09-28 22:24:42 [main] ERROR com.java.logback.examples.LogbackExample17 - Error Message
2017-09-28 22:24:42 [main] WARN  com.java.logback.examples.LogbackExample17 -  Warning Message
2017-09-28 22:24:42 [main] INFO  com.java.logback.examples.LogbackExample17 - Information Message
2017-09-28 22:24:42 [main] INFO  com.java.logback.examples.LogbackExample17 - Another Information Message
2017-09-28 22:24:42 [main] DEBUG com.java.logback.examples.LogbackExample17 - Debug Message
2017-09-28 22:24:42 [main] ERROR com.java.logback.examples.LogbackExample17 - The object is null!!
```

```
production.log
2017-09-28 22:24:42 ERROR com.java.logback.examples.LogbackExample17 - Error Message
2017-09-28 22:24:42 WARN  com.java.logback.examples.LogbackExample17 - Warning Message
2017-09-28 22:24:42 INFO  com.java.logback.examples.LogbackExample17 - Information Message
2017-09-28 22:24:42 INFO  com.java.logback.examples.LogbackExample17 - Another Information Message
2017-09-28 22:24:42 DEBUG com.java.logback.examples.LogbackExample17 - Debug Message
2017-09-28 22:24:42 ERROR com.java.logback.examples.LogbackExample17 - The object is null!!
```

Example 18: Conditional processing of configuration files: Multiple Configuration files based on a static property

In this example, we implement conditional processing constructs that decide which configuration file should be selected based on a property value. The configuration file is as follows:

```
logback.xml
<?xml version="1.0" encoding="UTF-8"?>
<configuration>
    <property scope="context" resource="app.properties" />
    <if condition='property("ENVIRONMENT").contains("DEV")'>
        <then>
            <include file="F:\workspace\Logback\src\logback-dev.xml" />
        </then>
    </if>
    <if condition='property("ENVIRONMENT").contains("PROD")'>
        <then>
            <include file="F:\workspace\Logback\src\logback-prod.xml" />
        </then>
    </if>
    <if condition='property("ENVIRONMENT").contains("UAT")'>
        <then>
            <include file="F:\workspace\Logback\src\logback-uat.xml" />
        </then>
    </if>
</configuration>
```

Three different configuration files have been defined based on the value of the property "ENVIRONMENT." This property is configured by the file app. properties.

Currently, this value is set to 'DEV.'

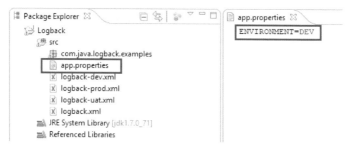

The three configuration files are defined at the same level as the logback. xml file as follows:

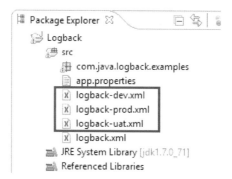

The contents of these files based on the target environment are as follows:

1.   Development Environment: logback-dev.xml

```
X logback-dev.xml  ⊠
  <included>
  <appender name="consoleAppender" class="ch.qos.logback.core.ConsoleAppender">
      <encoder>
          <pattern>%d{yyyy-MM-dd} [%thread] %-5level %logger{55} - %msg%n</pattern>
      </encoder>
  </appender>
  <root level="debug">
      <appender-ref ref="consoleAppender" />
  </root>
  </included>
```

For this environment, we define a simple console appender.

2.   Production Environment: logback-prod.xml

```
X logback-prod.xml
  <included>
  <appender name="consoleAppender" class="ch.qos.logback.core.ConsoleAppender">
      <encoder>
          <pattern>%d{yyyy-MM-dd HH:mm:ss} [%thread] %-5level %logger{55} - %msg%n</pattern>
      </encoder>
  </appender>
  <appender name="rollingFileAppender"
      class="ch.qos.logback.core.rolling.RollingFileAppender">
      <file>productionLog.log</file>
      <rollingPolicy class="ch.qos.logback.core.rolling.TimeBasedRollingPolicy">
          <!-- roll-over on a daily basis -->
          <fileNamePattern>productionLog.%d{yyyy-MM-dd-HH-mm}.log</fileNamePattern>
          <maxHistory>30</maxHistory>
      </rollingPolicy>
      <encoder>
          <pattern>%d{yyyy-MM-dd HH:mm:ss} [%thread] %-5level %logger{55} - %msg%n</pattern>
      </encoder>
  </appender>

  <root level="debug">
      <appender-ref ref="consoleAppender" />
      <appender-ref ref="rollingFileAppender" />
  </root>
  </included>
```

For the production environment, we define two appenders, a rolling file appender with a daily rolling policy and a console appender as well.

3.   UAT Environment: logback-uat.xml

```
X logback-uat.xml
  <included>
      <appender name="fileAppender" class="ch.qos.logback.core.FileAppender">
          <file>uat.log</file>
          <encoder>
              <pattern>%d{yyyy-MM-dd HH:mm:ss} %-5level %logger{55} - %msg %n </pattern>
          </encoder>
      </appender>
      <root level="INFO">
          <appender-ref ref="fileAppender" />
      </root>
  </included>
```

For this environment, we define a simple file appender.

The java class is as follows:

```
LogbackExample18.java
  package com.java.logback.examples;

  import org.slf4j.Logger;

  public class LogbackExample18 {

      public static void main(String[] args) throws InterruptedException {

          // get logger object
          Logger logger = LoggerFactory.getLogger(LogbackExample18.class);
          for (int i = 0; i < 5; i++) {
              // log messages
              logger.error("Error Message");
              logger.warn(" Warning Message");
              logger.info("Information Message");
              Thread.sleep(10000L);
          }
      }
  }
```

Now, based on the current value of the property 'ENVIRONMENT' which is set to 'DEV,' on execution of the program, the logs should be displayed on the console. This is exactly what happens as shown by the console output below:

```
Console 🔀     Javadoc   Declaration   Problems
<terminated> LogbackExample18 [Java Application] C:\Program Files\Java\jdk
2017-09-28 [main] ERROR com.java.logback.examples.LogbackExample18 - Error Message
2017-09-28 [main] WARN  com.java.logback.examples.LogbackExample18 -  Warning Message
2017-09-28 [main] INFO  com.java.logback.examples.LogbackExample18 -  Information Message
2017-09-28 [main] ERROR com.java.logback.examples.LogbackExample18 - Error Message
2017-09-28 [main] WARN  com.java.logback.examples.LogbackExample18 -  Warning Message
2017-09-28 [main] INFO  com.java.logback.examples.LogbackExample18 -  Information Message
2017-09-28 [main] ERROR com.java.logback.examples.LogbackExample18 - Error Message
2017-09-28 [main] WARN  com.java.logback.examples.LogbackExample18 -  Warning Message
2017-09-28 [main] INFO  com.java.logback.examples.LogbackExample18 -  Information Message
2017-09-28 [main] ERROR com.java.logback.examples.LogbackExample18 - Error Message
2017-09-28 [main] WARN  com.java.logback.examples.LogbackExample18 -  Warning Message
2017-09-28 [main] INFO  com.java.logback.examples.LogbackExample18 -  Information Message
2017-09-28 [main] ERROR com.java.logback.examples.LogbackExample18 - Error Message
2017-09-28 [main] WARN  com.java.logback.examples.LogbackExample18 -  Warning Message
2017-09-28 [main] INFO  com.java.logback.examples.LogbackExample18 -  Information Message
```

Now, we change the value of the property 'ENVIRONMENT' to 'PROD' and see what the output is.

On executing the program, the logs are now sent to the console as well as a file name productionLog.log as shown below.

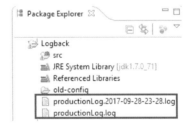

The contents are:

```
productionLog.2017-09-28-23-28.log 🔀
2017-09-28 23:28:01 [main] ERROR com.java.logback.examples.LogbackExample18 - Error Message
2017-09-28 23:28:01 [main] WARN  com.java.logback.examples.LogbackExample18 -  Warning Message
2017-09-28 23:28:01 [main] INFO  com.java.logback.examples.LogbackExample18 -  Information Message
2017-09-28 23:28:11 [main] ERROR com.java.logback.examples.LogbackExample18 - Error Message
2017-09-28 23:28:11 [main] WARN  com.java.logback.examples.LogbackExample18 -  Warning Message
2017-09-28 23:28:11 [main] INFO  com.java.logback.examples.LogbackExample18 -  Information Message
2017-09-28 23:28:21 [main] ERROR com.java.logback.examples.LogbackExample18 - Error Message
2017-09-28 23:28:21 [main] WARN  com.java.logback.examples.LogbackExample18 -  Warning Message
2017-09-28 23:28:21 [main] INFO  com.java.logback.examples.LogbackExample18 -  Information Message
2017-09-28 23:28:31 [main] ERROR com.java.logback.examples.LogbackExample18 - Error Message
2017-09-28 23:28:31 [main] WARN  com.java.logback.examples.LogbackExample18 -  Warning Message
2017-09-28 23:28:31 [main] INFO  com.java.logback.examples.LogbackExample18 -  Information Message
2017-09-28 23:28:41 [main] ERROR com.java.logback.examples.LogbackExample18 - Error Message
2017-09-28 23:28:41 [main] WARN  com.java.logback.examples.LogbackExample18 -  Warning Message
2017-09-28 23:28:41 [main] INFO  com.java.logback.examples.LogbackExample18 -  Information Message
```

```
productionLog.log 🔀
2017-09-28 23:28:51 [main] ERROR com.java.logback.examples.LogbackExample18 - Error Message
2017-09-28 23:29:51 [main] WARN  com.java.logback.examples.LogbackExample18 -  Warning Message
2017-09-28 23:29:51 [main] INFO  com.java.logback.examples.LogbackExample18 -  Information Message
```

The console output is the same as the log file output.

Further, if we change the value of the property to "UAT," a log file called uat.log is generated.

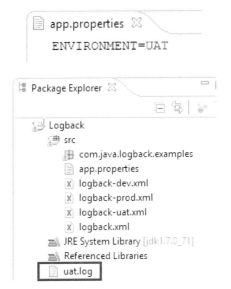

Its contents of the file uat.log are as follows:

```
uat.log
2017-09-28 23:37:07 ERROR com.java.logback.examples.LogbackExample18 - Error Message
2017-09-28 23:37:07 WARN  com.java.logback.examples.LogbackExample18 -  Warning Message
2017-09-28 23:37:07 INFO  com.java.logback.examples.LogbackExample18 - Information Message
2017-09-28 23:37:08 ERROR com.java.logback.examples.LogbackExample18 - Error Message
2017-09-28 23:37:08 WARN  com.java.logback.examples.LogbackExample18 -  Warning Message
2017-09-28 23:37:08 INFO  com.java.logback.examples.LogbackExample18 - Information Message
2017-09-28 23:37:09 ERROR com.java.logback.examples.LogbackExample18 - Error Message
2017-09-28 23:37:09 WARN  com.java.logback.examples.LogbackExample18 -  Warning Message
2017-09-28 23:37:09 INFO  com.java.logback.examples.LogbackExample18 - Information Message
2017-09-28 23:37:10 ERROR com.java.logback.examples.LogbackExample18 - Error Message
2017-09-28 23:37:10 WARN  com.java.logback.examples.LogbackExample18 -  Warning Message
2017-09-28 23:37:10 INFO  com.java.logback.examples.LogbackExample18 - Information Message
2017-09-28 23:37:11 ERROR com.java.logback.examples.LogbackExample18 - Error Message
2017-09-28 23:37:11 WARN  com.java.logback.examples.LogbackExample18 -  Warning Message
2017-09-28 23:37:11 INFO  com.java.logback.examples.LogbackExample18 - Information Message
```

In the current configuration (the main configuration file logback.xml) we have provided 3 if-conditions. But, we haven't considered the case when there is no match. In this case, the logger doesn't have a default NOP implementation as well because a configuration file (logback.xml) has been provided by the developer. Hence, it would be better to have a default condition to fall back on.

This can be done as follows:

```xml
<?xml version="1.0" encoding="UTF-8"?>
<configuration>
    <property scope="context" resource="app.properties" />
    <if condition='property("ENVIRONMENT").contains("DEV")'>
        <then>
            <include file="F:\workspace\Logback\src\logback-dev.xml" />
        </then>
    </if>
    <if condition='property("ENVIRONMENT").contains("PROD")'>
        <then>
            <include file="F:\workspace\Logback\src\logback-prod.xml" />
        </then>
    </if>
    <if condition='property("ENVIRONMENT").contains("UAT")'>
        <then>
            <include file="F:\workspace\Logback\src\logback-uat.xml" />
        </then>
    </if>
    <appender name="consoleAppender" class="ch.qos.logback.core.ConsoleAppender">
        <encoder>
            <pattern>%d{yyyy-MM-dd HH:mm:ss} [%thread] %-5level %logger{55} - %msg%n</pattern>
        </encoder>
    </appender>
    <root level="debug">
        <appender-ref ref="consoleAppender" />
    </root>
</configuration>
```

Here, we provide a default appender and root logger in case the all the conditions do not match. If none of the conditions are met, then the logger defaults to a console appender. But, it is important to note that if even one of the conditions is met, then the logs will be duplicated as we have provided a default console appender and root logger.

If we want to avoid this duplication, we can use the additivity parameter or the duplicate message filter as explained before.

Another way to avoid duplicate messages is to use the nested if-then-else-if clause in the configuration file as shown below:

```xml
<?xml version="1.0" encoding="UTF-8"?>
<configuration>
    <property scope="context" resource="app.properties" />
    <if condition='property("ENVIRONMENT").contains("DEV")'>
        <then>
            <include file="F:\workspace\Logback\src\logback-dev.xml" />
        </then>
        <else>
            <if condition='property("ENVIRONMENT").contains("PROD")'>
                <then>
                    <include file="F:\workspace\Logback\src\logback-prod.xml" />
                </then>
                <else>
                    <if condition='property("ENVIRONMENT").contains("UAT")'>
                        <then>
                            <include file="F:\workspace\Logback\src\logback-uat.xml" />
                        </then>
                        <else>
                            <include file="F:\workspace\Logback\src\logback-default.xml" />
                        </else>
                    </if>
                </else>
            </if>
        </else>
    </if>
</configuration>
```

Here, we add a nested if-then-else loop and provide a default configuration file if no condition matches. We add a new file called as logback-default.xml which implements a simple file appender.

This is shown below:

Now, if we execute the java program, a new file is created in the project structure as shown below:

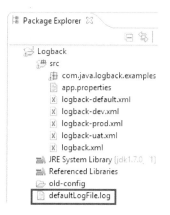

The contents of the file are same as before.

Example 19: Conditional Processing of Configuration File: Multiple configuration files based on System properties

In the previous example, we demonstrated the use of the conditional processing constructs where we read a property from a properties file and based on its value, we choose a configuration file.

This works well in case of a small and simple application. However, in case of large-scale applications that span over several environments and servers, there may be several properties specific to the Operating system that may need to be checked by the logging configuration prior to logging. In an environment that is large and complex, it becomes difficult to maintain a single file containing all the properties to be checked.

In such cases, system properties can be used. Generally, every large-scale application makes use of system properties to store the environment name or context. The logback logging functionality has the option of making use of the system property in its configuration. This is done with the help of the 'scope' element in the configuration files.

We set the scope to be 'system' and then recover the values of the environment variables.

This is shown below:

```xml
<?xml version="1.0" encoding="UTF-8"?>
<configuration>
    <property scope="system" />
    <if condition='property("ENVIRONMENT").contains("DEV")'>
        <then>
            <include file="F:\workspace\Logback\src\logback-dev.xml" />
        </then>
        <else>
            <if condition='property("ENVIRONMENT").contains("PROD")'>
                <then>
                    <include file="F:\workspace\Logback\src\logback-prod.xml" />
                </then>
                <else>
                    <if condition='property("ENVIRONMENT").contains("UAT")'>
                        <then>
                            <include file="F:\workspace\Logback\src\logback-uat.xml" />
                        </then>
                        <else>
                            <include file="F:\workspace\Logback\src\logback-default.xml" />
                        </else>
                    </if>
                </else>
            </if>
        </else>
    </if>
</configuration>
```

We keep the same configuration file as before but we change the scope to 'system.'

We go to the system variables and create a new variable called as 'ENVIRONMENT' with the vale 'DEV' as follows:

We save this value and execute the following java program:

```
LogbackExample19.java
    package com.java.logback.examples;

  + import org.slf4j.Logger;

    public class LogbackExample19 {
        public static void main(String[] args) throws InterruptedException {

            // get logger object
            Logger logger = LoggerFactory.getLogger(LogbackExample19.class);

            // log messages
            logger.error("Error Message");
            logger.warn(" Warning Message");
            logger.info("Information Message");


        }

    }
```

The output is as follows:

```
Console  Javadoc  Declaration  Problems
<terminated> LogbackExample19 [Java Application] C:\Program Files\Java\jdk1.7.0_71\bin\javaw.exe (29-Oct-2017 11:46:57 AM)
11:46:57,417 |-INFO in ch.qos.logback.classic.LoggerContext[default] - Could NOT find resource [logback-test.xml]
11:46:57,417 |-INFO in ch.qos.logback.classic.LoggerContext[default] - Could NOT find resource [logback.groovy]
11:46:57,417 |-INFO in ch.qos.logback.classic.LoggerContext[default] - Found resource [logback.xml] at [file:/F:/workspace/Logback/bin/logback.xml]
11:46:57,492 |-INFO in ch.qos.logback.classic.joran.action.ConfigurationAction - debug attribute not set
11:46:57,495 |-ERROR in ch.qos.logback.core.joran.action.PropertyAction - In <property> element, either the "file" attribute alone, or the "resource" element al
11:46:57,535 |-INFO in ch.qos.logback.core.joran.util.ConfigurationWatchListUtil@f0f7074 - Adding [file:/F:/workspace/Logback/src/logback-dev.xml] to configuration
11:46:57,836 |-INFO in ch.qos.logback.core.joran.action.AppenderAction - About to instantiate appender of type [ch.qos.logback.core.ConsoleAppender]
11:46:57,840 |-INFO in ch.qos.logback.core.joran.action.AppenderAction - Naming appender as [consoleAppender]
11:46:57,846 |-INFO in ch.qos.logback.core.joran.action.NestedComplexPropertyIA - Assuming default type [ch.qos.logback.classic.encoder.PatternLayoutEncoder]
11:46:57,898 |-INFO in ch.qos.logback.classic.joran.action.RootLoggerAction - Setting level of ROOT logger to DEBUG
11:46:57,899 |-INFO in ch.qos.logback.core.joran.action.AppenderRefAction - Attaching appender named [consoleAppender] to Logger[ROOT]
11:46:57,900 |-INFO in ch.qos.logback.classic.joran.action.ConfigurationAction - End of configuration.
11:46:57,901 |-INFO in ch.qos.logback.classic.joran.JoranConfigurator@3e9fd765 - Registering current configuration as safe fallback point

2017-10-29 [main] ERROR com.java.logback.examples.LogbackExample19 - Error Message
2017-10-29 [main] WARN  com.java.logback.examples.LogbackExample19 -  Warning Message
2017-10-29 [main] INFO  com.java.logback.examples.LogbackExample19 - Information Message
```

As seen from the above figure, the logback-dev.xml file has been picked as the configuration file based on the system property and the three log statements have been printed to console as configured in the logback-dev. xml.

Note that the logback-dev.xml file is the same file that we have used in example 18.

Example 20: HTML Layout

In this example, we implement a html file appender. This appender logs the log messages to an html file. The configuration is:

```
logback.xml
<?xml version="1.0" encoding="UTF-8"?>
<configuration>
    <appender name="fileHtmlAppender" class="ch.qos.logback.core.FileAppender">
    <file>log.html</file>
    <encoder class="ch.qos.logback.core.encoder.LayoutWrappingEncoder">
        <layout class="ch.qos.logback.classic.html.HTMLLayout">
            <pattern>%thread%level%logger%msg</pattern>
        </layout>
    </encoder>
</appender>
    <root level="DEBUG">
        <appender-ref ref="fileHtmlAppender" />
    </root>
</configuration>
```

The Java class used to test the above configuration is:

```
LogbackExample20.java
package com.java.logback.examples;

import org.slf4j.Logger;

public class LogbackExample20 {
    public static void main(String[] args) throws InterruptedException {

        // get logger object
        Logger logger = LoggerFactory.getLogger(LogbackExample20.class);

        // log messages
        logger.error("Error Message");
        logger.warn(" Warning Message");
        logger.info("Information Message");
        logger.debug("Debug Message");

    }

}
```

On execution, a new file named log.html is generated in the project structure and its contents are as follows:

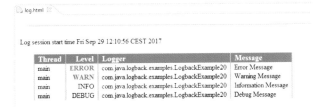

Log session start time Fri Sep 29 12:10:56 CEST 2017

Thread	Level	Logger	Message
main	ERROR	com.java.logback.examples.LogbackExample20	Error Message
main	WARN	com.java.logback.examples.LogbackExample20	Warning Message
main	INFO	com.java.logback.examples.LogbackExample20	Information Message
main	DEBUG	com.java.logback.examples.LogbackExample20	Debug Message

It is interesting to note that the color of the messages ERROR and WARN have been set to red by default.

Example 21: Programmatic Configuration of Logback: Console Appender

In this example, we configure logback programmatically with the use of a logger context object.

First, we get the logger context object and then we proceed to define an encoder and console appender.

Finally, we get the logger object and log message using the newly created console appender.

```
LogbackExample21.java

package com.java.logback.examples;
import org.slf4j.LoggerFactory;
import ch.qos.logback.classic.Level;
import ch.qos.logback.classic.Logger;
import ch.qos.logback.classic.LoggerContext;
import ch.qos.logback.classic.encoder.PatternLayoutEncoder;
import ch.qos.logback.core.ConsoleAppender;

class LogbackExample21 {

    public static void main(String[] args) {

        //get logger context
        LoggerContext loggerContext = (LoggerContext) LoggerFactory.getILoggerFactory();
        //create a PatternLayoutEncoder object
        PatternLayoutEncoder patternLayoutEncoder = new PatternLayoutEncoder();
        //set the context
        patternLayoutEncoder.setContext(loggerContext);
        //set the pattern
        patternLayoutEncoder.setPattern("%d{YYYY-MM-dd HH:mm:ss} %-5level - %msg%n");
        //start the encoder
        patternLayoutEncoder.start();

        //define a console appender
        ConsoleAppender consoleAppender = new ConsoleAppender();
        //set the context
        consoleAppender.setContext(loggerContext);
        //set its name
        consoleAppender.setName("consoleAppender");
        //set its pattern and start the appender
        consoleAppender.setEncoder(patternLayoutEncoder);
        consoleAppender.start();

        //get the logger object from the context
        Logger log = loggerContext.getLogger("Main");
        //set the additivity and Level of the logger
        log.setAdditive(false);
        log.setLevel(Level.DEBUG);
        //add the console appender to the logger
        log.addAppender(consoleAppender);

        //log messages on to the console
        log.info("Information Message");
        log.warn("Warning Message");
        log.debug("Debug Message");
    }
}
```

On execution, the output is as follows:

```
Console ✕    @ Javadoc   Declaration   Problems
<terminated> LogbackExample21 [Java Application] C:\Program Files\Ja
2017-09-29 13:00:36 INFO  - Information Message
2017-09-29 13:00:36 WARN  - Warning Message
2017-09-29 13:00:36 DEBUG - Debug Message
```

Example 22: Programmatic Configuration of Logback: File Appender

This example is similar to example 21, but here we programmatically generate a File Appender.

```java
import ch.qos.logback.classic.LoggerContext;
import ch.qos.logback.classic.encoder.PatternLayoutEncoder;
import ch.qos.logback.core.rolling.RollingFileAppender;
import ch.qos.logback.core.rolling.TimeBasedRollingPolicy;

class LogbackExample22 {

    public static void main(String[] args) {
        // get logger context
        LoggerContext loggerContext = (LoggerContext) LoggerFactory.getILoggerFactory();
        // create a PatternLayoutEncoder object
        PatternLayoutEncoder patternLayoutEncoder = new PatternLayoutEncoder();
        // set the context
        patternLayoutEncoder.setContext(loggerContext);
        // set the pattern
        patternLayoutEncoder.setPattern("%d{YYYY-MM-dd HH:mm:ss} %-5level - %msg%n");
        // start the encoder
        patternLayoutEncoder.start();
        // define a rolling file appender
        RollingFileAppender rollingFileAppender = new RollingFileAppender();
        // set the context
        rollingFileAppender.setContext(loggerContext);
        // name the appender
        rollingFileAppender.setName("Rolling File Appender");
        // set its pattern
        rollingFileAppender.setEncoder(patternLayoutEncoder);
        rollingFileAppender.setAppend(true);
        // define the location and name of the output log file
        rollingFileAppender.setFile("myLogFile.log");

        // Define a time based rolling policy
        TimeBasedRollingPolicy timeBasedRollingPolicy = new TimeBasedRollingPolicy();
        timeBasedRollingPolicy.setContext(loggerContext);
        timeBasedRollingPolicy.setParent(rollingFileAppender);
        timeBasedRollingPolicy.setFileNamePattern("myLogFile-%d{yyyy-MM-dd-HH}.log");
        timeBasedRollingPolicy.setMaxHistory(7);
        timeBasedRollingPolicy.start();
        //set the policy to the logger
        rollingFileAppender.setRollingPolicy(timeBasedRollingPolicy);
        rollingFileAppender.start();
        // get the logger object from the context
        Logger log = loggerContext.getLogger("Main");
        // set the additivity and Level of the logger
        log.setAdditive(false);
        log.setLevel(Level.DEBUG);
        // add the rolling file appender to the logger
        log.addAppender(rollingFileAppender);
        // log messages to a file
        log.info("Information Message");
        log.warn("Warning Message");
        log.debug("Debug Message");
    }
}
```

On executing this class, a log file called as myLogFile.log is created and its contents are as follows:

Example 23: Custom Filter

In this example, we implement a custom filter. We define our own custom filter by extending the filter class as follows:

```java
MyCustomFilter.java

    package com.java.logback.examples;

+   import ch.qos.logback.classic.spi.ILoggingEvent;

    public class MyCustomFilter extends Filter<ILoggingEvent> {

        @Override
        public FilterReply decide(ILoggingEvent event) {

            // we check if the message contains either 'Debug' or 'Error', the log
            // message will be printed
            if (event.getMessage().contains("Debug")
                    || event.getMessage().contains("Error")) {
                return FilterReply.ACCEPT;
            } else {
                return FilterReply.DENY;
            }

        }

    }
```

We configure the filter to accept all log messages that contain the value 'Debug' or 'Error" in it.

We use this filter in our configuration file as shown below:

```xml
logback.xml
    <?xml version="1.0" encoding="UTF-8"?>
    <configuration>
        <appender name="consoleAppender" class="ch.qos.logback.core.ConsoleAppender">
            <filter class="com.java.logback.examples.MyCustomFilter" />
            <encoder>
                <pattern>%d{yyyy-MM-dd HH:mm:ss} [%thread] %-5level %logger{55} - %msg%n</pattern>
            </encoder>
        </appender>

        <root level="DEBUG">
            <appender-ref ref="consoleAppender" />
        </root>
    </configuration>
```

The Java class used to test this custom filter is as follows:

```
📄 LogbackExample23.java ⊠
   package com.java.logback.examples;

   import org.slf4j.Logger;
   import org.slf4j.LoggerFactory;

   public class LogbackExample23 {

       public static void main(String[] args) throws InterruptedException {

           // get logger object
           Logger logger = LoggerFactory.getLogger(LogbackExample23.class);

           // log messages
           // only the messages containing the word 'Error' or 'Debug' will be logged
           logger.error("Error Message");
           logger.warn("Warning Message");
           logger.info("Information Message");
           logger.debug("Debug Message");
           logger.debug("Another Debug Message");
           // induce an exception
           int a[] = { 1, 2, 0 };
           try {
               a[3] = 2;
           } catch (Exception e) {
               logger.error("Error! Array Index is not within bounds");
           }
       }
   }
```

The output generated on the console is as follows:

```
📟 Console ⊠   @ Javadoc  🔍 Declaration  📋 Problems                    ■ ✕ ✖ | 🔈 🛢 🖉 🗐 | 🖵 🗆 ▾
<terminated> LogbackExample23 [Java Application] C:\Program Files\Java\jdk
2017-09-28 16:21:50 [main] ERROR com.java.logback.examples.LogbackExample23 - Error Message
2017-09-28 16:21:50 [main] DEBUG com.java.logback.examples.LogbackExample23 - Debug Message
2017-09-28 16:21:50 [main] DEBUG com.java.logback.examples.LogbackExample23 - Another Debug Message
2017-09-28 16:21:50 [main] ERROR com.java.logback.examples.LogbackExample23 - Error! Array Index is not within bounds
```

As we can see from the output, only the messages that contain the word 'Error' or 'Debug' have been printed on the console.

Example 24: Custom Layout Example

In this example, we implement a custom layout.

We first define our own custom layout class. This class is shown below:

```
📄 MyCustomLayout.java ⊠
   package com.java.logback.examples;
   import java.text.SimpleDateFormat;
   import java.util.Date;
   import ch.qos.logback.classic.spi.ILoggingEvent;
   import ch.qos.logback.core.CoreConstants;
   import ch.qos.logback.core.LayoutBase;

   public class MyCustomLayout extends LayoutBase<ILoggingEvent> {

       public String doLayout(ILoggingEvent event) {

           StringBuffer stringBuffer = new StringBuffer();
           // define a simple date formatter to format the timestamp extracted from
           // the event object
           SimpleDateFormat formatter = new SimpleDateFormat("dd/MM/yyyy hh:mm:ss");
           // append and format the date and time
           stringBuffer.append(formatter.format(new Date(event.getTimeStamp())));
           stringBuffer.append(" ");
           // retrieve the Level
           stringBuffer.append(event.getLevel());
           stringBuffer.append(" [");
           // retrieve the Thread name
           stringBuffer.append(event.getThreadName());
           stringBuffer.append("] ");
           // retrieve the Logger name
           stringBuffer.append(" [");
           stringBuffer.append(event.getLoggerName());
           stringBuffer.append("] ");
           stringBuffer.append(" - ");
           // retrieve the Log Message
           stringBuffer.append(event.getFormattedMessage());
           stringBuffer.append(CoreConstants.LINE_SEPARATOR);
           // return the formatted message
           return stringBuffer.toString();
       }
   }
```

Once we have defined our layout class, we configure our logback configuration file to use this layout as follows:

```xml
logback.xml
<?xml version="1.0" encoding="UTF-8"?>
<configuration>
    <appender name="consoleAppender" class="ch.qos.logback.core.ConsoleAppender">
        <encoder class="ch.qos.logback.core.encoder.LayoutWrappingEncoder">
            <layout class="com.java.logback.examples.MyCustomLayout" />
        </encoder>
    </appender>

    <root level="DEBUG">
        <appender-ref ref="consoleAppender" />
    </root>
</configuration>
```

The java class is as follows:

```java
LogbackExample24.java
package com.java.logback.examples;

import org.slf4j.Logger;

public class LogbackExample24 {

    public static void main(String[] args) {
        // get logger object
        Logger logger = LoggerFactory.getLogger(LogbackExample24.class);

        // log messages
        logger.error("Error Message");
        logger.warn(" Warning Message");
        logger.info("Information Message");
        logger.debug("Debug Message");
    }

}
```

When we run the above java class, the output generated is as follows:

```
Console    Javadoc    Declaration    Problems
<terminated> LogbackExample24 [Java Application] C:\Program Files\Java
29/09/2017 05:07:43 ERROR [main]  [com.java.logback.examples.LogbackExample24]  - Error Message
29/09/2017 05:07:43 WARN [main]   [com.java.logback.examples.LogbackExample24]  - Warning Message
29/09/2017 05:07:43 INFO [main]   [com.java.logback.examples.LogbackExample24]  - Information Message
29/09/2017 05:07:43 DEBUG [main]  [com.java.logback.examples.LogbackExample24]  - Debug Message
```

The output clearly shows that the custom format defined by us has been used to format the log messages.

Example 25: Parameterized Logging with Lambda Expressions

In this example, we show the use of parameterized logging with lambda expressions. We declare two interfaces and provide functional implementations for them using lambda expressions in our Java class.

The interfaces are:

```java
Interface1.java
package com.java.logback.examples;

public interface Interface1 {

    public String infoMessage();
}
```

```
J Interface2.java ⊠
    package com.java.logback.examples;

    public interface Interface2 {

        public String errorMessage();
    }
```

We use the following logback configuration:

```
x logback.xml ⊠
  <?xml version="1.0" encoding="UTF-8"?>
  <configuration>
    <appender name="consoleAppender" class="ch.qos.logback.core.ConsoleAppender">
      <encoder>
        <pattern>%d{yyyy-MM-dd HH:mm:ss} [%thread] %-5level %logger{36} - %msg%n</pattern>
      </encoder>
    </appender>
    <root level="trace">
      <appender-ref ref="consoleAppender" />
    </root>
  </configuration>
```

The java class below implements the interfaces as shown:

```
J LogbackExample25.java ⊠
    package com.java.logback.examples;

  + import org.slf4j.Logger;

    public class LogbackExample25 {

        public static void main(String[] args) {

            // get logger object
            Logger logger = LoggerFactory.getLogger(LogbackExample25.class);

            // log messages
            logger.warn("A Warning Message");
            logger.error("An Error Message");
            logger.trace("A Trace Message");

            // Provide functional implementation of the interface method
            // infoMessage()
            Interface1 int1 = () -> {
                return "The Application is stable.";
            };

            // Provide functional implementation of the interface method
            // errorMessage()
            Interface2 int2 = () -> {
                return "Attention! The application has crashed! ";
            };

            // Provide functional implementation of the interface method
            // infoMessage()
            Interface1 int3 = () -> {
                return "All operations are in order.";
            };

            // log parameterized messages
            logger.info("Information Message: {} ", int1.infoMessage());
            logger.info("Information Message 2: {} ", int3.infoMessage());
            logger.error("Error Message: {}", int2.errorMessage());
        }
    }
```

The log output generated on the console is shown below:

Example 26: Parameterized Logging with Lambda Expressions containing parameters

In this example, we take a step forward and use lambda expressions that take in parameters as well. We now use interfaces that accept parameters as follows:

```java
Interface3.java
    package com.java.logback.examples;

    public interface Interface3 {

        public String errorMessage(String message);
    }
```

```java
Interface4.java
    package com.java.logback.examples;

    public interface Interface4 {

        public int warningMessage(int count);
    }
```

The logback configuration that we have used is as follows:

```xml
logback.xml
    <?xml version="1.0" encoding="UTF-8"?>
    <configuration>
      <appender name="consoleAppender" class="ch.qos.logback.core.ConsoleAppender">
        <encoder>
         <pattern>%d{yyyy-MM-dd HH:mm:ss} [%thread] %-5level %logger{36} - %msg%n</pattern>
        </encoder>
      </appender>
      <root level="trace">
       <appender-ref ref="consoleAppender" />
      </root>
    </configuration>
```

The Java class used to test the parametrized lambda expressions is as follows:

```
📄 LogbackExample26.java ⊠
    package com.java.logback.examples;

  ⊖ import org.slf4j.Logger;
    import org.slf4j.LoggerFactory;

    public class LogbackExample26 {

  ⊖    public static void main(String[] args) {

            // get logger object
            Logger logger = LoggerFactory.getLogger(LogbackExample26.class);

            // log messages
            logger.warn("A Warning Message");
            logger.error("An Error Message");

            // Provide functional implementation of the interface method
            // errorMessage()
            Interface3 int3 = (message) -> message + "Parameter Missing";

            // Provide functional implementation of the interface method
            // warningMessage()
            Interface4 int4 = (count) -> count + 1;

            // log parameterized messages with parameters
            logger.error("Error Message: {} ", int3.errorMessage("Attention!"));
            logger.warn("Warning, file count is: {}", int4.warningMessage(4));

        }
    }
```

The output generated is as follows:

```
🖥 Console ⊠  🔎 Problems  ⊮ Javadoc  🔩 Declaration  🗂 Annotations  ⌇ Call Hierarchy
<terminated> LogbackExample26 [Java Application] C:\Program Files\java\
2017-11-30 19:06:34 [main] WARN  c.j.l.examples.LogbackExample26 - A Warning Message
2017-11-30 19:06:34 [main] ERROR c.j.l.examples.LogbackExample26 - An Error Message
2017-11-30 19:06:34 [main] ERROR c.j.l.examples.LogbackExample26 - Information Message: Attention!Parameter Missing
2017-11-30 19:06:34 [main] INFO  c.j.l.examples.LogbackExample26 - Error Message: 5
```

CHAPTER
5

SLF4J

CONTENTS

SLF4J is Simple Logging Façade for Java which is a framework or abstraction for logging that allows the user to plug-in the logging framework dynamically at deployment time. It provides a layer (SLF4J layer) of abstraction between the application and the underlying logging framework used (SLF4J manual, 2017).

This framework was created by Ceki Gulcu in 2004. The latest stable release is version 1.7.25 (SLF4J News, 2017).

SLF4J acts as a channel between the application and the underlying base logging framework of the application.

We have already seen SLF4J briefly in use in the previous chapter. It is simple to integrate into any java project. To use slf4j in your project, we need to add the slf4j-api.jar in the classpath of the project. In addition to this, the jars of the underlying framework must be provided as well.

In this chapter, in the upcoming sections, we shall take a look at the SLF4J in detail.

5.1. FEATURES AND ADVANTAGES OF SLF4J

Some advantages of using SLF4J are as follows (SLF4J manual, 2017):

1.   It provides the ability to select your logging framework at the time of application deployment.
2.   It offers binding for other logging frameworks such as log4j, logback, java util logging etc.
3.   It provides a tool to migrate java projects to slf4j.
4.   It is fast and supports parameterization of your logging information.
5.   It provides API jars to bridge legacy code from old logging frameworks.

5.2. SLF4J DOWNLOAD

To use slf4j in your java application, the slf4j package is required. It can be downloaded from the official SL4J downloads page

https://www.slf4j.org/download.html

Once downloaded, extract the contents of the compressed file. SLF4J package comes with several jar files that are known as binding jars that help support several logging frameworks such as java util logging, log4j, apache commons etc.

Some of the files are as follows:

These bindings are explained in the next sections.

5.3. SLF4J BINDINGS

SLF4J provides several jar files, also known as bindings in its distribution package.

The slf4j-jdk14-1.7.25.jar is a binding for java util logging, i.e., jdk 1.4 logging. The slf4j-jcl1.7.25.jar is a binding jar for Jakarta Commons Logging framework. The slf4j-log4j12-1.7.25.jar is the binding for the log4j 1.2 version.

The log4j-over-slf4j-1.7.25.jar provides binding for the log4j so that implements the log4j api. Using this jar, any java application has the possibility to migrate to slf4j without changing the code. In order to migrate a log4j dependent application to slf4j, it is sufficient to just replace the log4j. jar file with the log4j-over-slf4j file.

For ease of migration from jcl to slf4j the package has a jar file named jcl-over-slf4j.jar that implements the api of jcl but uses slf4j as the base.

Additionally, slf4j provides a slf4j-simple-1.7.25.jar binding that supports a simple logger. It sends logging events to the system. Err or the console. This logger outputs log message of level higher or above INFO. This simple uncomplicated binding can be used in case of small applications.

Further, a NOP (no-operation) binding is present in the slf4j package as well. This is the default logger that is invoked if no other binding is present in the application. This logger output the log events on to the console as well.

In case of logback, the logback-classic inherently implements slf4j's logger which means that using slf4j with logback incurs no overhead whatsoever in terms of memory and processing times (SLF4J manual, 2017).

Switching between logging frameworks is easy using slf4j. In order to change your logging framework, you need to simply add ONE binding to your classpath.

If your application uses java util logging, then you have two jars in your classpath: slf4j-api and slf4j-jdk1.4.jar

Now, if you want to replace this with logback, replace the slf4j-jdk1.4. by logback-classic.jar. For logback, you will also need to add the logback-core.jar as it forms the base of the logback-classic.jar.

The various bindings between SLF4J and various logging frameworks are explained by the image below:

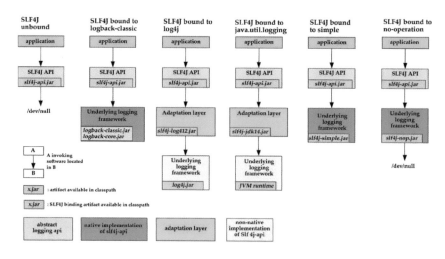

Figure 5.1: SLF4J bindings (SLF4J manual, 2017).

Now that we have seen the various bindings provided by slf4j, we proceed to see how they are implemented and used with other frameworks.

The next section discusses the Simple logger provided by SLF4J.

5.4. SIMPLE LOGGER

The SLF4J package has a simple logger in its package. This logger is a simple implementation of the slf4j logger interface that logs to the console or system. Err.

A few methods provided by this logger are:

Table 5.1: Method of Simple Logger (SLF4J 1.8.0-beta0 API, 2017)

Method	Description
void debug(String message)	This method logs a message of level debug.
void error(String message)	This method logs a message of level error.
void info(String message)	This method logs a message of level info.
void warn(String message)	This method logs a message of level warn.
void trace(String message)	This method logs a message of level trace.
void debug(String message, Throwable t)	This method logs a message of level debug, including an exception stack trace
void error(String message, Throwable t)	This method logs a message of level error, including an exception stack trace
void info(String message, Throwable t)	This method logs a message of level info, including an exception stack trace
void warn(String message, Throwable t)	This method logs a message of level warn, including an exception stack trace
void trace(String message, Throwable t)	This method logs a message of level trace, including an exception stack trace
String get Name()	This method returns the name of the logger.
void log(LoggingEvent e)	This method logs the logging event.
String render Level(int Level)	This method sets the level to the given level.
Boolean is Info Enabled()	This method returns true if info messages are enabled.
Boolean is Error Enabled()	This method returns true if error messages are enabled.
Boolean is Trace Enabled()	This method returns true if trace messages are enabled.
Boolean is Debug Enabled()	This method returns true if debug messages are enabled.
boolean isWarnEnabled()	This method returns true if warn messages are enabled.

In addition to the methods, some static string properties are provided by this class that help in configuring the logger. The properties are as follows:

Table 5.2: Simple Logger properties (SLF4J 1.8.0-beta0 API, 2017)

Property Name	Description
logfile	This is the target output. Possible options are file path, system.err or system.out
Cache Output Stream	If this is set to true, the output stream is cached.
Default Log Level	This can be debug, info, trace, error or warn. By default it is info.
Show Date Time	If this is set to true, the current date and time is printed along with the log message. It is false by default.
Date Time Format	This is used to set the date time to be used while formatting the log messages. By default, it is Simple Date Format of java.
Show Thread Name	This outputs the current thread name and is true by default.
Show Log Name	This property, if true prints the logger name along with the log message.
level In Brackets	This property is used to display the log level within square brackets. By default, it is false.
Show Short Log Name	This property if set to true shows the log name with the last component in the log message.

5.4.1. Examples Using Simple Logger

Example 1

In this example, we demonstrate the use of the slf4j simple logger. To use the slf4j simple logger, we first add slf4j-api.jar and slf4j-simple.jar to our class path as shown below:

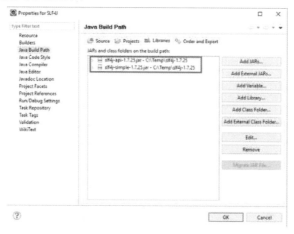

Now we proceed to write a simple java class that uses SLF4J simple logger to log messages.

```java
Example1.java
    package com.java.logging.slf4j.simpleLogger;

    import org.slf4j.Logger;
    import org.slf4j.LoggerFactory;

    public class Example1 {
        public static void main(String[] args) {
            //get the logger object from the LoggerFactory
            Logger logger = LoggerFactory.getLogger(Example1.class);

            //log messages
            logger.info("Information Message");
            logger.error("Error Message");
            logger.warn("Warning Message");
        }
    }
```

The output is as follows:

```
Console    @ Javadoc   Declaration   Problems
<terminated> Example1 [Java Application] C:\Program Files\Java\jdk
[main] INFO com.java.logging.slf4j.simpleLogger.Example1 - Information Message
[main] ERROR com.java.logging.slf4j.simpleLogger.Example1 - Error Message
[main] WARN com.java.logging.slf4j.simpleLogger.Example1 - Warning Message
```

By default, the simple logger is configured to display the logs as shown above. Also, the default level is set to info. But this can be configured which is shown in the next example.

Example 2

In this example, we configure the program to accept log messages of level trace and above.

The java class is as follows:

```java
Example2.java
    package com.java.logging.slf4j.simpleLogger;

    import org.slf4j.Logger;
    import org.slf4j.LoggerFactory;

    public class Example2 {
        public static void main(String[] args) {
            // get the logger object from the LoggerFactory
            Logger logger = LoggerFactory.getLogger(Example2.class);

            // log messages
            logger.info("Information Message");
            logger.error("Error Message");
            logger.warn("Warning Message");
            logger.debug("Debug Message");
            logger.trace("Trace Message");
        }
    }
```

Before we execute this class, we provide the following runtime parameter to the program:

When we run the program, we now get all the messages on the console, including the debug and warning messages.

```
Console ☒    @ Javadoc   Declaration   Problems
<terminated> Example2 [Java Application] C:\Program Files\Java\jdk
[main] INFO com.java.logging.slf4j.simpleLogger.Example2 - Information Message
[main] ERROR com.java.logging.slf4j.simpleLogger.Example2 - Error Message
[main] WARN com.java.logging.slf4j.simpleLogger.Example2 - Warning Message
[main] DEBUG com.java.logging.slf4j.simpleLogger.Example2 - Debug Message
[main] TRACE com.java.logging.slf4j.simpleLogger.Example2 - Trace Message
```

Example 3

In this example, we programmatically change the default level of the logger.

```java
package com.java.logging.slf4j.simpleLogger;

import org.slf4j.Logger;
import org.slf4j.LoggerFactory;

public class Example3 {
    public static void main(String[] args) {

        // set the DEFAULT LOG LEVEL TO DEBUG using the system property
        System.setProperty(org.slf4j.impl.SimpleLogger.DEFAULT_LOG_LEVEL_KEY,
            "DEBUG");

        // get the logger object from the LoggerFactory
        Logger logger = LoggerFactory.getLogger(Example3.class);

        // log messages
        logger.info("Information Message");
        logger.error("Error Message");
        logger.warn("Warning Message");
        logger.debug("Debug Message");
        // the trace message will not be printed as its priority is lower than
        // debug
        logger.trace("Trace Message");
    }
}
```

The output is as follows:

```
Console ☒    @ Javadoc   Declaration   Problems
<terminated> Example3 [Java Application] C:\Program Files\Java\jdk
[main] INFO com.java.logging.slf4j.simpleLogger.Example3 - Information Message
[main] ERROR com.java.logging.slf4j.simpleLogger.Example3 - Error Message
[main] WARN com.java.logging.slf4j.simpleLogger.Example3 - Warning Message
[main] DEBUG com.java.logging.slf4j.simpleLogger.Example3 - Debug Message
```

The output shows that all messages except the message of level trace have been printed.

Example 4

In this example, we make use of system properties to change the format of the log output.

The java class is as follows:

```java
Example4.java ☒
package com.java.logging.slf4j.simpleLogger;

import org.slf4j.Logger;
import org.slf4j.LoggerFactory;

public class Example4 {
    public static void main(String[] args) {

        // set the show date/time property to true using the system property
        System.setProperty(org.slf4j.impl.SimpleLogger.SHOW_DATE_TIME_KEY,
        "TRUE");
        // set the format for the date/time using the system property
        // DATE_TIME_FORMAT_KEY
        System.setProperty(org.slf4j.impl.SimpleLogger.DATE_TIME_FORMAT_KEY,
        "yyyy-MM-dd HH:mm:ss:SSS");

        // get the logger object from the LoggerFactory
        Logger logger = LoggerFactory.getLogger(Example4.class);

        // log messages
        logger.info("Information Message");
        logger.error("Error Message");
        logger.warn("Warning Message");
    }
}
```

The output is as follows:

```
Console ☒    @ Javadoc   Declaration   Problems              ☒ ☒ ☒ ☒
<terminated> Example4 [Java Application] C:\Program Files\Java\
2017-09-30 16:56:59:152 [main] INFO com.java.logging.slf4j.simpleLogger.Example4 - Information Message
2017-09-30 16:56:59:153 [main] ERROR com.java.logging.slf4j.simpleLogger.Example4 - Error Message
2017-09-30 16:56:59:153 [main] WARN com.java.logging.slf4j.simpleLogger.Example4 - Warning Message
```

Example 5

In this example, we configure the logger to output the logging information to a log file.

```
Example5.java

    package com.java.logging.slf4j.simpleLogger;

    import org.slf4j.Logger;
    import org.slf4j.LoggerFactory;

    public class Example5 {
        public static void main(String[] args) {

            // set the show date/time property to true using the system property
            System.setProperty(org.slf4j.impl.SimpleLogger.SHOW_DATE_TIME_KEY,
            "TRUE");
            // set the format for the date/time using the system property
            // DATE_TIME_FORMAT_KEY
            System.setProperty(org.slf4j.impl.SimpleLogger.DATE_TIME_FORMAT_KEY,
            "yyyy-MM-dd HH:mm:ss:SSS");

            // configure the logger to send the output to a log file by setting the
            // LOG_FILE_KEY value to a file name along with its path
            // here as we do not specify a path, the file will be generated in the
            // current directory
            System.setProperty(org.slf4j.impl.SimpleLogger.LOG_FILE_KEY,
            "logFile.log");

            // get the logger object from the LoggerFactory
            Logger logger = LoggerFactory.getLogger(Example5.class);

            // log messages
            logger.info("Information Message");
            logger.error("Error Message");
            logger.warn("Warning Message");
        }
    }
```

A file named as logFile.log is generated in the project directory as shown below:

The contents of this file are as follows:

```
logFile.log

2017-09-30 17:09:06:102 [main] INFO com.java.logging.slf4j.simpleLogger.Example4 - Information Message
2017-09-30 17:09:06:118 [main] ERROR com.java.logging.slf4j.simpleLogger.Example4 - Error Message
2017-09-30 17:09:06:118 [main] WARN com.java.logging.slf4j.simpleLogger.Example4 - Warning Message
```

Example 6

In this example, we configure the logger to display the log level within square brackets. We also configure the logger to print only the name of the last component of the logger. The java class is as follows:

```
📄 Example6.java ☒

    package com.java.logging.slf4j.simpleLogger;

    import org.slf4j.Logger;
    import org.slf4j.LoggerFactory;

    public class Example6 {
        public static void main(String[] args) {

            // display the log level in square brackets
            System.setProperty(org.slf4j.impl.SimpleLogger.LEVEL_IN_BRACKETS_KEY,
            "TRUE");
            // display only the last component of the logger name
            System.setProperty(org.slf4j.impl.SimpleLogger.SHOW_SHORT_LOG_NAME_KEY,
            "TRUE");

            // get the logger object from the LoggerFactory
            Logger logger = LoggerFactory.getLogger(Example6.class);

            // log messages
            logger.info("Information Message");
            logger.error("Error Message");
            logger.warn("Warning Message");
        }
    }
```

The output is as follows:

```
🖥 Console ☒    @ Javadoc  🔖 Declaration  📖 Problems
<terminated> Example6 [Java Application] C:\Program Files\Java\jdk
[main] [INFO] Example6 - Information Message
[main] [ERROR] Example6 - Error Message
[main] [WARN] Example6 - Warning Message
```

As we can see from the output, the level is printed with square brackets around it. Also, we can clearly note that the logger name is shorter and contains only the name of the final component of the complete logger name.

Example 7

We have so far seen how to configure the simple logging programmatically via system properties. But, it is possible to configure the SimpleLogger using a properties file as well.

Like other logging frameworks, Logger implementation of SimpleLogger also checks for a property file on startup. It checks for the presence of a resource named simplelogger.properties.

If no file is found and no properties are configured programmatically, the default logging option is to display the logs in relative time, with the level, thread name, logger and the message as shown in Example 1.

This example demonstrates the configuration of the SimpleLogger using a properties file.

We create a file called as simplelogger.properties in the project tree at the same level as the 'src' folder as shown below:

The contents of this file are as follows:

```
simplelogger.properties ⊠
    # SLF4J SimpleLogger configuration file

    # Default logging level for all instances of the logger
    org.slf4j.simpleLogger.defaultLogLevel=trace

    # Set to true if you want to output the name of the current thread
    org.slf4j.simpleLogger.showThreadName=false

    # Set to true if you want to display
    #the name of the  Logger instance in the output messages
    org.slf4j.simpleLogger.showLogName=true

    # Set to true if you want the only the name of the last
    #component of the logger to be included in the output messages
    org.slf4j.simpleLogger.showShortLogName=false
```

We set the log level to trace and configure the log output to include the thread name and the log name as well.

The java class is as follows:

```java
Example7.java ⊠
    package com.java.logging.slf4j.simpleLogger;

    import org.slf4j.Logger;
    import org.slf4j.LoggerFactory;

    public class Example7 {
        public static void main(String[] args) {

            // get the logger object from the LoggerFactory
            Logger logger = LoggerFactory.getLogger(Example7.class);

            // log messages
            logger.info("Information Message");
            logger.error("Error Message");
            logger.warn("Warning Message");
            logger.trace("Trace Message");
            try {
                int a = 0 / 0;
            } catch (Exception e) {
                logger.error("Cannot divide by zero!");
            }
        }
    }
```

The output is as follows:

```
🖥 Console 🌣    @ Javadoc 🔲 Declaration 🔲 Problems
<terminated> Example7 [Java Application] C:\Program Files\Java\jdk
[main] INFO com.java.logging.slf4j.simpleLogger.Example7 - Information Message
[main] ERROR com.java.logging.slf4j.simpleLogger.Example7 - Error Message
[main] WARN com.java.logging.slf4j.simpleLogger.Example7 - Warning Message
[main] TRACE com.java.logging.slf4j.simpleLogger.Example7 - Trace Message
[main] ERROR com.java.logging.slf4j.simpleLogger.Example7 - Cannot divide by zero!
```

Example 8

In the previous example, we saw how to configure the SLF4J Simple Logger logger via a properties file. In this example, we configure the logger display format to output the logs in YYYY-dd-mm format along with the name of the day of the week and the time zone.

```
📄 simplelogger.properties 🌣
# SLF4J SimpleLogger configuration file

# Default logging level for all instances of the logger
org.slf4j.simpleLogger.defaultLogLevel=debug

# Set to true if you want to output the name of the current thread
org.slf4j.simpleLogger.showThreadName=false

# Set to true if you want to display
#the name of the  Logger instance in the output messages
org.slf4j.simpleLogger.showLogName=true

# Set to true if you want the only the name of the last
#component of the logger to be included in the output messages
org.slf4j.simpleLogger.showShortLogName=false

#Set to true if you want to display the log level with brackets around it
org.slf4j.SimpleLogger.levelInBrackets=true

# Set to true if you want to include the current
#date and time in the output messages
#By default it is false
org.slf4j.simpleLogger.showDateTime=true

# Set the date and time format that will be used to format the output messages.
# The pattern used to set the date and time format is the same as
#that is used in java.text.SimpleDateFormat.
# If no format is specified or if the specified format is invalid,
#the following default format is used: yyyy-MM-dd HH:mm:ss:SSS Z.
org.slf4j.simpleLogger.dateTimeFormat=E, yyyy-MM-dd HH:mm:ss zzzz
```

We configure the logger to hide the thread name, display the log level in brackets and format the log message with the current date and time.

The format we use is: E, yyyy-MM-dd HH:mm:ss zzzz which is a simple Dat Format accepted by the java.text. Simple Date Format class.

Here E displays the name of the day of the week; Monday for instance. The yyyy-MM-dd HH:mm:ss displays the year day month along with the current time in hh:mm:ss. The parameter **zzzz** stands for the time zone in the full format.

The java class is as follows:

```
Example8.java 

  package com.java.logging.slf4j.simpleLogger;

  import org.slf4j.Logger;
  import org.slf4j.LoggerFactory;

  public class Example8 {
      public static void main(String[] args) {

          // get the logger object from the LoggerFactory
          Logger logger = LoggerFactory.getLogger(Example8.class);

          // log messages
          logger.info("Information Message");
          logger.error("Error Message");
          logger.warn("Warning Message");
          logger.debug("Debug Message");
          // induce an Exception
          try {
              Integer x = null;
              x.byteValue();
          } catch (NullPointerException e) {
              logger.error("Null Object!");
          }
      }
  }
```

The output is as follows:

```
Console     Javadoc    Declaration    Problems
<terminated> Example8 [Java Application] C:\Program Files\Java\jdk
Sat, 2017-09-30 19:38:35 Central European Summer Time INFO com.java.logging.slf4j.simpleLogger.Example8 - Information Message
Sat, 2017-09-30 19:38:35 Central European Summer Time ERROR com.java.logging.slf4j.simpleLogger.Example8 - Error Message
Sat, 2017-09-30 19:38:35 Central European Summer Time WARN com.java.logging.slf4j.simpleLogger.Example8 - Warning Message
Sat, 2017-09-30 19:38:35 Central European Summer Time DEBUG com.java.logging.slf4j.simpleLogger.Example8 - Debug Message
Sat, 2017-09-30 19:38:35 Central European Summer Time ERROR com.java.logging.slf4j.simpleLogger.Example8 - Null Object!
```

As shown by the output, the day of the week, along with the current date and time and the complete time zone has been added to the log messages.

5.5. USING SLF4J WITH OTHER LOGGING FRAMEWORKS

In the previous section, we briefly saw the slf4j-simple logging api and its implementation.

In this section, we take a look at the use of SLF4J with other logging framewotks.

1. SFL4j and Java Util Logging

To use SLF4J with java util logging as the underlying or base logging framework, we add the following jars to our classpath:

-slf4j-api.jar

-slf4j-jdk1.4.jar

This is shown below:

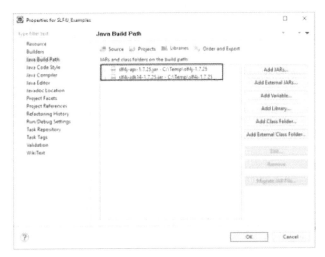

Note that only one binding jar can be present at any given moment in a project. This means that in addition to the slf4j-api.jar, only ONE more binding jar (a binding for a single framework) must be present. If many bindings are present, then the configuration doesn't take place.

The java class is as shown below:

```java
Example1.java

import org.slf4j.Logger;
import org.slf4j.LoggerFactory;

public class Example1 {
    public static void main(String[] args) {
        // get the logger object from the LoggerFactory
        Logger logger = LoggerFactory.getLogger(Example1.class);

        // log messages
        logger.info("Information Message");
        logger.error("Error Message");
        logger.warn("Warning Message");
    }
}
```

The logger needs to be configured as per the logging framework that we wish to use. In this case, it is the java.util.logging. Hence, we need to provide a configuration file named as logging.properties. We use a logging. properties file that is placed in the resources folder. For this example, the default file that is provided by the java.util.logging package has been used.

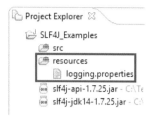

To execute the java program, we need to provide the location of the configuration file as follows:

The output generated is as follows:

```
Console 23    @ Javadoc    Declaration    Problems
<terminated> Example1 (1) [Java Application] C:\Program Files\Java
Sat Sep 30 22:48:13 CEST 2017 Example1 main
INFO: Information Message
Sat Sep 30 22:48:13 CEST 2017 Example1 main
SEVERE: Error Message
Sat Sep 30 22:48:13 CEST 2017 Example1 main
WARNING: Warning Message
```

If we look closely at the format of the output, it is the same output as generated using the java logging framework. This indicates that slf4j is using the java util logging framework as its underlying logging framework.

2. SLF4J and log4j2

To implement SLF4J with log4j logger, we follow the steps as explained in the previous example. The difference, in this case, is that we use the slf4j-log4j12 bindings. Let us use the same java class and the same project as before. Firstly we remove the slf4j-jdk1.4.jar binding.

We now proceed to add the slf4j binding jars to the class path.

In case of log4j, the slf4j-api.jar is dependent on the following jars to configure the application to use log4j as its logging framework.

- log4j-core.jar
- log4j-api.jar
- slf4j-log4j-impl.jar

The slf4j-log4j-impl.jar allows is the binding jar that allows your applications to be coded to use log4j2 as the logging framework implementation.

For older log4j versions (1.2 and older), the binding jar is the slf4j-log4j12.jar along with the following jars:

- log4j-core.jar
- log4j-api.jar
- slf4j-api

We add the jar required to configure log4j2 as our logging framework as shown below:

We click on OK and we have now completed the task of adding bindings.

As we are using log4j as the logging framework, we need to configure our project to use log4j. Hence, we add a simple log4j2.xml file in our class path as follows:

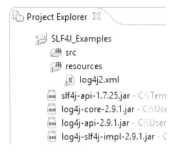

The contents of this file are as follows:

```
[X] log4j2.xml ☒
    <?xml version="1.0" encoding="UTF-8"?>
    <Configuration status="WARN">
        <Appenders>
            <Console name="console" target="SYSTEM_OUT">
                <PatternLayout pattern="[%-5level] %d{yyyy-MM-dd HH:mm:ss.SSS} [%t] %c{1} - %msg%n"/>
            </Console>
        </Appenders>
        <Loggers>
            <Root level="info" additivity="false">
                <AppenderRef ref="console"/>
            </Root>
        </Loggers>
    </Configuration>
```

The java class is the same as before:

```
[J] Example1.java ☒
    import org.slf4j.Logger;
    import org.slf4j.LoggerFactory;

    public class Example1 {
        public static void main(String[] args) {
            // get the logger object from the LoggerFactory
            Logger logger = LoggerFactory.getLogger(Example1.class);

            // log messages
            logger.info("Information Message");
            logger.error("Error Message");
            logger.warn("Warning Message");
        }
    }
```

Now, we execute the java program. The following output clearly shows that the pattern has changed and that log42.xml configuration file has been used to configure the log output.

```
🖵 Console ☒    @ Javadoc  🔍 Declaration  🔍 Problems
<terminated> Example1 (2) [Java Application] C:\Program Files\Java\jdk
[INFO ] 2017-09-30 10:04:33.464 [main] Example1 - Information Message
[ERROR] 2017-09-30 10:04:33.464 [main] Example1 - Error Message
[WARN ] 2017-09-30 10:04:33.464 [main] Example1 - Warning Message
```

3. SLF4J and Logback

We have so far taken a look at the use of slf4j with log4j and the java util logging frameworks.

In this section, we shall see the use of slf4j with logback.

As logback natively implements slf4j, this combination is extremely easy to implement and configure.

Similar to the previous 2 examples, we remove the existing bindings.

Then, we proceed to add the bindings required for the logback framework.

In case of logback, in addition to the slf4j-api.jar, we need the logback-classic.jar as it implements the slf4j logger api. But, logback-classic is in turn dependent on logback-core.jar. Hence, we need to add that jar to our classpath as well.

Hence, in total, we require 3 jar files to configure slf4j with logback. They are:

-    slf4j-api.jar

-    logback-classic.jar

-    logback-core.jar

We add them to our class path by right-clicking on the project-> Build Path-> Configure Build Path.

Next, we add a logback.xml configuration file to configure our application to use logback as its logging framework.

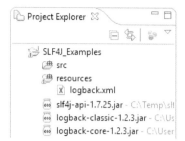

The contents of this file are as follows:

```xml
[X] logback.xml ⊠
    <?xml version="1.0" encoding="UTF-8"?>
<configuration>
    <appender name="consoleAppender" class="ch.qos.logback.core.ConsoleAppender">
        <encoder>
            <pattern>%d{yyyy-MM-dd HH:mm:ss} [%thread] %-5level %logger{55} - %msg%n</pattern>
        </encoder>
    </appender>

    <root level="debug">
        <appender-ref ref="consoleAppender" />
    </root>
</configuration>
```

The java class stays the same as before.

```java
[J] Example1.java ⊠

    import org.slf4j.Logger;
    import org.slf4j.LoggerFactory;

    public class Example1 {
        public static void main(String[] args) {
            // get the logger object from the LoggerFactory
            Logger logger = LoggerFactory.getLogger(Example1.class);

            // log messages
            logger.info("Information Message");
            logger.error("Error Message");
            logger.warn("Warning Message");
        }
    }
```

The output is as follows:

```
🖥 Console ⊠    @ Javadoc  🔍 Declaration  🔍 Problems
<terminated> Example1 (2) [Java Application] C:\Program Files\Java\jdk
2017-09-30 10:56:31 [main] INFO  Example1 - Information Message
2017-09-30 10:56:31 [main] ERROR Example1 - Error Message
2017-09-30 10:56:31 [main] WARN  Example1 - Warning Message
```

As shown by the output, the logback configuration file has been used to format the log messages.

5.6. COMMON SLF4J ERRORS

5.6.1. SLF4J NOP

In slf4j, if no binding is found then the slf4j-api.jar will default to a No-Operation implementation and reject all log messages (SLF4J 1.8.0-beta0 API, 2017)

Consider the same project that we have used for the previous example. We remove theslf4j-simple.jar and just leave the slf4j-api.jar on the classpath as follows:

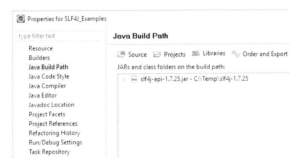

Now, we try to execute the following java class:

```java
import org.slf4j.Logger;
import org.slf4j.LoggerFactory;

public class Example1 {
    public static void main(String[] args) {
        // get the logger object from the LoggerFactory
        Logger logger = LoggerFactory.getLogger(Example1.class);

        // log messages
        logger.info("Information Message");
        logger.error("Error Message");
        logger.warn("Warning Message");
    }
}
```

We get the following warning messages on the console:

```
Console    @ Javadoc    Declaration    Problems
<terminated> Example1 (2) [Java Application] C:\Program Files\Java\jdk
SLF4J: Failed to load class "org.slf4j.impl.StaticLoggerBinder".
SLF4J: Defaulting to no-operation (NOP) logger implementation
SLF4J: See http://www.slf4j.org/codes.html#StaticLoggerBinder for further details.
```

In order to fix this issue, the easiest way is to configure your program to use a logging framework. Once you add the required bindings, the above warning disappears and the application starts logging as per the underlying logging configuration

5.6.2. Multiple Bindings on the Classpath

This is yet another common error that occurs quite frequently.

Sometimes, during the course of development, developers switch between multiple logging frameworks. Hence, sometimes it may happen that we leave the old bindings on the framework. In this case, the logging does not work properly.

Consider that your project was configured to use logback for logging purposes. In this case, the following jars are present on your classpath:

-     slf4j-api.jar
-     logback-classic.jar
-     logback-core.jar

Now, you wish to configure your project to use log4j2. You proceed to add the following jars to your classpath:

-     log4j-core.jar
-     log4j-api.jar
-     slf4j-log4j-impl.jar
-     slf4j-api.jar

But, you forget to remove the previous jar files. Now, your classpath looks like this:

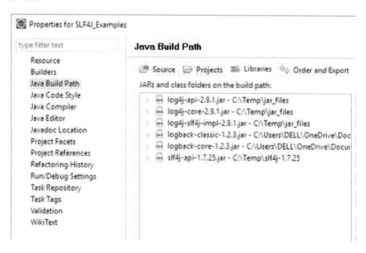

When you execute the java program, we get the following warning messages:

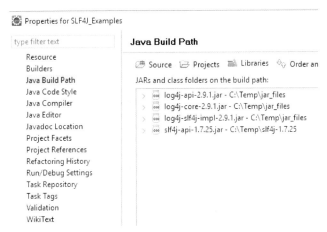

To fix this issue, we simply remove the old bindings and compile our class again.

On execution of the java class, we now get the desired output as shown below:

5.7. MIGRATING YOUR PROJECT TO SLF4J

The SLF4J package comes with a migrator tool that helps migrate projects that use other logging frameworks to use slf4j as the façade for logging.

This is done using the slf4j-migrator.jar provided in the slf4j distribution package.

Consider a project that is using log4j as its logging framework as shown below:

The project consists of a sole java class called Example1.java and has the log4j2.xml configuration file along with the log4j-api and log4j-core jar files in the classpath.

The java class makes use of the log4j log Manager to get the logger object.

```java
import org.apache.logging.log4j.LogManager;
import org.apache.logging.log4j.Logger;

public class Example1 {
    public static void main(String[] args) {
        //get the logger object from the LogManager
        Logger logger = LogManager.getLogger(Example1.class);
        // log messages
        logger.info("Information Message");
        logger.error("Error Message");
        logger.warn("Warning Message");
    }
}
```

To migrate this project to slf4j we first go to the directory where the slf4j-migrate jar is present and open a command prompt at this location

We execute the jar file using the command line as follows:

```
Microsoft Windows [Version 10.0.15063]
(c) 2017 Microsoft Corporation. All rights reserved.

c:\Temp>cd slf4j-1.7.25

c:\Temp\slf4j-1.7.25>java -jar slf4j-migrator-1.7.25.jar
Starting SLF4J Migrator
```

A simple dialog box is displayed as follows:

We specify the path of our log4j project and select the checkbox. We click on the button 'Migrate Project to SLF4J.'

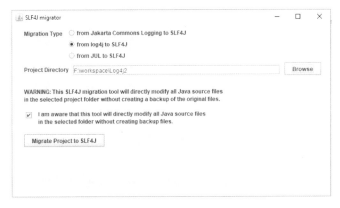

The dialog is updated as follows:

As we can see, it has found the java file in the project and modified the java file to use slf4j.

We now go back to eclipse and take a look at our java class.

```
Example1.java ⊠

 import org.apache.logging.log4j.LogManager;
 import org.apache.logging.log4j.Logger;

 public class Example1 {
     public static void main(String[] args) {

         //get the logger object from the LogManager
         Logger logger = LoggerFactory.getLogger(Example1.class);
         // log messages
         logger.info("Information Message");
         logger.error("Error Message");
         logger.warn("Warning Message");
     }
 }
```

As shown in the image above the contents of the java file have been modified. Now it uses the Logger Factory in slf4j.

But, it gives us an error as the compiler is unable to recognize 'Logger Factory.'

This is because the migrator does the task of migrating the code, not adding slf4j bindings to your classpath.

The bindings need to be handled by the end users. As we are migrating from log4j2 to slf4j we add the following jars to our project:

- slf4j-log4j-impl.jar

- slf4j-api.jar

The log4j-core and log4j-api jar are already present on the classpath. Once we add these jar files and import the slf4j logger instead of the log4j logger and re-build our project, the error is gone.

```
Example1.java ⊠
import org.slf4j.Logger;
import org.slf4j.LoggerFactory;

public class Example1 {
    public static void main(String[] args) {

        // get the logger object from the LogManager
        Logger logger = LoggerFactory.getLogger(Example1.class);
        // log messages
        logger.info("Information Message");
        logger.error("Error Message");
        logger.warn("Warning Message");
    }
}
```

In this example, we modified only a single java file. Hence, the use of the migrator doesn't seem practical. It may seem cumbersome and complex to use the migrator as the project we have used is a very small project where the migration can be done manually.

But, this is not the case in many applications. Imagine a large-scale application with over a thousand java files that implement a logger. In such projects, it becomes tedious to change the java classes manually. In such scenarios, the migrator is extremely useful and practical and helps save time and manpower.

CHAPTER
6

TINY LOG

CONTENTS

6.1. INTRODUCTION

Tiny log is a lightweight logging framework for Java and android applications. It is open source, distributed under the Apache License 2.0 and was released in August 2012 (tinylog, 2017). The very first version to be released was **version 0.6.** The latest stable version **is 1.2.**

Some of the useful features of this framework are as follows (tinylog, 2017):

- It is lightweight and has a very small size. The jar file has a size of 94KB.
- It is easy to configure and use. Like most logging frameworks it can be configured using a properties file, system properties or programmatically.
- It makes use of precompiled patterns which optimizes the performance making it fast.
- TinyLog supports multithreaded applications.
- It provides bindings for a number of different logging frameworks such as Apache Commons Logging, Log4j1.x, and slf4j as well.

6.2. DOWNLOAD

Tiny log is fairly simple to install. First, we need to download the tinylog. jar file

It can be found at the following location:

http://www.tinylog.org/download

Once we download the zip file, we extract its contents.

As we can see, the tinylog jar file is very small and has a size of 92 KB. To use in in a Java project, we simply add it to the project build path. The configuration will be discussed in the next section.

6.3. COMPONENTS OF TINY LOG

The Tiny Log framework is not complex and has minimal components that work together to provide logging functionality.

It has 2 main components: Logger, Level, Writers, and Configurator.

6.3.1. Logger

The logger is the main component of this framework. The logger is the component that is used to generate the log events. In tiny log, the logger is a static class.

Some of the important methods of this class are as follows:

Table 6.1: Logger Methods (**tinylog 1.2.** API, 2017).

Method	Description
Configurator getConfiguration()	This method returns a copy of the current tinylog configuration.
Level getLevel()	This method returns the current global log level.
Level getLevel(String string)	This method returns the level for a class or a package.
void debug(String message)	This method logs a debug message.
void info(String message)	This method logs an information message.
void error(String message)	This method logs an error message.
void warn(String message)	This method logs a warn message.
void trace(String message)	This method logs a trace message.
void debug(Throwable t)	This method logs a debug message with the stack trace.
void info(Throwable t)	This method logs an info message with the stack trace.
void error(Throwable t)	This method logs an error message with the stack trace.
void warn(Throwable t)	This method logs a warn message with the stack trace.
void trace(Throwable t)	This method logs a trace message with the stack trace.
void debug(Throwable t, String message, Object…arguments)	This method logs a debug message with the stack trace and the given arguments
void info(Throwable t, String message, Object…arguments)	This method logs an info message with the stack trace and the given arguments

void error(Throwable t, String message, Object…arguments)	This method logs an error message with the stack trace and the given arguments
void warn(Throwable t, String message, Object…arguments)	This method logs a warning message with the stack trace and the given arguments
void trace(Throwable t, String message, Object…arguments)	This method logs a trace message with the stack trace and the given arguments

6.3.2. Level

Similar to other logging frameworks, tinylog makes use of a level class that holds the various levels used by the logger to log the messages.

This class consists of an enumeration of the following log levels:

-DEBUG

-TRACE

-INFO

-ERROR

-WARN

The order of their priority is:

TRACE<DEBUG<INFO<WARN<ERROR

By default, tiny log is configured to log messages of level INFO and above.

This means that the debug and trace messages are ignored by the logger.

6.3.3. Writers

In tiny log, the writers are analogous to appenders and print the log messages to the desired location/destination such as console, file etc. (tiny **log 1.2.** API, 2017).

The following writers are provided by tiny log:

1.   Console Writer: This writer writes the log messages on to the console.

2.   File Writer: This writer writes the log messages to a file.

3.   Rolling File Writer: This writer is like a Rolling File Appender and rolls out (rotates) the log files.

Once a certain condition is met (size/ time for example) a new file is created and the old one is backed-up. Tiny log provides a **labeler** that is used to name the log files that are rotated. The labeler is analogous to a file name pattern in logback/log4j. Also, rolling **policies** are provided that help define when to create/roll out a new file. Policies are analogous to Triggering policies used in logback.

Similar to other frameworks used for logging, the labeler and the policies go hand in hand.

Tiny Log comes with the following labelers:

- Count Labeler: This labeler is used to label the rolled out files in a sequential way starting from 0 such as file.0.log, file.1.log and so on. To configure this labeler the keyword 'count' must be used in the configuration.

- Process Id Labeler: This particular labeler is used to label the rolled out files with the current process id such as file.1234.log. The keyword 'pid' is used to configure this labeler.

- Time Stamp Labeler: This labeler is used to label the rolled-out files with the timestamp. This timestamp is generally a date format as specified by the Simple Date Format. The keyword 'timestamp' is used to configure this labeler for the writer.

TinyLog has the following Policies:

- Hourly Policy: This rolling policy rotates log files on an hourly basis. The keyword to be used in the configuration is 'hourly.'

- Daily: This rolling policy rotates log files on a daily basis. The keyword to be used in the configuration is 'daily.'

- Weekly: This rolling policy rotates log files on a weekly basis. The keyword to be used in the configuration is 'weekly.'

- Monthly: This rolling policy rotates log files on a monthly basis. The keyword to be used in the configuration is 'monthly.'

- Yearly: This rolling policy rotates log files on a yearly basis. The keyword to be used in the configuration is 'yearly.'

- Size Policy: This rolling policy rotates log files based on the size of the log file. A roll-out happens when the given file size is reached. The keyword to be used in the configuration is 'size.' Example: tinylog. writer. policies= size: 1KB.

- Count Policy: This policy is used to rotate the log files based on the count of the total number of log entries in the log file. The keyword to be used during configuration is 'count.'

Example: tinylog. writer. policies = count: 10

- Startup Policy: This policy rolls out a new file each time the application is started. The keyword that should be used is 'startup.' This is the default policy set up for the rolling file writer. If no other policy is configured, then the startup policy is activated by tiny log.

4. JDBC Writer: This writer writes the log messages to an SQL database table.

This writer supports writing of logs to the database in batch mode as well. Moreover, in case of losses of connections, tinylog supports the reestablishment of the lost connection. The configuration for the logger is the same configuration that is used in case of the configuration of jdbc with the url, sid, and hostname. The username and password (if any) for the database can be configured as well.

Using the jdbc writer the following values can be logged (tinylog, 2017)

Parameter Name	Description
DATE	The date and time pertaining to the log
THREAD_ID	The identifier of the current thread
THREAD_NAME	The name of the current thread
RENDERED_LOG_ENTRY	The final value of the rendered log entry used for text format
PROCESS_ID	The process id of the application
CLASS	The fully qualified name of the class
CLASS_NAME	The name of the class without its package name that generated the log request
METHOD	The name of the method that generated the log request
PACKAGE	The package that issues the log requests
MESSAGE	The log message
LINE	The line number that generated the log request
EXCEPTION	Exception (if any) thrown by the program
LEVEL	The level of the log entry
CONTEXT	The values set within the logging context
FILE	The name of the java source file that generated the log request

5. Shared File Writer: This writer is used to share a file among several logger instances. This is generally used in a multithreaded context.

6. Logcat Writer: This writer is used to log messages in an Android system/context.

TinyLog provides a Writer interface which is implemented by all the above writer classes.

The methods provided by this interface are as follows (tinylog, 2017):

Table 6.2: Writer Interface Methods (**tinylog 1.2.** API, 2017)

Method	Description
void write(LogEntry logEntry)	This method writes a log entry/message to its destination.
void init(Configuration configuration)	This method is used to initialize the writer.
Set<LogEntryValue> getRequiredLogEntryValues()	This method returns all the values of the log entries that are needed by the writer.
void flush()	This method flushes out the writer and outputs any residual buffer data.
void close()	This method closes the current writer and frees all the resources it occupies from memory.

6.3.4. Configurator

The configurator is used to configure the TinyLog Logger (tinylog 1.2 API, 2017). Some of the use methods provided by this class are as follows:

Table 6.3: Configurator class methods (tinylog 1.2 API, 2017)

Method	Description
Configurator add Writer (Writer writer)	This method adds a writer to output the log entries.
Configurator add Writer (Writer, Level level)	This method adds a writer to output the log entries and set the given level for the writer.
Configurator add Writer (Writer, Level, String pattern)	This method adds a writer to output the log entries, sets the given level for the writer and sets the given pattern for the writer.

Boolean activate ()	This method is used to activate the tinylog configuration.
static Configurator current Config ()	This method returns a new configuration based on the current configuration.
static Configurator default Config ()	This method returns a new configuration based on the default tinylog configuration.
static Configurator from File (File file)	This method loads the tinylog properties from a file on the system.
static Configurator from Resource (String file)	This method loads the tinylog properties from a file on the classpath.
Configurator level l(Level level)	This method sets the log level severity.
Configurator remove All Writers ()	This method removes all the writers.
Configurator remove Writer (Writer writer)	This method removes the specified writer.
Configurator writer (Writer writer)	This method sets the given parameter as the writer

In addition to the above components, another important part of the tinylog configuration is the format used for logging.

The format decides the way in which the logs will be printed on the destination. Tinylog uses placeholders '{}' to specify the elements present in the log format.

The default format is the following (tinylog, 2017):

"{date:yyyy-MM-dd   HH:mm:ss}   [{thread}]   {class}.{method} ()\n{level}: {message}."

By default, the date and time are printed followed by the current thread name, followed by the fully qualified class name and method name on the first line. On the next line, the level of the message and the message is printed.

The various placeholders and their meaning are provided in the table below:

Table 6.4: Place Holder Descriptions (tinylog, 2017)

Place Holder Name	Description
{class}	The fully qualified name of the class that logged the message.
{class_name}	The name of the class (not the full package name) that logged the message.
{date}	The date and time the logging request took place. It is compatible with SimpleDateFormat in Java.
{file}	Name of the java source file which issued the log request
{line}	Line number in the java class where the log was invoked.
{message}	The log message
{method}	The name of method that invoked the log message.
{package}	The name of the package that invoked the logging request.
{level}	The log level of the message.
{pid}	The process ID of the java application.
{thread}	The name of the current thread.
{thread_id}	The ID of the current thread that invoked the log message.
{context:key}	Key-value pair taken at runtime (Thread-safe)

6.4. CONFIGURATION

In the previous section, we took a brief look at the components of tinylog. We shall now proceed to configure tinylog for our java applications.

The first step is to add the tinylog.jar file on the classpath of our project.

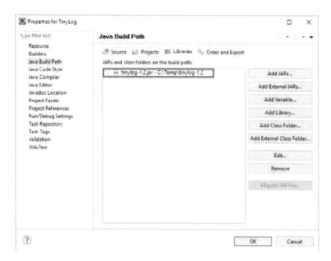

We now proceed to add the logging configuration. In tinylog, this can be done in three ways:

-    Via a tinylog. properties file

-    Via system properties

-    Via Java API

We shall take a look at all of these ways.

1.   Configuration using properties file

This is the most common way of configuring logging functionality for java projects. We provide a simple tinylog. Properties file with the parameters that we wish to configure such as level, pattern, etc.

Similar to log4j and logback, the properties file must be placed in either the resources folder or in the src folder of your project.

This is shown below:

We have created a file named tinylog.properties in the source folder. In this file, we simply configure a console writer.

We proceed to write a java class to test the configuration. It is as follows:

```
J TinyLogExample.java ⊠
   package com.java.logging.tinylog;

   //import the static logger
   import org.pmw.tinylog.Logger;

   public class TinyLogExample {
       public static void main(String[] args) {

           // log messages
           Logger.info("Information Message");
           Logger.warn("Warning Message");
           Logger.error("Error Message");
       }

   }
```

On execution of the above class, we get the log output as shown below:

```
🖳 Console ⊠   @ Javadoc  🔍 Declaration  🔲 Problems
<terminated> TinyLogExample [Java Application] C:\Program Files\Java\
2017-09-30 21:11:31 [main] com.java.logging.tinylog.TinyLogExample.main()
INFO: Information Message
2017-09-30 21:11:31 [main] com.java.logging.tinylog.TinyLogExample.main()
WARNING: Warning Message
2017-09-30 21:11:31 [main] com.java.logging.tinylog.TinyLogExample.main()
ERROR: Error Message
```

The format shown above is the default output format of tinylog.

2.   Configuration using the System properties

The system properties can be used to configure the tinylog logging configuration for a java project.

This is done via the VM parameters tab in Eclipse.

Consider the following java class:

```
J TinyLogConfig.java ⊠
   package com.java.logging.tinylog;

   //import the static logger
   import org.pmw.tinylog.Logger;

   public class TinyLogConfig {
       public static void main(String[] args) {

           // log messages
           Logger.info("Information Message");
           Logger.warn("Warning Message");
           Logger.error("Error Message");
           Logger.debug("Debug Message");
       }

   }
```

To configure the tinylog parameters, we right click on the java class and click on Run As-> Run Configurations.

We open the arguments tab and provide our logging configuration in the VM arguments section as follows:

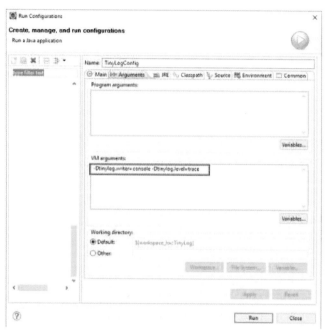

We add the parameters that we wish to configure and click on 'Run.'

The output of the program is as follows:

```
Console ⊠    @ Javadoc  Declaration  Problems
<terminated> TinyLogConfig [Java Application] C:\Program Files\Java\jdk
2017-09-30 21:31:48 [main] com.java.logging.tinylog.TinyLogConfig.main()
INFO: Information Message
2017-09-30 21:31:48 [main] com.java.logging.tinylog.TinyLogConfig.main()
WARNING: Warning Message
2017-09-30 21:31:48 [main] com.java.logging.tinylog.TinyLogConfig.main()
DEBUG: Debug Message
2017-09-30 21:31:48 [main] com.java.logging.tinylog.TinyLogConfig.main()
ERROR: Error Message
```

In the above output, messages of level debug have been printed as well. This means that the configuration provided by using the system properties has been configured for the class.

3.   Configuration using API

Tinylog provides the end users with the ability to configure the logging programmatically as well. This can be done with the help of the Configurator class and is shown by the class TinyLogConfigurator.java below:

```
TinyLogConfigurator.java

    package com.java.logging.tinylog;

    //import the Configurator
    import org.pmw.tinylog.Configurator;
    //import the static logger
    import org.pmw.tinylog.Logger;
    import org.pmw.tinylog.Level;
    import org.pmw.tinylog.writers.ConsoleWriter;

    public class TinyLogConfigurator {
        public static void main(String[] args) {

            // get the default configuration
            // set the writer as the ConsoleWriter
            // set the level to TRACE
            // activate the configuration
            Configurator.defaultConfig().writer(new ConsoleWriter())
                    .level(Level.TRACE).activate();

            // log messages
            Logger.info("Information Message");
            Logger.warn("Warning Message");
            Logger.error("Error Message");
            Logger.debug("Debug Message");
            Logger.trace("Trace Message");
        }
    }
```

On execution of this class, we get the following output:

```
Console    Javadoc   Declaration   Problems
<terminated> TinyLogConfigurator [Java Application] C:\Program Files\Java\jdk
2017-09-30 21:42:27 [main] com.java.logging.tinylog.TinyLogConfigurator.main()
INFO: Information Message
2017-09-30 21:42:27 [main] com.java.logging.tinylog.TinyLogConfigurator.main()
WARNING: Warning Message
2017-09-30 21:42:27 [main] com.java.logging.tinylog.TinyLogConfigurator.main()
ERROR: Error Message
2017-09-30 21:42:27 [main] com.java.logging.tinylog.TinyLogConfigurator.main()
DEBUG: Debug Message
2017-09-30 21:42:27 [main] com.java.logging.tinylog.TinyLogConfigurator.main()
TRACE: Trace Message
```

The output shows that the default format has been used and the logs have been printed on the console. Also, the level has been set to trace as we have configured and hence the logs of level debug and trace have been sent to the console as well.

6.5. EXAMPLES

Example 1: Simple Console Writer

In this example, we demonstrate the use of a simple console writer using tinylog. We used a properties file to configure our application to use tinylog.

The properties file is as follows:

```
tinylog.properties ⌗
tinylog.writer = console
tinylog.writer.format = {date:yyyy-MM-dd HH:mm:ss} {thread} {level}: {message}
tinylog.level=trace
```

We configure our application use the console writer with the level trace. The format of the log messages is as shown above.

The java class is as follows:

```
TinyLogExample1.java ⌗
package com.java.logging.tinylog;

//import the static logger
import org.pmw.tinylog.Logger;

public class TinyLogExample1 {

    public static void main(String[] args) {
        // log messages
        Logger.trace("Trace Message");
        Logger.info("Information Message");
        Logger.warn("Warning Message");
        Logger.error("Error Message");
        Logger.debug("Debug Message");

    }
}
```

The output is:

```
Console ⌗    @ Javadoc   Declaration   Problems
<terminated> TinyLogExample1 [Java Application] C:\Program Files\Java\jdk
2017-09-30 22:38:41 main WARNING: Warning Message
2017-09-30 22:38:41 main ERROR: Error Message
2017-09-30 22:38:41 main TRACE: Trace Message
2017-09-30 22:38:41 main INFO: Information Message
2017-09-30 22:38:41 main DEBUG: Debug Message
```

Example 2: Simple File Writer

This example demonstrates the File Writer in tinylog. We use a properties file to configure our application to write log messages to a file.

The properties file is as follows:

```
tinylog.properties ⌗
#Set the writer to file
tinylog.writer = file
#specify the format of the output messages
tinylog.writer.format = {date:yyyy-MM-dd HH:mm:ss} {thread} [{package}] {level}: {message}
#specify the filename and path
tinylog.writer.filename=myLogFile.log
#specify the level of the writer
tinylog.level=debug
```

The java class is the following:

```
TinyLogExample2.java
    package com.java.logging.tinylog;

    //import the static logger
    import org.pmw.tinylog.Logger;

    public class TinyLogExample2 {

        public static void main(String[] args) {
            // log messages
            Logger.trace("Trace Message");
            Logger.info("Information Message");
            Logger.warn("Warning Message");
            Logger.error("Error Message");
            Logger.debug("Debug Message");

        }
    }
```

On execution of the above class, a new file called as myLogFile.log is generated in the project structure as shown below:

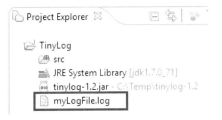

The contents of this file are as follows:

```
myLogFile.log
2017-09-30 22:50:08 main [com.java.logging.tinylog] INFO: Information Message
2017-09-30 22:50:08 main [com.java.logging.tinylog] WARNING: Warning Message
2017-09-30 22:50:08 main [com.java.logging.tinylog] ERROR: Error Message
2017-09-30 22:50:08 main [com.java.logging.tinylog] DEBUG: Debug Message
```

Example 3: Rolling File Writer based on size

This example shows the use of a rolling file writer that rolls log files on the basis of size. We make use of a properties file to configure our application. We define the labeler to be the count labeler and the policy to be a size policy as shown by the tinylog. properties file below:

```
tinylog.properties
#Set the writer to file
tinylog.writer = rollingfile
#specify the format of the output messages
tinylog.writer.format = {date:yyyy-MM-dd HH:mm:ss} {thread} [{package}] {level}: {message}
#specify the filename and path
tinylog.writer.filename=myLogFile.log
#specify the number of backups
tinylog.writer.backups=5
#specify the labeler
tinylog.writer.label=count
#set the writing policy to size
tinylog.writer.policies = size: 2KB
#specify the level of the writer
tinylog.level=trace
```

The java class is as follows:

```java
TinyLogExample3.java

package com.java.logging.tinylog;

//import the static logger
import org.pmw.tinylog.Logger;

public class TinyLogExample3 {

    public static void main(String[] args) {
        // log messages in a loop
        for (int i = 0; i < 10; i++) {

            Logger.trace("Trace Message");
            Logger.info("Information Message");
            Logger.warn("Warning Message");
            Logger.error("Error Message");
            Logger.debug("Debug Message");
        }
    }
}
```

When we run the java class, two files are generated as shown below:

```
Project Explorer

TinyLog
    src
    JRE System Library [jdk1.7.0_71]
    tinylog-1.2.jar - C:\Temp\tinylog-1.2
    myLogFile.0.log
    myLogFile.log
```

The contents of the log files are as follows:

myLogFile0.log

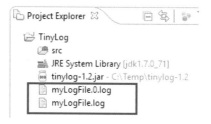

```
myLogFile.0.log

2017-09-30 23:13:41 main [com.java.logging.tinylog] TRACE: Trace Message
2017-09-30 23:13:41 main [com.java.logging.tinylog] INFO: Information Message
2017-09-30 23:13:41 main [com.java.logging.tinylog] WARNING: Warning Message
2017-09-30 23:13:41 main [com.java.logging.tinylog] ERROR: Error Message
2017-09-30 23:13:41 main [com.java.logging.tinylog] DEBUG: Debug Message
2017-09-30 23:13:41 main [com.java.logging.tinylog] TRACE: Trace Message
2017-09-30 23:13:41 main [com.java.logging.tinylog] INFO: Information Message
2017-09-30 23:13:41 main [com.java.logging.tinylog] WARNING: Warning Message
2017-09-30 23:13:41 main [com.java.logging.tinylog] ERROR: Error Message
2017-09-30 23:13:41 main [com.java.logging.tinylog] DEBUG: Debug Message
2017-09-30 23:13:41 main [com.java.logging.tinylog] TRACE: Trace Message
2017-09-30 23:13:41 main [com.java.logging.tinylog] INFO: Information Message
2017-09-30 23:13:41 main [com.java.logging.tinylog] WARNING: Warning Message
2017-09-30 23:13:41 main [com.java.logging.tinylog] ERROR: Error Message
2017-09-30 23:13:41 main [com.java.logging.tinylog] DEBUG: Debug Message
2017-09-30 23:13:41 main [com.java.logging.tinylog] TRACE: Trace Message
2017-09-30 23:13:41 main [com.java.logging.tinylog] INFO: Information Message
2017-09-30 23:13:41 main [com.java.logging.tinylog] WARNING: Warning Message
2017-09-30 23:13:41 main [com.java.logging.tinylog] ERROR: Error Message
2017-09-30 23:13:41 main [com.java.logging.tinylog] DEBUG: Debug Message
2017-09-30 23:13:41 main [com.java.logging.tinylog] TRACE: Trace Message
2017-09-30 23:13:41 main [com.java.logging.tinylog] INFO: Information Message
2017-09-30 23:13:41 main [com.java.logging.tinylog] WARNING: Warning Message
2017-09-30 23:13:41 main [com.java.logging.tinylog] ERROR: Error Message
2017-09-30 23:13:41 main [com.java.logging.tinylog] DEBUG: Debug Message
2017-09-30 23:13:41 main [com.java.logging.tinylog] TRACE: Trace Message
2017-09-30 23:13:41 main [com.java.logging.tinylog] INFO: Information Message
```

myLogFile.log

```
myLogFile.log
2017-09-30 23:13:41 main [com.java.logging.tinylog] WARNING: Warning Message
2017-09-30 23:13:41 main [com.java.logging.tinylog] ERROR: Error Message
2017-09-30 23:13:41 main [com.java.logging.tinylog] DEBUG: Debug Message
2017-09-30 23:13:41 main [com.java.logging.tinylog] TRACE: Trace Message
2017-09-30 23:13:41 main [com.java.logging.tinylog] INFO: Information Message
2017-09-30 23:13:41 main [com.java.logging.tinylog] WARNING: Warning Message
2017-09-30 23:13:41 main [com.java.logging.tinylog] ERROR: Error Message
2017-09-30 23:13:41 main [com.java.logging.tinylog] DEBUG: Debug Message
2017-09-30 23:13:41 main [com.java.logging.tinylog] TRACE: Trace Message
2017-09-30 23:13:41 main [com.java.logging.tinylog] INFO: Information Message
2017-09-30 23:13:41 main [com.java.logging.tinylog] WARNING: Warning Message
2017-09-30 23:13:41 main [com.java.logging.tinylog] ERROR: Error Message
2017-09-30 23:13:41 main [com.java.logging.tinylog] DEBUG: Debug Message
2017-09-30 23:13:41 main [com.java.logging.tinylog] TRACE: Trace Message
2017-09-30 23:13:41 main [com.java.logging.tinylog] INFO: Information Message
2017-09-30 23:13:41 main [com.java.logging.tinylog] WARNING: Warning Message
2017-09-30 23:13:41 main [com.java.logging.tinylog] ERROR: Error Message
2017-09-30 23:13:41 main [com.java.logging.tinylog] DEBUG: Debug Message
2017-09-30 23:13:41 main [com.java.logging.tinylog] TRACE: Trace Message
2017-09-30 23:13:41 main [com.java.logging.tinylog] INFO: Information Message
2017-09-30 23:13:41 main [com.java.logging.tinylog] WARNING: Warning Message
2017-09-30 23:13:41 main [com.java.logging.tinylog] ERROR: Error Message
2017-09-30 23:13:41 main [com.java.logging.tinylog] DEBUG: Debug Message
```

Example 4: Rolling File Writer based on count

In the previous example, we saw how to configure the rolling file writer on the basis of the size of the log files. Now, we try to understand how to roll files based on the count of the log messages.

The properties file is as follows:

```
tinylog.properties
#Set the writer to file
tinylog.writer = rollingfile
#specify the format of the output messages
tinylog.writer.format = {date:yyyy-MM-dd HH:mm:ss} {thread} [{level}]: {message}
#specify the filename and path
tinylog.writer.filename=myLogFile.log
#specify the number of backups
tinylog.writer.backups=5
#specify the labeler
tinylog.writer.label=count
#set the writing policy to count
tinylog.writer.policies = count : 15
#specify the level of the writer
tinylog.level=debug
```

The java class is as follows:

```java
TinyLogExample4.java
package com.java.logging.tinylog;

//import the static logger
import org.pmw.tinylog.Logger;

public class TinyLogExample4 {

    public static void main(String[] args) {
        // log messages in a loop
        for (int i = 0; i < 15; i++) {

            Logger.info("Information Message");
            Logger.warn("Warning Message");
            Logger.error("Error Message");
            Logger.debug("Debug Message");
        }
    }
}
```

When we run the class, 4 files are generated in the project tree which is shown below:

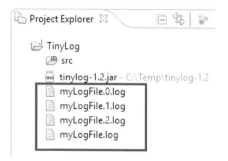

The contents of the files are as follows:

myLogFile0.log and myLogFile1.log

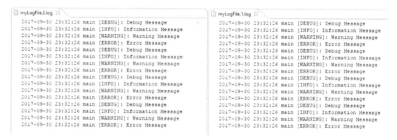

myLogFile2.log and myLogFile.log

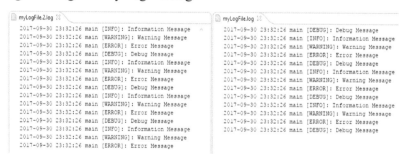

The files myLogFile0.log, myLogFile1.log, and myLogFile2.log each have 15 entries. As the file myLogFile.log was created the last, it has the remaining log entries.

Example 5: Loading the Configuration File

Sometimes, the configuration file or the properties file may not be present in the current project directory. In such cases, we have the possibility of loading the properties file in tinylog.

This can be done in two ways: using a system property or programmatically. In this example, we demonstrate how to load the properties file using the system property.

The properties file is configured to output to the console as shown below:

```
tinylog.properties
#Set the writer to file
tinylog.writer = console
#specify the format of the output messages
tinylog.writer.format = {date:yyyy-MM-dd HH:mm:ss} {thread} [{level}]: {message}
#specify the level of the writer
tinylog.level=debug
```

This file is located in C:\ Temp, a location that is not the current classpath.

The java class is the following:

```
TinyLogExample5.java
package com.java.logging.tinylog;

//import the static logger
import org.pmw.tinylog.Logger;

public class TinyLogExample5 {

    public static void main(String[] args) {

        // log messages in a loop
        Logger.info("Information Message");
        Logger.warn("Warning Message");
        Logger.error("Error Message");
        Logger.debug("Debug Message");
    }
}
```

Before running the class, we now provide the system property in the Run Configurations> VM Arguments tab as follows:

We add the property 'tinylog.configuration' and specify the fully qualified path of the configuration file.

We click on run to execute the class.

The output is as follows:

```
Console ⊠    @ Javadoc   Declaration   Problems
<terminated> TinyLogExample5 [Java Application] C:\Program Files\Java\jdk
2017-10-01 00:18:08 main [INFO]: Information Message
2017-10-01 00:18:08 main [WARNING]: Warning Message
2017-10-01 00:18:08 main [ERROR]: Error Message
2017-10-01 00:18:08 main [DEBUG]: Debug Message
```

Example 6: Loading the configuration file programmatically

In the example, we load the tinylog.properties file, which is present in C:\Temp using the Configutator API.

The contents of the properties file are:

```
tinylog.properties ⊠
#Set the writer to file
tinylog.writer = console
#specify the format of the output messages
tinylog.writer.format = {date:yyyy-MM-dd HH:mm:ss} {thread} [{level}]: {message}
#specify the level of the writer
tinylog.level=debug
```

The java class is as follows:

```
TinyLogExample6.java ⊠
    package com.java.logging.tinylog;

    //import the static logger
    import java.io.File;
    import java.io.IOException;

    import org.pmw.tinylog.Configurator;
    import org.pmw.tinylog.Logger;

    public class TinyLogExample6 {

        public static void main(String[] args) throws IOException {

            // get the configuration file path in a File object
            File file = new File("C:\\TEMP\\tinylog.properties");

            // use the configurator class to load the properties file
            Configurator.fromFile(file);

            // log messages in a loop
            Logger.info("Information Message");
            Logger.warn("Warning Message");
            Logger.error("Error Message");
            Logger.debug("Debug Message");
        }
    }
```

In this class, we create an object of type File that holds the path to the properties file. Then, we input this file as a parameter to the Configurator's fromFile() method that reads the file and configures the logging as per the configuration specified in the properties file.

On executing the above class, we get the following output:

```
Console ⊠    @ Javadoc  Declaration  Problems
<terminated> TinyLogExample6 [Java Application] C:\Program Files\Java\jdk
2017-10-01 08:12:03 main [INFO]: Information Message
2017-10-01 08:12:03 main [WARNING]: Warning Message
2017-10-01 08:12:03 main [ERROR]: Error Message
2017-10-01 08:12:03 main [DEBUG]: Debug Message
```

Example 7: Configuring log level based on class

In this example, we configure our application to have different log levels at the global Wand class level.

We set the global level to be info. This means that unless specified otherwise, the log level across the application is set to 'info.' Now, we set the level using another parameter (the @ parameter) and specify another level for a particular class as shown in the file below:

```
tinylog.properties ⊠
#Set the writer to file
tinylog.writer = console
#specify the format of the output messages
tinylog.writer.format = {date:yyyy-MM-dd HH:mm:ss} {thread} [{level}]: {message}
#specify the global level of the writer
tinylog.level=info
#specify a log level for a particular class
tinylog.level@TinylogExample7=debug
```

The java class is as follows:

```
TinyLogExample7.java ⊠
//import the static logger
import java.io.IOException;

import org.pmw.tinylog.Logger;

public class TinyLogExample7 {

    public static void main(String[] args) throws IOException {

        // log messages in a loop
        // all the messages will be printed on the console as the log level for
        // the class is set to debug
        Logger.info("Information Message");
        Logger.warn("Warning Message");
        Logger.error("Error Message");
        Logger.debug("Debug Message");
        // call a method in another class
        Example.writeLog();
    }
}

class Example {

    static void writeLog() {
        // the debug message will not be printed as the global log level is info
        Logger.debug("Debug Message Test");
        // this message will be printed
        Logger.info("Information Message: In class Example");
    }
}
```

In the above class, we have another non-public class that is present within the same package. In the main class TinyLogExample7, the level is set to debug, hence all the log messages are allowed and printed to the console.

However, in the non-public class Example, the level is not debug. The global log level is applicable in this case; which is info. Hence, the debug message is not seen in the output which is shown below:

```
Console ⊠    @ Javadoc   Declaration   Problems
<terminated> TinyLogExample7 [Java Application] C:\Program Files\Java\jdk
2017-10-01 09:12:35 main [INFO]: Information Message
2017-10-01 09:12:35 main [WARNING]: Warning Message
2017-10-01 09:12:35 main [ERROR]: Error Message
2017-10-01 09:12:35 main [INFO]: Information Message: In class Example
```

We can see clearly that the class Example is outside the scope of the class 'TinyLogEcample7' and hence the debug message is not printed as the global log level is set for this class.

Example 8: Configuring Log Level based on Package

Previously, we have seen how to configure a separate log level based on the class. In this example, we take a look at how to do the same at a package level.

In this example, we set different log levels based on different packages. We create three different packages, each with a java class, in our project as shown below:

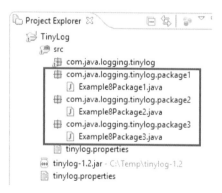

The classes in package2 and package3 consist of a static method writeLog() that logs messages. We call this method from the main class which is '**Example8Package1.java.**'

The three classes are as follows:

Exampl8Package1.java:

```java
Example8Package1.java
    package com.java.logging.tinylog.package1;

    import org.pmw.tinylog.Logger;

    import com.java.logging.tinylog.package2.Example8Package2;
    import com.java.logging.tinylog.package3.Example8Package3;

    public class Example8Package1 {

        public static void main(String[] args) {

            // log messages
            Logger.warn("Warning Message: Package 1");
            Logger.error("Error Message: Package 1");
            Logger.debug("Debug Message: Package 1");
            Logger.info("Information Message: Package 1");

            // call methods from different packages
            Example8Package2.writeLog();
            Example8Package3.writeLog();

        }

    }
```

Example8Package2.java

```java
Example8Package2.java
    package com.java.logging.tinylog.package2;

    import org.pmw.tinylog.Logger;

    public class Example8Package2 {

        public static void writeLog() {

            // log messages.
            // only error and warning message will be logged as the level for this
            // package is set to warning
            Logger.info("Information Message: Package 2");
            Logger.warn("Warning Message: Package 2");
            Logger.warn("Another Warning Message: Package 2");
            Logger.error("Error Message: Package 2");

        }

    }
```

Example8Package3.java

```java
Example8Package3.java
    package com.java.logging.tinylog.package3;

    import org.pmw.tinylog.Logger;

    public class Example8Package3 {

        public static void writeLog() {

            // log messages
            // only the error messages will be printed on the console as the log
            // level for this package is set to error
            Logger.warn("Warning Message: Package 3");
            Logger.error("Error Message: Package 3");
            Logger.error("Another Error Message: Package 3");

        }

    }
```

The configuration file as shown below:

```
📄 tinylog.properties ⊠
    #Set the writer to file
    tinylog.writer = console
    #specify the format of the output messages
    tinylog.writer.format = {date:yyyy-MM-dd HH:mm:ss} {thread} [{level}]: {message}
    #specify the global level of the writer
    tinylog.level=info
    #specify a log level for a particular package
    tinylog.level@com.java.logging.tinylog.package1=debug
    tinylog.level@com.java.logging.tinylog.package2=warning
    tinylog.level@com.java.logging.tinylog.package3=error
```

In the configuration file, we set the log level debug for package1, warning for package2 and error for package3.

On execution of the main class Example8Package1, the output displays all the log messages of level debug and higher for package1, warning and higher for package2 and only error message for package3 as shown below:

```
🖥 Console ⊠    @ Javadoc  🔍 Declaration  📋 Problems
<terminated> Example8Package1 [Java Application] C:\Program Files\Java\jdk
2017-10-01 10:07:45 main [WARNING]: Warning Message: Package 1
2017-10-01 10:07:45 main [DEBUG]: Debug Message: Package 1
2017-10-01 10:07:45 main [INFO]: Information Message: Package 1
2017-10-01 10:07:45 main [ERROR]: Error Message: Package 1
2017-10-01 10:07:45 main [WARNING]: Warning Message: Package 2
2017-10-01 10:07:45 main [WARNING]: Another Warning Message: Package 2
2017-10-01 10:07:45 main [ERROR]: Error Message: Package 2
2017-10-01 10:07:45 main [ERROR]: Error Message: Package 3
2017-10-01 10:07:45 main [ERROR]: Another Error Message: Package 3
```

As the output clearly shows, only messages of warning and above are displayed on the console for Package2 and messages of level error are displayed for package3.

Example 9: Configuring the Package Log level programmatically.

In the previous example, we configured different log levels for different packages via the configuration file tinylog.properties.

But, the same setup can be done using the TinyLog API as well.

The properties file is as follows:

```
📄 tinylog.properties ⊠
    #Set the writer to file
    tinylog.writer = console
    #specify the format of the output messages
    tinylog.writer.format = {date:yyyy-MM-dd HH:mm:ss} {thread} [{level}]: {message}
    #specify the global level of the writer
    tinylog.level=info
```

We have 3 packages similar to the previous example with 3 java classes; one in each package.

We can make use of the configurator class as follows to set the level at the package scope.

```
Example9Package1.java

package com.java.logging.tinylog.package1;

import org.pmw.tinylog.Configurator;
import org.pmw.tinylog.Level;
import org.pmw.tinylog.Logger;

import com.java.logging.tinylog.package2.Example8Package2;
import com.java.logging.tinylog.package3.Example8Package3;

public class Example9Package1 {

    public static void main(String[] args) {

        // use the configurator to set the log level for each package
        Configurator.currentConfig()
        .level("com.java.logging.tinylog.package1", Level.INFO)
        .activate();
        Configurator.currentConfig()
        .level("com.java.logging.tinylog.package2", Level.ERROR)
        .activate();
        Configurator.currentConfig()
        .level("com.java.logging.tinylog.package3", Level.WARNING)
        .activate();

        // log messages
        Logger.warn("Warning Message: Package 1");
        Logger.error("Error Message: Package 1");
        // the debug message is not printed
        Logger.debug("Debug Message: Package 1");
        Logger.info("Information Message: Package 1");

        // call methods from different packages
        Example8Package2.writeLog();
        Example8Package3.writeLog();

    }
}
```

The class Example9Package2.java is as follows:

```
Example9Package2.java

package com.java.logging.tinylog.package2;

import org.pmw.tinylog.Logger;

public class Example9Package2 {

    public static void writeLog() {

        // log messages
        // only error messages will be logged as the level for this package is
        // set to error
        Logger.warn("Warning Message: Package 2");
        Logger.warn("Another Warning Message: Package 2");
        Logger.error("Error Message: Package 2");
        Logger.error("Another Error Message: Package 2");

    }
}
```

Class Exampl9Package3.java

```
Example9Package3.java ⋈
   package com.java.logging.tinylog.package3;

   import org.pmw.tinylog.Logger;

   public class Example9Package3 {

      public static void writeLog() {

         // log messages
         // only the error and warning messages will be printed on the console as
         // the log level for this package is set to error
         Logger.warn("Warning Message: Package 3");
         Logger.error("Error Message: Package 3");
         Logger.error("Another Error Message: Package 3");
      }

   }
```

On executing the main class 'Example9Package1, the output we get is:

```
Console ⋈    @ Javadoc   Declaration   Problems
<terminated> Example9Package1 [Java Application] C:\Program Files\Java\jdk
2017-10-01 10:39:10 main [WARNING]: Warning Message: Package 1
2017-10-01 10:39:10 main [INFO]: Information Message: Package 1
2017-10-01 10:39:10 main [ERROR]: Error Message: Package 1
2017-10-01 10:39:10 main [ERROR]: Error Message: Package 2
2017-10-01 10:39:10 main [WARNING]: Warning Message: Package 3
2017-10-01 10:39:10 main [ERROR]: Error Message: Package 3
2017-10-01 10:39:10 main [ERROR]: Another Error Message: Package 3
```

The above output shows the project has been configured to use different log levels as per the package name. The class in package1 prints log messages of level INFO and above and hence the debug message is not printed to the console. The same goes for package2. It has been configured to accept only error messages and hence only a single log message of type error is seen on the console.

Finally, in case of package 3, all the messages have been printed on the console as their level is either error or warning, which is the level that we have configured for this package using the Configurator class.

Example10: Parameterized Logging

In this example, we demonstrate the use of parameterized logging in Tinylog. It is similar to that of logback. We use curly brackets {} to provide the parameters.

In addition to simple parameterized logging, we implement the use of choices in order to display different messages based on the value of a parameter.

We consider the following configuration file:

```
📄 tinylog.properties ☒
   #Set the writer to file
   tinylog.writer = console
   #specify the global level of the writer
   tinylog.level=trace
```

The java class that we use to implement and test parametrized logging is as follows:

```
📄 TinyLogExample10.java ☒
   package com.java.logging.tinylog;

   import org.pmw.tinylog.Logger;

   public class TinyLogExample10 {

      public static void main(String[] args) {
         int x = 2;
         int y = 5;
         // logging with a single parameter
         Logger.debug("Debugging the input parameters. Value of x is {} ", x);
         Logger.debug("Debugging the input parameters. Value of y is {} ", y);

         // logging with multiple parameters
         Logger.debug("Debugging the input parameters:- Parameter 1: {}, Parameter 2: {}", x, y);

         // logging with multiple parameters and placeholder values
         Logger.debug("Debugging the input parameters 2:- Parameter 1: {0}, Parameter 2: {1}", x, y);

         // parameterized logging with choice
         // we have 3 choices for the value of i- 0, 1 or 1
         // Based on the value, the appropriate log message is selected and
         // printed on the console
         for (int i = 0; i < 3; i++)
            Logger.trace("There {0#exists no class|1#is one class|1<are {} classes}", i);
      }
   }
```

On execution of the above class, we get the following output:

```
🖥 Console ☒  📋 Problems  @ Javadoc  🔍 Declaration  📑 Annotations
<terminated> TinyLogExample10 [Java Application] C:\Program Files\java
2017-11-06 16:25:57 [main] com.java.logging.tinylog.TinyLogExample10.main()
DEBUG: Debugging the input parameters. Value of x is 2
2017-11-06 16:25:57 [main] com.java.logging.tinylog.TinyLogExample10.main()
DEBUG: Debugging the input parameters. Value of y is 5
2017-11-06 16:25:57 [main] com.java.logging.tinylog.TinyLogExample10.main()
DEBUG: Debugging the input parameters:- Parameter 1: 2, Parameter 2: 5
2017-11-06 16:25:57 [main] com.java.logging.tinylog.TinyLogExample10.main()
DEBUG: Debugging the input parameters 2:- Parameter 1: 2, Parameter 2: 15
2017-11-06 16:25:57 [main] com.java.logging.tinylog.TinyLogExample10.main()
TRACE: There exists no class
2017-11-06 16:25:57 [main] com.java.logging.tinylog.TinyLogExample10.main()
TRACE: There is one class
2017-11-06 16:25:57 [main] com.java.logging.tinylog.TinyLogExample10.main()
TRACE: There are 2 classes
```

As the output shows, log messages with the parameter values have been printed on the console. Additionally, we can see that a different log message is printed based on the value of the variable i.

For the value 0, the message printed is: There exists no class

For the value 1, the message printed is: There is one class

For the value 2, the message printed is: There are 2 classes

Example 11: Limiting the stack trace

In this example, we see how to limit the length of the stack trace that is printed with the exceptions.

Consider the following initial configuration:

```
tinylog.properties ✕
    #Set the writer to file
    tinylog.writer = console
    #specify the global level of the writer
    tinylog.level=debug
```

The java class used to test this configuration is as follows:

```java
TinyLogExample11.java ✕
    package com.java.logging.tinylog;

    import org.pmw.tinylog.Logger;

    public class TinyLogExample11 {

        public static void main(String[] args) {

            // logging with a single parameter
            Logger.trace("Trace Message");
            Logger.error("Error Message");
            Logger.warn("Warning Message");

            // throw an exception
            // the detailed stack trace will not be printed on the console
            Logger.error(new NullPointerException());

            // induce an exception
            try {
                int c = 10 / 0;
                System.out.println(c);
            } catch (ArithmeticException e) {
                Logger.error("Cannot divivde by zero!" + e);
            }

        }
    }
```

On execution, we see the complete stack trace as shown below:

```
Console ✕   Problems   @ Javadoc   Declaration   Annotations
<terminated> TinyLogExample12 [Java Application] C:\Program Files\java
2017-11-08 12:50:17 [main] com.java.logging.tinylog.TinyLogExample12.main()
ERROR: Error Message
2017-11-08 12:50:17 [main] com.java.logging.tinylog.TinyLogExample12.main()
WARNING: Warning Message
2017-11-08 12:50:17 [main] com.java.logging.tinylog.TinyLogExample12.main()
ERROR: java.lang.NullPointerException
        at com.java.logging.tinylog.TinyLogExample12.main(TinyLogExample12.java:21)
2017-11-08 12:50:17 [main] com.java.logging.tinylog.TinyLogExample12.main()
ERROR: Cannot divivde by zero!java.lang.ArithmeticException: / by zero
```

If we want to reduce or hide the complete stack trace, this can be done using the stacktrace property of tinylog. This is shown below:

```
tinylog.properties ✕
    #Set the writer to file
    tinylog.writer = console
    #specify the global level of the writer
    tinylog.level=debug
    tinylog.stacktrace=0
```

Here, we limit the stacktrace to 0. This means that no details of the stack trace will be provided in the logs.

Now, on the execution of the same java class as before, we get the following output:

```
Console ⊠   Problems   @ Javadoc   Declaration   Annotations
<terminated> TinyLogFxample11 [Java Application] C:\Program Files\java
2017-11-07 16:37:04 [main] com.java.logging.tinylog.TinyLogExample11.main()
ERROR: Error Message
2017-11-07 16:37:04 [main] com.java.logging.tinylog.TinyLogExample11.main()
WARNING: Warning Message
2017-11-07 16:37:04 [main] com.java.logging.tinylog.TinyLogExample11.main()
ERROR: java.lang.NullPointerException
2017-11-07 16:37:04 [main] com.java.logging.tinylog.TinyLogExample11.main()
ERROR: Cannot divivde by zero!java.lang.ArithmeticException: / by zero
```

As seen from the output, the stack trace has not been printed on the console.

By default the value of the 'tinylog.stacktrace' the parameter is set to 40. To have a stack trace without any limits on the size, this value should be set to -1.

Example 12: Manipulating the Message format using the min-size parameter

In this example, we demonstrate the use of the min-size parameter to manipulate the format of the log message output.

The configuration used is as follows:

```
tinylog.properties ⊠
#Set the writer to file
tinylog.writer = console
#specify the global level of the writer
tinylog.level=trace
#specify the format of the output messages
tinylog.writer.format = {date:yyyy-MM-dd HH:mm:ss} [{thread}] {{level}|min-size=9}:{message}
```

The Java class used to test is as follows:

```
TinyLogExample13.java ⊠
package com.java.logging.tinylog;

import org.pmw.tinylog.Logger;

public class TinyLogExample13 {

    public static void main(String[] args) {

        // log messages
        Logger.trace("Trace Message");
        Logger.error("Error Message");
        Logger.warn("Warning Message");
        // induce an exception
        try {
            int c = 10 / 0;
            System.out.println(c);
        } catch (ArithmeticException e) {
            Logger.error("Cannot divivde by zero!" + e);
        }

    }
}
```

The output is as follows:

```
Console 🔲   Problems  @ Javadoc  Declaration  Annotations
<terminated> TinyLogExample13 [Java Application] C:\Program Files\java
2017-11-08 13:21:24 [main] ERROR    :Error Message
2017-11-08 13:21:24 [main] WARNING  :Warning Message
2017-11-08 13:21:24 [main] TRACE    :Trace Message
2017-11-08 13:21:24 [main] ERROR    :Cannot divivde by zero!java.lang.ArithmeticException: / by zero
```

Example 14: Manipulating the log message format using indentations

In this example, we modify the log output message by adding indentations to it. This is shown in the configuration below:

```
tinylog.properties 🔲
#Set the writer to file
tinylog.writer = console
#specify the global level of the writer
tinylog.level=trace
#specify the format of the output messages
tinylog.writer.format = {date:yyyy-MM-dd HH:mm:ss} [{thread}] {{level}|min-size=9}:{message|indent=18}
```

The test java class is as follows:

```java
TinyLogExample14.java 🔲
package com.java.logging.tinylog;

import org.pmw.tinylog.Logger;

public class TinyLogExample14 {

    public static void main(String[] args) {

        // log messages
        Logger.error("Error Message");
        Logger.warn("Warning Message");

        // throw exceptions
        Logger.debug(new NullPointerException("Value is null!"));
        Logger.debug(new ArithmeticException("Cannot divide by zero!"));
        Logger.debug(new IllegalArgumentException("Cannot invoke an object on a null method!"));
        Logger.error(new ArrayIndexOutOfBoundsException("The index is out of bounds!"));

    }
}
```

The output is:

```
Console 🔲   Problems  @ Javadoc  Declaration  Annotations
<terminated> TinyLogExample14 [Java Application] C:\Program Files\java
2017-11-08 13:33:26 [main] ERROR    :Error Message
2017-11-08 13:33:26 [main] WARNING  :Warning Message
2017-11-08 13:33:26 [main] ERROR    :java.lang.ArrayIndexOutOfBoundsException: The index is out of bounds!
                                      at com.java.logging.tinylog.TinyLogExample14.main(TinyLogExample14.java:17)
2017-11-08 13:33:26 [main] DEBUG    :java.lang.NullPointerException: Value is null!
                                      at com.java.logging.tinylog.TinyLogExample14.main(TinyLogExample14.java:14)
2017-11-08 13:33:26 [main] DEBUG    :java.lang.ArithmeticException: Cannot divide by zero!
                                      at com.java.logging.tinylog.TinyLogExample14.main(TinyLogExample14.java:15)
2017-11-08 13:33:26 [main] DEBUG    :java.lang.IllegalArgumentException: Cannot invoke an object on a null method!
                                      at com.java.logging.tinylog.TinyLogExample14.main(TinyLogExample14.java:16)
```

Example 15: Multiple formats per writer

Here, we use different formats for the output logs based on the type of writer.

The configuration is as follows:

```
tinylog.properties
#specify the global log level
tinylog.level=debug

#Define a writer
tinylog.writer1 = console
#specify the format of the output messages
tinylog.writer1.format = {date:yyyy-MM-dd HH:mm:ss} {level}:{message}

#Define another writer
tinylog.writer2 = file
tiylog.writer2.filename = myLogFile.txt
#specify the format of the output messages
tinylog.writer2.format = {date:yyyy-MM-dd HH:mm:ss} {class}.{method}() [{thread}] {level}:{message}
```

The java class:

```java
TinyLogExample15.java
package com.java.logging.tinylog;

import org.pmw.tinylog.Logger;

public class TinyLogExample15 {

    public static void main(String[] args) {

        // log messages
        Logger.error("Error Message");
        Logger.warn("Warning Message");
        Logger.debug("Debug Message");
        Logger.trace("Trace Message");
        Logger.info("Information Message");

        Logger.error("Another Error Message");
        Logger.warn("Another Warning Message");
        Logger.debug("Another Debug Message");
        Logger.trace("Another Trace Message");
        Logger.info("Another Information Message");

        // throw exceptions
        Logger.debug(new NullPointerException());
        Logger.debug(new ArithmeticException("Cannot divide by zero!"));

    }
}
```

The output generated on the console is as follows:

```
Console    Markers    Properties    Servers    Data Source Explorer    Snippets    Annotation
<terminated> TinyLogExample15 [Java Application] C:\Program Files (x86)\java
2017-11-14 ERROR:Error Message
2017-11-14 WARNING:Warning Message
2017-11-14 ERROR:Another Error Message
2017-11-14 WARNING:Another Warning Message
2017-11-14 DEBUG:Debug Message
2017-11-14 INFO:Information Message
2017-11-14 DEBUG:Another Debug Message
2017-11-14 INFO:Another Information Message
2017-11-14 DEBUG:java.lang.NullPointerException
        at com.java.logging.tinylog.TinyLogExample15.main(TinyLogExample15.java:23)
2017-11-14 DEBUG:java.lang.ArithmeticException: Cannot divide by zero!
        at com.java.logging.tinylog.TinyLogExample15.main(TinyLogExample15.java:24)
```

A new file is created in the project structure as follows:

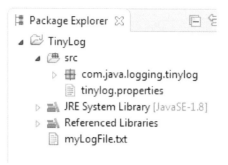

The output of the second writer is as follows:

```
myLogFile.txt 
2017-11-14 13:03:46 com.java.logging.tinylog.TinyLogExample15.main() [main] ERROR:Error Message
2017-11-14 13:03:46 com.java.logging.tinylog.TinyLogExample15.main() [main] WARNING:Warning Message
2017-11-14 13:03:46 com.java.logging.tinylog.TinyLogExample15.main() [main] DEBUG:Debug Message
2017-11-14 13:03:46 com.java.logging.tinylog.TinyLogExample15.main() [main] INFO:Information Message
2017-11-14 13:03:46 com.java.logging.tinylog.TinyLogExample15.main() [main] ERROR:Another Error Message
2017-11-14 13:03:46 com.java.logging.tinylog.TinyLogExample15.main() [main] WARNING:Another Warning Message
2017-11-14 13:03:46 com.java.logging.tinylog.TinyLogExample15.main() [main] DEBUG:Another Debug Message
2017-11-14 13:03:46 com.java.logging.tinylog.TinyLogExample15.main() [main] INFO:Another Information Message
2017-11-14 13:03:46 com.java.logging.tinylog.TinyLogExample15.main() [main] DEBUG:java.lang.NullPointerException
    at com.java.logging.tinylog.TinyLogExample15.main(TinyLogExample15.java:23)
2017-11-14 13:03:46 com.java.logging.tinylog.TinyLogExample15.main() [main] DEBUG:java.lang.ArithmeticException: Cannot divide by zero!
    at com.java.logging.tinylog.TinyLogExample15.main(TinyLogExample15.java:24)
```

Example 16: Adding a FileWriter Programmatically

In this example, we take a look at how to define a file writer programmatically within the java code.

We make use of the Configurator class.

We call the writer() method and provide it with the parameters to configure a file writer as shown below:

```
TinyLogExample16.java 
    package com.java.logging.tinylog;

   import org.pmw.tinylog.Configurator;

    public class TinyLogExample16 {

        public static void main(String[] args) {

            // call the writer() method to configure a new writer
            Configurator.defaultConfig().writer(new FileWriter("fileWriterLog.txt")).
            level(Level.TRACE).activate();

            // log messages
            Logger.error("Error Message");
            Logger.warn("Warning Message");
            Logger.debug("Debug Message");
            Logger.trace("Trace Message");
            Logger.info("Information Message");
        }
    }
```

The above class creates a new file as shown below:

The contents of this file are as follows:

```
fileWriterLog.txt
2017-11-14 13:55:42 [main] com.java.logging.tinylog.TinyLogExample16.main()
ERROR: Error Message
2017-11-14 13:55:42 [main] com.java.logging.tinylog.TinyLogExample16.main()
WARNING: Warning Message
2017-11-14 13:55:42 [main] com.java.logging.tinylog.TinyLogExample16.main()
DEBUG: Debug Message
2017-11-14 13:55:42 [main] com.java.logging.tinylog.TinyLogExample16.main()
TRACE: Trace Message
2017-11-14 13:55:42 [main] com.java.logging.tinylog.TinyLogExample16.main()
INFO: Information Message
```

Example 17: Add a FileWriter Using the VM Parameters

In this example, we configure a simple file writer by use of the VM parameters in eclipse.

Consider the following Java class:

```java
TinyLogExample17.java
package com.java.logging.tinylog;

import org.pmw.tinylog.Logger;

public class TinyLogExample17 {

    public static void main(String[] args) {

        // log messages
        Logger.error("Error Message");
        Logger.warn("Warning Message");
        Logger.debug("Debug Message");
        Logger.info("Information Message");

        // induce exceptions
        try {
            int x = 1 / 0;
            System.out.println(x);
        } catch (ArithmeticException e) {
            Logger.error("Cannot divide by zero! " + e);
        }

        Integer y = null;

        try {
            y.toString();
        } catch (NullPointerException e) {
            Logger.error("Null value encountered! " + e);
        }

    }
}
```

To add the log configuration, we right click on the class body and go to 'Run Configurations.' We navigate to the Arguments tab and add our log configuration as shown in the upcoming screenshots:

We add the configuration parameters to the vm arguments tab as follows:

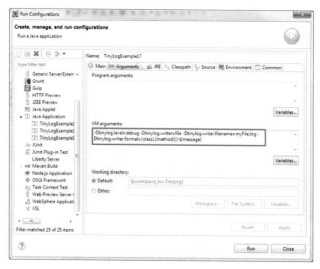

We now click on 'Run' to launch the java program.

On execution, a new file is generated as shown below:

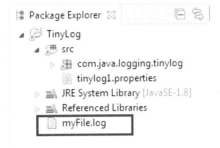

The contents of this file are:

```
myFile.log
com.java.logging.tinylog.TinyLogExample17.main()    Error Message
com.java.logging.tinylog.TinyLogExample17.main()    Warning Message
com.java.logging.tinylog.TinyLogExample17.main()    Debug Message
com.java.logging.tinylog.TinyLogExample17.main()    Information Message
com.java.logging.tinylog.TinyLogExample17.main()    Cannot divide by zero! java.lang.ArithmeticException: / by zero
com.java.logging.tinylog.TinyLogExample17.main()    Null value encountered! java.lang.NullPointerException
```

Example 18: Configuring a Rolling File Writer Programmatically

In this example, we programmatically define and configure a rolling file writer. The java class is:

```java
TinyLogExample18.java
package com.java.logging.tinylog;

import org.pmw.tinylog.Configurator;
import org.pmw.tinylog.Level;
import org.pmw.tinylog.Logger;
import org.pmw.tinylog.labelers.TimestampLabeler;
import org.pmw.tinylog.policies.StartupPolicy;
import org.pmw.tinylog.writers.RollingFileWriter;

public class TinyLogExample18 {

    public static void main(String[] args) {
        // use the writer method to define a new rolling file writer with a
        // timestamp labeler and a startup policy
        // a new log file will be created at startup
        Configurator
            .currentConfig()
            .writer(new RollingFileWriter("rollingLogFile.log", 5,
                    new TimestampLabeler(), new StartupPolicy()))
            .activate();

        Configurator.currentConfig().level(Level.TRACE).activate();

        for (int i = 0; i < 2; i++) {
            Logger.trace("Trace Message");
            Logger.info("Information Message");
            Logger.warn("Warning Message");
            Logger.error("Error Message");
            Logger.debug("Debug Message");
        }
    }
}
```

We execute this class 2 times and each time we execute this class, a new file is created as shown below:

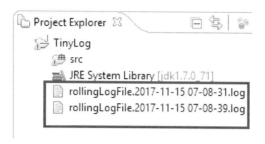

```
rollingLogFile.2017-11-15 07-08-31.log  ⊠

2017-11-15 07:08:31 [main] com.java.logging.tinylog.TinyLogExample18.main()
TRACE: Trace Message
2017-11-15 07:08:31 [main] com.java.logging.tinylog.TinyLogExample18.main()
INFO: Information Message
2017-11-15 07:08:31 [main] com.java.logging.tinylog.TinyLogExample18.main()
WARNING: Warning Message
2017-11-15 07:08:31 [main] com.java.logging.tinylog.TinyLogExample18.main()
ERROR: Error Message
2017-11-15 07:08:31 [main] com.java.logging.tinylog.TinyLogExample18.main()
DEBUG: Debug Message
2017-11-15 07:08:31 [main] com.java.logging.tinylog.TinyLogExample18.main()
TRACE: Trace Message
2017-11-15 07:08:31 [main] com.java.logging.tinylog.TinyLogExample18.main()
INFO: Information Message
2017-11-15 07:08:31 [main] com.java.logging.tinylog.TinyLogExample18.main()
WARNING: Warning Message
2017-11-15 07:08:31 [main] com.java.logging.tinylog.TinyLogExample18.main()
ERROR: Error Message
2017-11-15 07:08:31 [main] com.java.logging.tinylog.TinyLogExample18.main()
DEBUG: Debug Message
```

```
rollingLogFile.2017-11-15 07-08-39.log  ⊠

2017-11-15 07:08:39 [main] com.java.logging.tinylog.TinyLogExample18.main()
TRACE: Trace Message
2017-11-15 07:08:39 [main] com.java.logging.tinylog.TinyLogExample18.main()
INFO: Information Message
2017-11-15 07:08:39 [main] com.java.logging.tinylog.TinyLogExample18.main()
WARNING: Warning Message
2017-11-15 07:08:39 [main] com.java.logging.tinylog.TinyLogExample18.main()
ERROR: Error Message
2017-11-15 07:08:39 [main] com.java.logging.tinylog.TinyLogExample18.main()
DEBUG: Debug Message
2017-11-15 07:08:39 [main] com.java.logging.tinylog.TinyLogExample18.main()
TRACE: Trace Message
2017-11-15 07:08:39 [main] com.java.logging.tinylog.TinyLogExample18.main()
INFO: Information Message
2017-11-15 07:08:39 [main] com.java.logging.tinylog.TinyLogExample18.main()
WARNING: Warning Message
2017-11-15 07:08:39 [main] com.java.logging.tinylog.TinyLogExample18.main()
ERROR: Error Message
2017-11-15 07:08:39 [main] com.java.logging.tinylog.TinyLogExample18.main()
DEBUG: Debug Message
```

Example 19: Configuring a Rolling File Writer Using VM parameters

In this example, we configure a rolling file writer with the help of the VM parameters in eclipse. The java class is:

```
TinyLogExample19.java ⊠

    package com.java.logging.tinylog;

    import org.pmw.tinylog.Logger;

    public class TinyLogExample19 {

        public static void main(String[] args) {

            // log messages
            for (int i = 0; i < 5; i++) {
                Logger.trace("Trace Message");
                Logger.info("Information Message");
                Logger.warn("Warning Message");
                Logger.error("Error Message");
                Logger.debug("Debug Message");
            }
        }
    }
```

We add the rolling file parameters in the VM arguments tab as shown below:

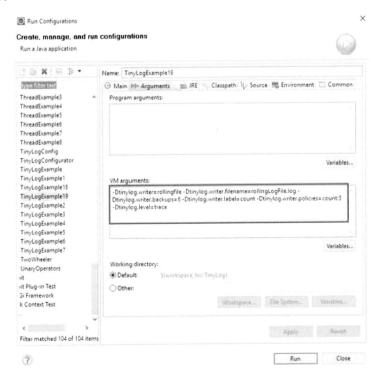

We click on run. On execution of the class, log files are rolled over after the count of the log entries reaches 5.

This is shown below:

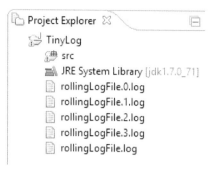

The contents of the files are as follows:

```
rollingLogFile.0.log ⊠
    2017-11-15 22:54:49 [main] com.java.logging.tinylog.TinyLogExample19.main()
    WARNING: Warning Message
    2017-11-15 22:54:49 [main] com.java.logging.tinylog.TinyLogExample19.main()
    ERROR: Error Message
    2017-11-15 22:54:49 [main] com.java.logging.tinylog.TinyLogExample19.main()
    DEBUG: Debug Message
    2017-11-15 22:54:49 [main] com.java.logging.tinylog.TinyLogExample19.main()
    TRACE: Trace Message
    2017-11-15 22:54:49 [main] com.java.logging.tinylog.TinyLogExample19.main()
    INFO: Information Message
    2017-11-15 22:54:49 [main] com.java.logging.tinylog.TinyLogExample19.main()
    WARNING: Warning Message
```

```
rollingLogFile.1.log ⊠
    2017-11-15 22:54:49 [main] com.java.logging.tinylog.TinyLogExample19.main()
    INFO: Information Message
    2017-11-15 22:54:49 [main] com.java.logging.tinylog.TinyLogExample19.main()
    WARNING: Warning Message
    2017-11-15 22:54:49 [main] com.java.logging.tinylog.TinyLogExample19.main()
    ERROR: Error Message
    2017-11-15 22:54:49 [main] com.java.logging.tinylog.TinyLogExample19.main()
    DEBUG: Debug Message
    2017-11-15 22:54:49 [main] com.java.logging.tinylog.TinyLogExample19.main()
    TRACE: Trace Message
    2017-11-15 22:54:49 [main] com.java.logging.tinylog.TinyLogExample19.main()
    INFO: Information Message
```

```
rollingLogFile.2.log ⊠
    2017-11-15 22:54:49 [main] com.java.logging.tinylog.TinyLogExample19.main()
    TRACE: Trace Message
    2017-11-15 22:54:49 [main] com.java.logging.tinylog.TinyLogExample19.main()
    INFO: Information Message
    2017-11-15 22:54:49 [main] com.java.logging.tinylog.TinyLogExample19.main()
    WARNING: Warning Message
    2017-11-15 22:54:49 [main] com.java.logging.tinylog.TinyLogExample19.main()
    ERROR: Error Message
    2017-11-15 22:54:49 [main] com.java.logging.tinylog.TinyLogExample19.main()
    DEBUG: Debug Message
    2017-11-15 22:54:49 [main] com.java.logging.tinylog.TinyLogExample19.main()
    TRACE: Trace Message
```

```
rollingLogFile.3.log ⌗
  2017-11-15 22:54:49 [main] com.java.logging.tinylog.TinyLogExample19.main()
  TRACE: Trace Message
  2017-11-15 22:54:49 [main] com.java.logging.tinylog.TinyLogExample19.main()
  INFO: Information Message
  2017-11-15 22:54:49 [main] com.java.logging.tinylog.TinyLogExample19.main()
  WARNING: Warning Message
  2017-11-15 22:54:49 [main] com.java.logging.tinylog.TinyLogExample19.main()
  ERROR: Error Message
  2017-11-15 22:54:49 [main] com.java.logging.tinylog.TinyLogExample19.main()
  DEBUG: Debug Message
```

```
rollingLogFile.log ⌗
  2017-11-15 22:54:49 [main] com.java.logging.tinylog.TinyLogExample19.main()
  ERROR: Error Message
  2017-11-15 22:54:49 [main] com.java.logging.tinylog.TinyLogExample19.main()
  DEBUG: Debug Message
```

Example 20: Multiple Writers using VM parameters

In this example, we define and configure multiple writers using the eclipse VM parameters. The java class is:

```java
TinyLogExample20.java ⌗
package com.java.logging.tinylog;

import org.pmw.tinylog.Logger;

public class TinyLogExample20 {

    public static void main(String[] args) {

        // log messages in a loop
        for (int i = 0; i < 5; i++) {

            Logger.error("Error Message");
            Logger.warn("Warning Message");
            Logger.debug("Debug Message");
            Logger.info("Information Message");
        }
    }
}
```

We add the configuration statements for two writers as follows:

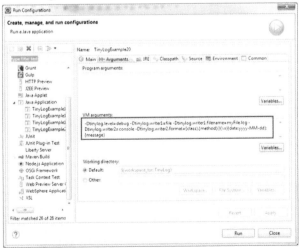

On execution of the class, the following output is seen on the console:

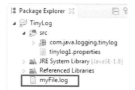

A new file is created as follows:

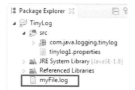

The contents of the file are as follows:

```
myFile.log
2017-11-16 14:42:10 [main] com.java.logging.tinylog.TinyLogExample20.main()
ERROR: Error Message
2017-11-16 14:42:10 [main] com.java.logging.tinylog.TinyLogExample20.main()
WARNING: Warning Message
2017-11-16 14:42:10 [main] com.java.logging.tinylog.TinyLogExample20.main()
DEBUG: Debug Message
2017-11-16 14:42:10 [main] com.java.logging.tinylog.TinyLogExample20.main()
INFO: Information Message
2017-11-16 14:42:10 [main] com.java.logging.tinylog.TinyLogExample20.main()
ERROR: Error Message
2017-11-16 14:42:10 [main] com.java.logging.tinylog.TinyLogExample20.main()
WARNING: Warning Message
2017-11-16 14:42:10 [main] com.java.logging.tinylog.TinyLogExample20.main()
DEBUG: Debug Message
2017-11-16 14:42:10 [main] com.java.logging.tinylog.TinyLogExample20.main()
INFO: Information Message
2017-11-16 14:42:10 [main] com.java.logging.tinylog.TinyLogExample20.main()
ERROR: Error Message
2017-11-16 14:42:10 [main] com.java.logging.tinylog.TinyLogExample20.main()
WARNING: Warning Message
2017-11-16 14:42:10 [main] com.java.logging.tinylog.TinyLogExample20.main()
DEBUG: Debug Message
2017-11-16 14:42:10 [main] com.java.logging.tinylog.TinyLogExample20.main()
INFO: Information Message
2017-11-16 14:42:10 [main] com.java.logging.tinylog.TinyLogExample20.main()
ERROR: Error Message
2017-11-16 14:42:10 [main] com.java.logging.tinylog.TinyLogExample20.main()
WARNING: Warning Message
2017-11-16 14:42:10 [main] com.java.logging.tinylog.TinyLogExample20.main()
DEBUG: Debug Message
2017-11-16 14:42:10 [main] com.java.logging.tinylog.TinyLogExample20.main()
INFO: Information Message
2017-11-16 14:42:10 [main] com.java.logging.tinylog.TinyLogExample20.main()
ERROR: Error Message
2017-11-16 14:42:10 [main] com.java.logging.tinylog.TinyLogExample20.main()
WARNING: Warning Message
2017-11-16 14:42:10 [main] com.java.logging.tinylog.TinyLogExample20.main()
DEBUG: Debug Message
2017-11-16 14:42:10 [main] com.java.logging.tinylog.TinyLogExample20.main()
INFO: Information Message
```

Example 21: Multiple Rolling File Writers using VM parameters

In this example, we demonstrate the configuration of multiple rolling file writers using the eclipse VM parameters. The java class is as follows:

```java
TinyLogExample21.java
package com.java.logging.tinylog;

import org.pmw.tinylog.Logger;

public class TinyLogExample21 {

    public static void main(String[] args) {

        // log messages in a loop
        //the log messages will be logged in two different files
        for (int i = 0; i < 5; i++) {

            Logger.error("Error Message");
            Logger.warn("Warning Message");
            Logger.info("Information Message");

        }
    }
}
```

We add the configurations for 2 different rolling file writers; one that has a startup policy and another that has a size based policy as shown below:

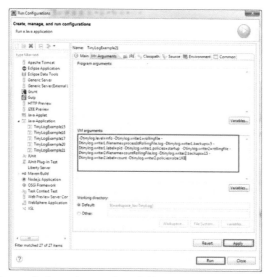

On execution of the class, the following 3 files are created in the hierarchy:

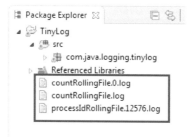

On a second and third execution of the class, additional log files based on the rolling policy 'startup' are generated as shown below:

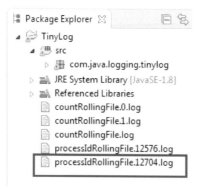

The contents of the log files are as follows:

📄 processIdRollingFile.12576.log ⊠

```
2017-11-16 15:15:58 [main] com.java.logging.tinylog.TinyLogExample21.main()
ERROR: Error Message
2017-11-16 15:15:58 [main] com.java.logging.tinylog.TinyLogExample21.main()
WARNING: Warning Message
2017-11-16 15:15:58 [main] com.java.logging.tinylog.TinyLogExample21.main()
INFO: Information Message
2017-11-16 15:15:58 [main] com.java.logging.tinylog.TinyLogExample21.main()
ERROR: Error Message
2017-11-16 15:15:58 [main] com.java.logging.tinylog.TinyLogExample21.main()
WARNING: Warning Message
2017-11-16 15:15:58 [main] com.java.logging.tinylog.TinyLogExample21.main()
INFO: Information Message
2017-11-16 15:15:58 [main] com.java.logging.tinylog.TinyLogExample21.main()
ERROR: Error Message
2017-11-16 15:15:58 [main] com.java.logging.tinylog.TinyLogExample21.main()
WARNING: Warning Message
2017-11-16 15:15:58 [main] com.java.logging.tinylog.TinyLogExample21.main()
INFO: Information Message
2017-11-16 15:15:58 [main] com.java.logging.tinylog.TinyLogExample21.main()
ERROR: Error Message
2017-11-16 15:15:58 [main] com.java.logging.tinylog.TinyLogExample21.main()
WARNING: Warning Message
2017-11-16 15:15:58 [main] com.java.logging.tinylog.TinyLogExample21.main()
INFO: Information Message
2017-11-16 15:15:58 [main] com.java.logging.tinylog.TinyLogExample21.main()
ERROR: Error Message
2017-11-16 15:15:58 [main] com.java.logging.tinylog.TinyLogExample21.main()
WARNING: Warning Message
2017-11-16 15:15:58 [main] com.java.logging.tinylog.TinyLogExample21.main()
INFO: Information Message
```

📄 processIdRollingFile.12704.log ⊠

```
2017-11-16 15:18:18 [main] com.java.logging.tinylog.TinyLogExample21.main()
ERROR: Error Message
2017-11-16 15:18:18 [main] com.java.logging.tinylog.TinyLogExample21.main()
WARNING: Warning Message
2017-11-16 15:18:18 [main] com.java.logging.tinylog.TinyLogExample21.main()
INFO: Information Message
2017-11-16 15:18:18 [main] com.java.logging.tinylog.TinyLogExample21.main()
ERROR: Error Message
2017-11-16 15:18:18 [main] com.java.logging.tinylog.TinyLogExample21.main()
WARNING: Warning Message
2017-11-16 15:18:18 [main] com.java.logging.tinylog.TinyLogExample21.main()
INFO: Information Message
2017-11-16 15:18:18 [main] com.java.logging.tinylog.TinyLogExample21.main()
ERROR: Error Message
2017-11-16 15:18:18 [main] com.java.logging.tinylog.TinyLogExample21.main()
WARNING: Warning Message
2017-11-16 15:18:18 [main] com.java.logging.tinylog.TinyLogExample21.main()
INFO: Information Message
2017-11-16 15:18:18 [main] com.java.logging.tinylog.TinyLogExample21.main()
ERROR: Error Message
2017-11-16 15:18:18 [main] com.java.logging.tinylog.TinyLogExample21.main()
WARNING: Warning Message
2017-11-16 15:18:18 [main] com.java.logging.tinylog.TinyLogExample21.main()
INFO: Information Message
2017-11-16 15:18:18 [main] com.java.logging.tinylog.TinyLogExample21.main()
ERROR: Error Message
2017-11-16 15:18:18 [main] com.java.logging.tinylog.TinyLogExample21.main()
WARNING: Warning Message
2017-11-16 15:18:18 [main] com.java.logging.tinylog.TinyLogExample21.main()
INFO: Information Message
```

📄 countRollingFile.0.log ⊠

```
2017-11-16 15:15:58 [main] com.java.logging.tinylog.TinyLogExample21.main()
WARNING: Warning Message
2017-11-16 15:15:58 [main] com.java.logging.tinylog.TinyLogExample21.main()
INFO: Information Message
2017-11-16 15:15:58 [main] com.java.logging.tinylog.TinyLogExample21.main()
ERROR: Error Message
2017-11-16 15:15:58 [main] com.java.logging.tinylog.TinyLogExample21.main()
WARNING: Warning Message
2017-11-16 15:15:58 [main] com.java.logging.tinylog.TinyLogExample21.main()
INFO: Information Message
2017-11-16 15:18:18 [main] com.java.logging.tinylog.TinyLogExample21.main()
ERROR: Error Message
2017-11-16 15:18:18 [main] com.java.logging.tinylog.TinyLogExample21.main()
WARNING: Warning Message
2017-11-16 15:18:18 [main] com.java.logging.tinylog.TinyLogExample21.main()
INFO: Information Message
2017-11-16 15:18:18 [main] com.java.logging.tinylog.TinyLogExample21.main()
ERROR: Error Message
2017-11-16 15:18:18 [main] com.java.logging.tinylog.TinyLogExample21.main()
WARNING: Warning Message
```

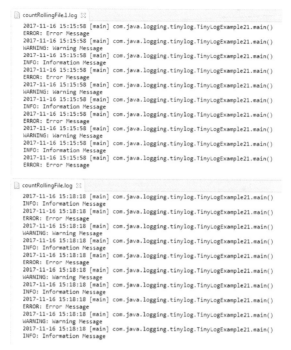

Example 22: Lambda Expressions

In this example, we demonstrate the use of lambda expressions in logging. In order to start, we first need to download version 1.3 of tinylog as the version 1.2 does not support lambda expressions.

We download the version 1.3 from the tinylog downloads page:

http://www.tinylog.org/download

We add the tinylog-1.3.1.jar file to our classpath as shown below:

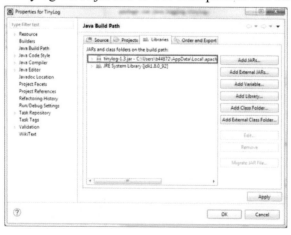

We define 2 simple interfaces that we shall implement in the form of lambda expressions in our class. The interfaces are as follows:

```
J Interface1.java ⊠
    package com.java.logging.tinylog;

    interface Interface1 {
        String message();
    }
```

```
J Interface2.java ⊠
    package com.java.logging.tinylog;

    public interface Interface2 {

        int calculate(int a, int b);
    }
```

We use the following java class to log messages using lambda expressions:

```
J TinyLogExample22.java ⊠
    package com.java.logging.tinylog;

    + import org.pmw.tinylog.Configurator;

    public class TinyLogExample22 {

        public static void main(String[] args) {

            // call the writer() method to configure a new console writer
            Configurator.defaultConfig().writer(new ConsoleWriter()).level(Level.TRACE).activate();
            // log regular messages
            Logger.error("Error Message");
            Logger.warn("Warning Message");
            Logger.info("Information Message");

            // log messages using lambda expressions

            // Provide functional implementation of the interface method message()
            Interface1 int1 = () -> {
                return "The application is stable. No issues to report";
            };

            // Log Messages using Interface1
            // log message with only parameters
            Logger.info(int1.message());
            // log message with a message description and parameters
            Logger.info("Application Information Message : " + int1.message());

            // Provide functional implementation of the interface method message()
            Interface2 int2 = (a, b) -> {
                return a + b;
            };

            // Log Messages using Interface2
            // log message with only parameters
            Logger.info(int2.calculate(5, 10));
            // log message with a message description and parameters
            Logger.info("The value returned is : " + int2.calculate(15, 10));
        }
    }
```

The output generated is as follows:

```
Console ⊠   Problems  @ Javadoc   Declaration   Annotations
<terminated> TinyLogExample22 [Java Application] C:\Program Files\java\jdk1.8.0_92\bin\javaw.exe (16 nov. 2017 à
2017-11-16 16:11:51 [main] com.java.logging.tinylog.TinyLogExample22.main()
ERROR: Error Message
2017-11-16 16:11:51 [main] com.java.logging.tinylog.TinyLogExample22.main()
WARNING: Warning Message
2017-11-16 16:11:51 [main] com.java.logging.tinylog.TinyLogExample22.main()
INFO: Information Message
2017-11-16 16:11:51 [main] com.java.logging.tinylog.TinyLogExample22.main()
INFO: The application is stable. No issues to report
2017-11-16 16:11:51 [main] com.java.logging.tinylog.TinyLogExample22.main()
INFO: Application Information Message : The application is stable. No issues to report
2017-11-16 16:11:51 [main] com.java.logging.tinylog.TinyLogExample22.main()
INFO: 15
2017-11-16 16:11:51 [main] com.java.logging.tinylog.TinyLogExample22.main()
INFO: The value returned is : 25
```

Example 23: Shared File Writer

In this example, we implement a shared file writer which can be shared by multiple threads. This writer is used in a multithreaded context. We add the writer using the Configurator class as shown below:

```java
package com.java.logging.tinylog;

import org.pmw.tinylog.Configurator;
import org.pmw.tinylog.Level;
import org.pmw.tinylog.Logger;
import org.pmw.tinylog.writers.ConsoleWriter;
import org.pmw.tinylog.writers.SharedFileWriter;

public class TinyLogExample23 {

    public static void main(String[] args) {

        // call the writer() method to configure a new console writer
        Configurator.defaultConfig().writer(new ConsoleWriter()).level(Level.TRACE).activate();

        // add a shared writer in addition to the console writer using the
        // addWriter() method
        Configurator.currentConfig().addWriter(new SharedFileWriter("myLogFile.txt", true)).activate();

        // log regular messages
        Logger.error("Error Message");
        Logger.warn("Warning Message");
        Logger.info("Information Message");
        Logger.debug("Debug Message");
    }
}
```

The output generated on the console is as follows:

```
Console ⊠   Problems  @ Javadoc   Declaration   Annotations
<terminated> TinyLogExample23 [Java Application] C:\Program Files\java\jdk1.8.0_92\bin\javaw.exe
2017-11-16 16:58:29 [main] com.java.logging.tinylog.TinyLogExample23.main()
ERROR: Error Message
2017-11-16 16:58:29 [main] com.java.logging.tinylog.TinyLogExample23.main()
INFO: Information Message
2017-11-16 16:58:29 [main] com.java.logging.tinylog.TinyLogExample23.main()
DEBUG: Debug Message
2017-11-16 16:58:29 [main] com.java.logging.tinylog.TinyLogExample23.main()
WARNING: Warning Message
```

A new file is created as follows:

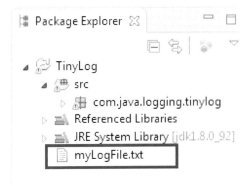

The contents of the file are as follows:

```
myLogFile.txt  ⌧
2017-11-16 16:58:29 [main] com.java.logging.tinylog.TinyLogExample23.main()
ERROR: Error Message
2017-11-16 16:58:29 [main] com.java.logging.tinylog.TinyLogExample23.main()
WARNING: Warning Message
2017-11-16 16:58:29 [main] com.java.logging.tinylog.TinyLogExample23.main()
INFO: Information Message
2017-11-16 16:58:29 [main] com.java.logging.tinylog.TinyLogExample23.main()
DEBUG: Debug Message
```

Example 24: Writing Thread

This configuration is used to execute the writers in another thread than the existing thread.

A new thread is created in addition to the main thread that does the logging for the application. The java class is as follows:

```java
TinyLogExample24.java  ⌧
package com.java.logging.tinylog;

import org.pmw.tinylog.Configurator;
import org.pmw.tinylog.Logger;

public class TinyLogExample24 {

    public static void main(String[] args) {

        // use the writingThread() method of the configurator class to specify
        // the priority of the thread that writes the logs
        Configurator.currentConfig().writingThread("main", 1).activate();

        // log messages to the console
        Logger.error("Error Message");
        Logger.warn("Warning Message");
        Logger.info("Information Message");
        Logger.debug("Debug Message");
    }
}
```

The output generated is as follows:

```
Console ☒  Problems  @ Javadoc  Declaration  Annotations
<terminated> TinyLogExample24 [Java Application] C:\Program Files\java\jdk1.8.0_92\bin\javaw.exe
2017-11-16 17:58:43 [main] com.java.logging.tinylog.TinyLogExample24.main()
ERROR: Error Message
2017-11-16 17:58:43 [main] com.java.logging.tinylog.TinyLogExample24.main()
INFO: Information Message
2017-11-16 17:58:43 [main] com.java.logging.tinylog.TinyLogExample24.main()
WARNING: Warning Message
```

Example 25: Hourly Rolling File Appender

In this example, we implement an hourly rolling file appender. We add a sleep statement to force a rollover of log files. The java class is as follows:

```java
TinyLogExample25.java ☒
    package com.java.logging.tinylog;

    import org.pmw.tinylog.Logger;

    public class TinyLogExample25 {

        public static void main(String[] args) throws InterruptedException {

            // log messages
            for (int i = 0; i < 4; i++) {

                Logger.error("Error Message");
                Logger.warn("Warning Message");
                Logger.info("Information Message");

                // sleep for 25 minutes
                Thread.sleep(900000);
            }
        }
    }
```

The configuration for the rolling file appender is done via the VM parameters in eclipse:

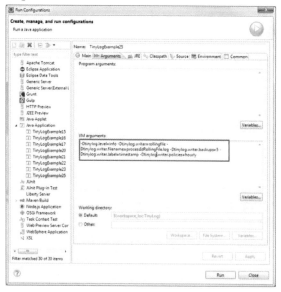

On execution of the class, 2 files are generated as follows:

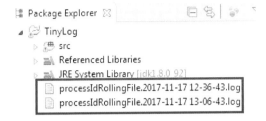

The contents of the files are as follows:

```
processIdRollingFile.2017-11-17 12-36-43.log

2017-11-17 12:36:43 [main] com.java.logging.tinylog.TinyLogExample25.main()
ERROR: Error Message
2017-11-17 12:36:43 [main] com.java.logging.tinylog.TinyLogExample25.main()
WARNING: Warning Message
2017-11-17 12:36:43 [main] com.java.logging.tinylog.TinyLogExample25.main()
INFO: Information Message
2017-11-17 12:51:43 [main] com.java.logging.tinylog.TinyLogExample25.main()
ERROR: Error Message
2017-11-17 12:51:43 [main] com.java.logging.tinylog.TinyLogExample25.main()
WARNING: Warning Message
2017-11-17 12:51:43 [main] com.java.logging.tinylog.TinyLogExample25.main()
INFO: Information Message
```

```
processIdRollingFile.2017-11-17 13-06-43.log

2017-11-17 13:06:43 [main] com.java.logging.tinylog.TinyLogExample25.main()
ERROR: Error Message
2017-11-17 13:06:43 [main] com.java.logging.tinylog.TinyLogExample25.main()
WARNING: Warning Message
2017-11-17 13:06:43 [main] com.java.logging.tinylog.TinyLogExample25.main()
INFO: Information Message
2017-11-17 13:21:43 [main] com.java.logging.tinylog.TinyLogExample25.main()
ERROR: Error Message
2017-11-17 13:21:43 [main] com.java.logging.tinylog.TinyLogExample25.main()
WARNING: Warning Message
2017-11-17 13:21:43 [main] com.java.logging.tinylog.TinyLogExample25.main()
INFO: Information Message
```

Example 26: Daily Rolling File Appender

In this example, we implement a daily rolling file appender. The java class is as follows:

```java
TinyLogExample26.java

package com.java.logging.tinylog;

import org.pmw.tinylog.Logger;

public class TinyLogExample26 {

    public static void main(String[] args) throws InterruptedException {

        // log messages
        for (int i = 0; i < 4; i++) {

            Logger.error("Error Message");
            Logger.warn("Warning Message");

        }
    }
}
```

The configuration for the rolling file appender is done using the eclipse vm parameters as follows:

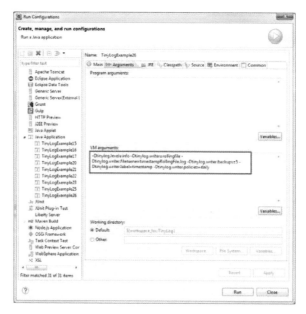

In order to generate different files, we change the date manually during the execution of the class.

On execution of the class, two files are created as follows:

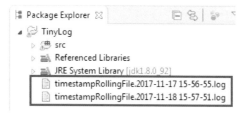

The contents of the file are as follows:

```
timestampRollingFile.2017-11-17 15-56-55.log  ✕
2017-11-17 15:56:55 [main] com.java.logging.tinylog.TinyLogExample26.main()
ERROR: Error Message
2017-11-17 15:56:55 [main] com.java.logging.tinylog.TinyLogExample26.main()
WARNING: Warning Message
2017-11-17 15:56:55 [main] com.java.logging.tinylog.TinyLogExample26.main()
ERROR: Error Message
2017-11-17 15:56:55 [main] com.java.logging.tinylog.TinyLogExample26.main()
WARNING: Warning Message
2017-11-17 15:56:55 [main] com.java.logging.tinylog.TinyLogExample26.main()
ERROR: Error Message
2017-11-17 15:56:55 [main] com.java.logging.tinylog.TinyLogExample26.main()
WARNING: Warning Message
2017-11-17 15:56:55 [main] com.java.logging.tinylog.TinyLogExample26.main()
ERROR: Error Message
2017-11-17 15:56:55 [main] com.java.logging.tinylog.TinyLogExample26.main()
WARNING: Warning Message
```

```
timestampRollingFile.2017-11-18 15-57-51.log

2017-11-18 15:57:51 [main] com.java.logging.tinylog.TinyLogExample26.main()
ERROR: Error Message
2017-11-18 15:57:51 [main] com.java.logging.tinylog.TinyLogExample26.main()
WARNING: Warning Message
2017-11-18 15:57:51 [main] com.java.logging.tinylog.TinyLogExample26.main()
ERROR: Error Message
2017-11-18 15:57:51 [main] com.java.logging.tinylog.TinyLogExample26.main()
WARNING: Warning Message
2017-11-18 15:57:51 [main] com.java.logging.tinylog.TinyLogExample26.main()
ERROR: Error Message
2017-11-18 15:57:51 [main] com.java.logging.tinylog.TinyLogExample26.main()
WARNING: Warning Message
2017-11-18 15:57:51 [main] com.java.logging.tinylog.TinyLogExample26.main()
ERROR: Error Message
2017-11-18 15:57:51 [main] com.java.logging.tinylog.TinyLogExample26.main()
WARNING: Warning Message
```

If we wish to implement a yearly rolling file appender, the process is the same. We proceed to provide the 'yearly' parameter as follows:

We add a sleep () statement in the java class as follows:

```java
TinyLogExample26.java

package com.java.logging.tinylog;

import org.pmw.tinylog.Logger;

public class TinyLogExample26 {

    public static void main(String[] args) throws InterruptedException {

        // log messages
        for (int i = 0; i < 2; i++) {

            Logger.error("Error Message");
            Logger.warn("Warning Message");
            //add a sleep message
            Thread.sleep(900000);

        }
    }
}
```

We change the year manually while the application waits as follows:

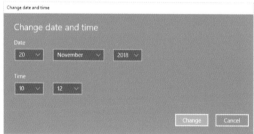

And click on OK.

The output is as follows:

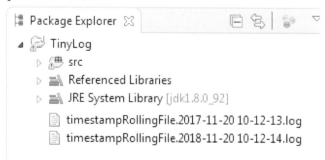

The contents of these files are as follows:

📄 timestampRollingFile.2017-11-20 10-12-13.log ☒

```
2017-11-20 10:12:13 [main] com.java.logging.tinylog.TinyLogExample26.main()
ERROR: Error Message
2017-11-20 10:12:13 [main] com.java.logging.tinylog.TinyLogExample26.main()
WARNING: Warning Message
```

📄 timestampRollingFile.2018-11-20 10-12-14.log ☒

```
2018-11-20 10:42:13 [main] com.java.logging.tinylog.TinyLogExample26.main()
ERROR: Error Message
2018-11-20 10:42:13 [main] com.java.logging.tinylog.TinyLogExample26.main()
WARNING: Warning Message
```

Example 27: Custom File Writer

In this example, we implement a customized file writer. The class is as follows:

```java
package com.java.logging.tinylog;

import java.io.OutputStream;
import java.util.EnumSet;
import java.util.Set;
import java.io.BufferedOutputStream;
import java.io.FileOutputStream;
import org.pmw.tinylog.Configuration;
import org.pmw.tinylog.LogEntry;
import org.pmw.tinylog.writers.LogEntryValue;
import org.pmw.tinylog.writers.PropertiesSupport;
import org.pmw.tinylog.writers.Property;
import org.pmw.tinylog.writers.VMShutdownHook;
import org.pmw.tinylog.writers.Writer;

// extend the writer class and provide the PropertiesSupport parameter
@PropertiesSupport(name = "CustomWriter", properties = { @Property(name = "fileName", type = String.class) })
public class CustomWriter implements Writer {

    private OutputStream stream;
    String fileName;

    public CustomWriter(final String fileName) {
        this.fileName = fileName;
    }

    @Override
    public void close() throws Exception {

        // unregister the writer and close the stream
        VMShutdownHook.unregister(this);
        stream.close();
    }

    @Override
    public void flush() throws Exception {
        stream.flush();
    }

    @Override
    public void init(Configuration arg0) throws Exception {
        // define a buffered stream for the writer and register the writer
        stream = new BufferedOutputStream(new FileOutputStream(fileName));
        VMShutdownHook.register(this);
    }

    @Override
    public void write(LogEntry logEntry) throws Exception {
        // write the logs to the file using output stream
        String entry = logEntry.getRenderedLogEntry();
        stream.write(entry.getBytes());
    }

    @Override
    public Set<LogEntryValue> getRequiredLogEntryValues() {
        // get the log entries required by the writer
        return EnumSet.of(LogEntryValue.LEVEL, LogEntryValue.RENDERED_LOG_ENTRY);
    }
}
```

In order to register the custom writer class, we need to register it in the 'org. pmw tiny log. writers.' We first create this file in the META-INF/ services folder as follows:

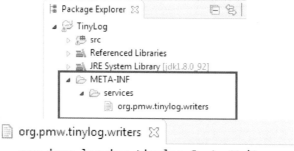

```
org.pmw.tinylog.writers ⊠

com.java.logging.tinylog.CustomWriter
```

The java class is as follows:

```java
TinyLogExample27.java ⊠

    package com.java.logging.tinylog;

⊕ import org.pmw.tinylog.Configurator;

    public class TinyLogExample27 {

        public static void main(String[] args) {

            // configure the class to use the custom writer
            Configurator.defaultConfig().writer(new CustomWriter("logFile.txt")).activate();

            // log messages to the console
            Logger.error("Error Message");
            Logger.warn("Warning Message");
            Logger.info("Information Message");
            Logger.debug("Debug Message");
        }

    }
```

When we execute the class, a new file is created as follows:

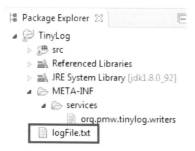

The contents of the file are as follows:

```
logFile.txt ⊠

2017-11-17 17:33:10 [main] com.java.logging.tinylog.TinyLogExample27.main()
ERROR: Error Message
2017-11-17 17:33:10 [main] com.java.logging.tinylog.TinyLogExample27.main()
WARNING: Warning Message
2017-11-17 17:33:10 [main] com.java.logging.tinylog.TinyLogExample27.main()
INFO: Information Message
```

Example 28: Custom Console Writer

In this example, we define a custom console writer as follows:

```
CustomConsoleWriter.java

package com.java.logging.tinylog;

import java.util.EnumSet;
import java.util.Set;
import java.io.PrintStream;

import org.pmw.tinylog.Configuration;
import org.pmw.tinylog.LogEntry;
import org.pmw.tinylog.writers.LogEntryValue;
import org.pmw.tinylog.writers.PropertiesSupport;
import org.pmw.tinylog.writers.Property;
import org.pmw.tinylog.writers.VMShutdownHook;
import org.pmw.tinylog.writers.Writer;

//extend the writer class and provide the PropertiesSupport parameter with the
//stream as an optional parameter
@PropertiesSupport(name = "CustomConsoleWriter", properties = {
        @Property(name = "stream", type = String.class, optional = true) })
public class CustomConsoleWriter implements Writer {

    private PrintStream stream;
    String fileName;

    public CustomConsoleWriter() {
        stream = System.out;
    }

    @Override
    public void close() throws Exception {

        // unregister the writer and close the stream
        VMShutdownHook.unregister(this);
        stream.close();
    }

    @Override
    public void flush() throws Exception {
        stream.flush();
    }

    @Override
    public void init(Configuration arg0) throws Exception {
        // provide no implementation
    }

    @Override
    public void write(LogEntry logEntry) throws Exception {
        // write the logs to the console using print stream
        String entry = logEntry.getRenderedLogEntry();
        stream.write(entry.getBytes());
    }

    @Override
    public Set<LogEntryValue> getRequiredLogEntryValues() {
        // get the log entries required by the writer
        return EnumSet.of(LogEntryValue.RENDERED_LOG_ENTRY);
    }
}
```

We modify the writer's file as follows:

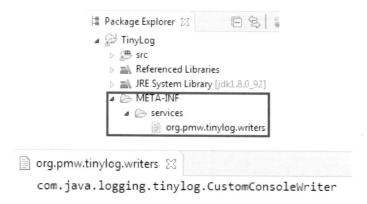

The Java class used to test the custom console writer is as follows:

```
TinyLogExample28.java
package com.java.logging.tinylog;

import org.pmw.tinylog.Configurator;

public class TinyLogExample28 {

    public static void main(String[] args) {

        // configure the class to use the custom console writer
        Configurator.defaultConfig().writer(new CustomConsoleWriter()).level(Level.TRACE).activate();

        // log messages to the console
        Logger.error("Error Message");
        Logger.warn("Warning Message");
        Logger.info("Information Message");
        Logger.debug("Debug Message");
        Logger.trace("Trace Message");

        // throw an exception
        // the detailed stack trace will be printed on the console
        Logger.error(new NullPointerException());

        // induce an exception
        try {
            int a = 10 / 0;
            System.out.println(a);
        } catch (ArithmeticException e) {
            Logger.error("Cannot divivde by zero!" + e);
        }

    }

}
```

The output generated on the console is as follows:

```
Console    Problems   @ Javadoc   Declaration   Annotations   Call Hierarchy
<terminated> TinyLogExample28 [Java Application] C:\Program Files\java\jdk1.8.0_92\bin\javaw.exe (20 nov. 201
2017-11-20 11:46:53 [main] com.java.logging.tinylog.TinyLogExample28.main()
ERROR: Error Message
2017-11-20 11:46:53 [main] com.java.logging.tinylog.TinyLogExample28.main()
WARNING: Warning Message
2017-11-20 11:46:53 [main] com.java.logging.tinylog.TinyLogExample28.main()
INFO: Information Message
2017-11-20 11:46:53 [main] com.java.logging.tinylog.TinyLogExample28.main()
DEBUG: Debug Message
2017-11-20 11:46:53 [main] com.java.logging.tinylog.TinyLogExample28.main()
TRACE: Trace Message
2017-11-20 11:46:53 [main] com.java.logging.tinylog.TinyLogExample28.main()
ERROR: java.lang.NullPointerException
        at com.java.logging.tinylog.TinyLogExample28.main(TinyLogExample28.java:23)
2017-11-20 11:46:53 [main] com.java.logging.tinylog.TinyLogExample28.main()
ERROR: Cannot divivde by zero!java.lang.ArithmeticException: / by zero
```

We can further configure multiple customized writers. This can be done by adding the different writers in the **org.pmw.tinylog.writers** file located in the META-INF\services folder.

```
📄 org.pmw.tinylog.writers ⊠
    com.java.logging.tinylog.CustomConsoleWriter
    com.java.logging.tinylog.CustomWriter
```

We add the Custom Writer previously explained in Example 27. This is a custom file writer.

We can add several writers one after the other. We can modify the java class to use multiple writers as follows:

```
📄 TinyLogExample28.java ⊠
    package com.java.logging.tinylog;

  + import org.pmw.tinylog.Configurator;

    public class TinyLogExample28 {

        public static void main(String[] args) {
            // configure the class to use the custom console writer
            Configurator.defaultConfig().writer(new CustomConsoleWriter()).level(Level.TRACE).activate();
            Configurator.currentConfig().addWriter(new CustomWriter("myLogFile.log")).level(Level.TRACE).activate();

            // log messages to the console
            Logger.error("Error Message");
            Logger.warn("Warning Message");
            Logger.info("Information Message");
            Logger.debug("Debug Message");
            Logger.trace("Trace Message");

            // throw an exception
            // the detailed stack trace will be printed on the console
            Logger.error(new NullPointerException());

            // induce an exception
            try {
                int a = 10 / 0;
                System.out.println(a);
            } catch (ArithmeticException e) {
                Logger.error("Cannot divide by zero!" + e);
            }

        }

    }
```

Now, the above class implements two custom writers: File and Console. On execution of the file a new file is created by the file writer as follows:

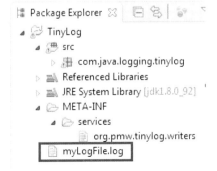

The contents of this file are as follows:

```
📄 myLogFile.log ⋈
2017-11-20 13:25:12 [main] com.java.logging.tinylog.TinyLogExample28.main()
ERROR: Error Message
2017-11-20 13:25:12 [main] com.java.logging.tinylog.TinyLogExample28.main()
WARNING: Warning Message
2017-11-20 13:25:12 [main] com.java.logging.tinylog.TinyLogExample28.main()
INFO: Information Message
2017-11-20 13:25:12 [main] com.java.logging.tinylog.TinyLogExample28.main()
DEBUG: Debug Message
2017-11-20 13:25:12 [main] com.java.logging.tinylog.TinyLogExample28.main()
TRACE: Trace Message
2017-11-20 13:25:12 [main] com.java.logging.tinylog.TinyLogExample28.main()
ERROR: java.lang.NullPointerException
    at com.java.logging.tinylog.TinyLogExample28.main(TinyLogExample28.java:24)
2017-11-20 13:25:12 [main] com.java.logging.tinylog.TinyLogExample28.main()
ERROR: Cannot divide by zero!java.lang.ArithmeticException: / by zero
```

The output displayed on the console is as follows:

```
🖥 Console ⋈  📋 Problems  @ Javadoc  📄 Declaration  📎 Annotations  📲 Call Hierarchy
<terminated> TinyLogExample28 [Java Application] C:\Program Files\java\jdk1.8.0_92\bin\javaw.exe (20 nov. 20
2017-11-20 13:25:12 [main] com.java.logging.tinylog.TinyLogExample28.main()
ERROR: Error Message
2017-11-20 13:25:12 [main] com.java.logging.tinylog.TinyLogExample28.main()
WARNING: Warning Message
2017-11-20 13:25:12 [main] com.java.logging.tinylog.TinyLogExample28.main()
INFO: Information Message
2017-11-20 13:25:12 [main] com.java.logging.tinylog.TinyLogExample28.main()
DEBUG: Debug Message
2017-11-20 13:25:12 [main] com.java.logging.tinylog.TinyLogExample28.main()
TRACE: Trace Message
2017-11-20 13:25:12 [main] com.java.logging.tinylog.TinyLogExample28.main()
ERROR: java.lang.NullPointerException
        at com.java.logging.tinylog.TinyLogExample28.main(TinyLogExample28.java:24)
2017-11-20 13:25:12 [main] com.java.logging.tinylog.TinyLogExample28.main()
ERROR: Cannot divide by zero!java.lang.ArithmeticException: / by zero
```

Example 29: Tiny Binding with slf4j

In this example, we demonstrate the use of slf4j with tinylog. TinyLog provides a binding jar that can be found at the following link:

http://www.tinylog.org/download

We download the jar and add it to the classpath. In addition to the binding jar, we need to add the standard slfj-api.jar which is required to use the slf4j logging framework. We add the tinylog.jar as we are going to be using the tinylog framework as the underlying framework.

The jar files in the classpath are as follows:

The java class is as follows:

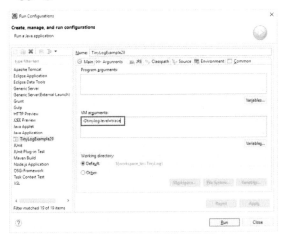

```java
package com.java.logging.tinylog;

//import slf4j Logger and LoggerFactory
import org.slf4j.Logger;
import org.slf4j.LoggerFactory;

public class TinyLogExample29 {

    public static void main(String[] args) {

        //get the logger
        Logger logger = LoggerFactory.getLogger(TinyLogExample29.class);

        //log messages
        logger.debug("Debug Message");
        logger.info("Information Message");
        logger.warn("Warning Message");
        logger.error("Error Message");

        logger.error("Exception: " + new ArithmeticException());
        logger.error("Another Exception: " + new ArrayIndexOutOfBoundsException());
        logger.error("One more Exception: " + new IllegalArgumentException());

    }
}
```

We set the logging level to trace as shown below:

We click on run to execute the java class.

The logs are directed to the console by default as we have not specified any fixed destination for the logs. If we wish to specify additional writers, a configuration specific to tinylog such as a properties file, or vm setting or a configuration using API must be done.

The output displayed on the console is as follows:

```
Console 23   Problems  @ Javadoc  Declaration
<terminated> TinyLogExample29 [Java Application] C:\Program Files\Java
2017-11-25 18:27:08 [main] com.java.logging.tinylog.TinyLogExample29.main()
DEBUG: Debug Message
2017-11-25 18:27:08 [main] com.java.logging.tinylog.TinyLogExample29.main()
INFO: Information Message
2017-11-25 18:27:08 [main] com.java.logging.tinylog.TinyLogExample29.main()
WARNING: Warning Message
2017-11-25 18:27:08 [main] com.java.logging.tinylog.TinyLogExample29.main()
ERROR: Error Message
2017-11-25 18:27:08 [main] com.java.logging.tinylog.TinyLogExample29.main()
ERROR: Exception: java.lang.ArithmeticException
2017-11-25 18:27:08 [main] com.java.logging.tinylog.TinyLogExample29.main()
ERROR: Another Exception: java.lang.ArrayIndexOutOfBoundsException
2017-11-25 18:27:08 [main] com.java.logging.tinylog.TinyLogExample29.main()
ERROR: One more Exception: java.lang.IllegalArgumentException
```

Example 30: Null Writer

In this example, we define a null writer. This writer rejects all log messages. The java class is as follows:

```java
TinyLogExample31.java 23

package com.java.logging.tinylog;

//get the Logger
import org.pmw.tinylog.Logger;

public class TinyLogExample31 {

    public static void main(String[] args) {

        // log messages
        Logger.debug("Debug Message");
        Logger.info("Information Message");
        Logger.warn("Warning Message");
        Logger.error("Error Message");

        Logger.error("Exception: " + new ArithmeticException());
        Logger.error("Another Exception: " + new ArrayIndexOutOfBoundsException());
        Logger.error("One more Exception: " + new IllegalArgumentException());

    }
}
```

We set the writers to null as follows:

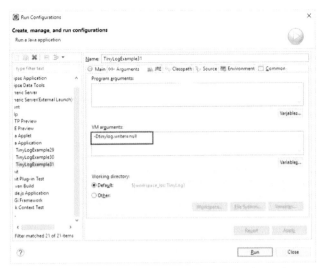

On execution of the class, no output is displayed on the console as this setting discards all the log entries.

```
Console ⊠  Problems  @ Javadoc  Declaration
<terminated> TinyLogExample31 [Java Application] C:\Program Files\Java\
```

Example 31: Logging to an HTML File

In this example, we configure the logger to log to an html file. The test java class is as follows:

```java
TinyLogExample31.java ⊠

package com.java.logging.tinylog;

import org.pmw.tinylog.Logger;

public class TinyLogExample31 {

    public static void main(String[] args) {

        // log messages in a loop
        for (int i = 0; i < 5; i++) {

            Logger.error("Error Message");
            Logger.warn("Warning Message");
            Logger.info("Information Message");
            Logger.debug("Debug Message");

        }
    }
}
```

The configuration is done with the help of the eclipse vm arguments as shown below:

The output generated on the console is as follows:

```
Console   Problems   Javadoc   Declaration   Annotations   Call Hierarchy
<terminated> TinyLogExample31 [Java Application] C:\Program Files\java
2017-11-29 15:28:01 [main] com.java.logging.tinylog.TinyLogExample31.main()
ERROR: Error Message
2017-11-29 15:28:01 [main] com.java.logging.tinylog.TinyLogExample31.main()
WARNING: Warning Message
2017-11-29 15:28:01 [main] com.java.logging.tinylog.TinyLogExample31.main()
ERROR: Error Message
2017-11-29 15:28:01 [main] com.java.logging.tinylog.TinyLogExample31.main()
WARNING: Warning Message
2017-11-29 15:28:01 [main] com.java.logging.tinylog.TinyLogExample31.main()
ERROR: Error Message
2017-11-29 15:28:01 [main] com.java.logging.tinylog.TinyLogExample31.main()
WARNING: Warning Message
2017-11-29 15:28:01 [main] com.java.logging.tinylog.TinyLogExample31.main()
ERROR: Error Message
2017-11-29 15:28:01 [main] com.java.logging.tinylog.TinyLogExample31.main()
WARNING: Warning Message
2017-11-29 15:28:01 [main] com.java.logging.tinylog.TinyLogExample31.main()
ERROR: Error Message
2017-11-29 15:28:01 [main] com.java.logging.tinylog.TinyLogExample31.main()
WARNING: Warning Message
2017-11-29 15:28:01 [main] com.java.logging.tinylog.TinyLogExample31.main()
INFO: Information Message
2017-11-29 15:28:01 [main] com.java.logging.tinylog.TinyLogExample31.main()
INFO: Information Message
2017-11-29 15:28:01 [main] com.java.logging.tinylog.TinyLogExample31.main()
INFO: Information Message
2017-11-29 15:28:01 [main] com.java.logging.tinylog.TinyLogExample31.main()
INFO: Information Message
2017-11-29 15:28:01 [main] com.java.logging.tinylog.TinyLogExample31.main()
INFO: Information Message
```

A new file called 'myLogFile37624.html' is generated as shown below:

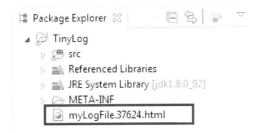

We open this file to view its contents using the web browser in eclipse as shown below:

C:\Users\ workspace\TinyLog\myLogFile.37624.html

file:///C:/Users/ workspace/TinyLog/myLogFile.37624.html

2017-11-29 15:22:09 [main] com.java.logging.tinylog.TinyLogExample31.main() ERROR: Error Message 2017-11-29 15:22:09 [main] com.java.logging.tinylog.TinyLogExample31.main() WARNING: Warning Message 2017-11-29 15:22:09 [main] com.java.logging.tinylog.TinyLogExample31.main() INFO: Information Message 2017-11-29 15:22:09 [main] com.java.logging.tinylog.TinyLogExample31.main() ERROR: Error Message 2017-11-29 15:22:09 [main] com.java.logging.tinylog.TinyLogExample31.main() WARNING: Warning Message 2017-11-29 15:22:09 [main] com.java.logging.tinylog.TinyLogExample31.main() INFO: Information Message 2017-11-29 15:22:09 [main] com.java.logging.tinylog.TinyLogExample31.main() ERROR: Error Message 2017-11-29 15:22:09 [main] com.java.logging.tinylog.TinyLogExample31.main() WARNING: Warning Message 2017-11-29 15:22:09 [main] com.java.logging.tinylog.TinyLogExample31.main() INFO: Information Message 2017-11-29 15:22:09 [main] com.java.logging.tinylog.TinyLogExample31.main() ERROR: Error Message 2017-11-29 15:22:09 [main] com.java.logging.tinylog.TinyLogExample31.main() WARNING: Warning Message 2017-11-29 15:22:09 [main] com.java.logging.tinylog.TinyLogExample31.main() INFO: Information Message 2017-11-29 15:22:09 [main] com.java.logging.tinylog.TinyLogExample31.main() ERROR: Error Message 2017-11-29 15:22:09 [main] com.java.logging.tinylog.TinyLogExample31.main() WARNING: Warning Message com.java.logging.tinylog.TinyLogExample31.main() INFO: Information Message

CHAPTER
7

SUMMARY

In this book, we have seen 4 different logging frameworks and one Logging Framework Facade so far.

We started with the traditional and simple Java Logging Framework. We studied the architecture and components that form the core of this logging framework. We saw how to implement this framework by means of several simple examples. We discovered that this framework has no configuration overhead as it is embedded within the JRE itself. As it is part of the default Java JRE package, no special installation procedures need to be initiated. However, we came upon certain drawbacks to the use of this framework such as security issues and serialization problems. Additionally, the performance offered by this framework as per benchmark analysis performed by several platforms suggest that it up to 10 times more slower when compared to others frameworks (Benchmarking Java Logging Frameworks, 2017).

The next framework that we studied was the third-party (Apache) log4j2 logging framework. We explored its unique architecture, the components that make up the architecture and its configuration. We examined its capabilities by testing it via a sufficient amount of simple and easy examples that extensively use the API provided by this framework.

We found out that this framework is quite powerful and easy to configure, understand and implement. Several unique features such as logging to databases, asynchronous logging and logging over networks are offered by log4j2. Benchmark analysis hints that this framework performs well when compared to other Java frameworks. It performs at a level that is more or less the same as logback and can be implemented by all types of applications small and large alike (Sitepoint, 2017).

We then moved on to yet another third-party framework named logback which was launched by QOS as a successor to the framework log4j, also written by the same author that developed log4j, Ceki Gülcü. In the same manner, as we proceeded for the previous two logging frameworks, we analyzed and learned the core architecture and components of the Logback logging framework. With the help of several samples, we examined in detail the means to implement and use this framework for our java applications.

We came to the realization that this framework is almost as powerful as log4j and also that has certain perks in terms of features when compared with its predecessor. This framework ups the ante by providing useful and practical features such as condition processing of configuration files, automation in terms of rolling of files, exception handling, native SLF4J implementation, etc. to name a few (Gülcü and Pennec, 2011).

Moving forward, we took a turn to probe and examine SLF4J, a façade for logging frameworks, which raises the stakes and brings the story of the logging frameworks to a whole new level. Developed by Ceki Gülcü yet again, this framework offers the Java developers and users' community the chance to select their desired logging framework at the time of deployment. Needless to say, this framework clearly has an edge in the market of logging frameworks. It offers the prospect of hand-picking a logging framework based on the needs of the application which change rapidly and hence offers a massive advantage to developers and clients alike. With its wide array of bindings and support for several logging frameworks, it has risen up to be one of the most popular logging frameworks that are used by Java applications.

Although this framework offers several benefits, it has a slight inconvenience: it is only as fast as the logging framework it uses. Hence, the choice of the underlying base logging framework should be made prudently. Studies and benchmarking of various combinations SLF4J and log4j2, SLF4J and logback, SLF4J and Java Util logging indicates that the best combination among the three is SLF4J in combination with logback (Benchmarking Java Logging Frameworks, 2017).

Lastly, we revisited another small yet strong and sturdy framework called TinyLog. A simplistic framework with a simple design for logging, TinyLog is a one to keep an eye out for. Notwithstanding the fact that TinyLog does not offer all the incredible features offered by logback and log4j, it somewhat evens the field by achieving fast performance as described in the benchmark analysis (tinylog: Benchmark, 2017).

Granted that TinyLog is leaps and bounds behind the popularly used logging frameworks such as logback, log4j, JCL etc. in terms of support, use, community, and features, but it is one framework to watch out for. This framework bodes well for applications that wish to use a fast and lightweight alternative to the traditional logging frameworks.

The following table provides a comparison of the logging frameworks that we have studied in this book based on important parameters such as performance, powerful features, community support, maintenance, etc.

Framework Parameter	JUL	LOG4J	Logback	TinyLog
Log Levels	7 levels: info, config, fine, finer, finest, severe, warning	6 levels: info, error, warn, debug, trace, fatal	5 levels: error, warn, info, debug, trace	5 levels: Error, warn, trace, info, debug
Logging over Networks	Weak capabilities	Strong features	Strong features	Extremely limited functionality
Online community	Moderately large community	Strong online community and support	Extremely wide community and strong support	Small community but the good support provided
Actively maintained	No	No	Yes	Yes
Performance (asynchronous) (Benchmarking Java Logging Frameworks, 2017)	Weak as compared to the other 3 frameworks	Definitely better than JUL but slightly slower than logback	Very good performance as compared to JUL and logback	Offers the best performance (tinylog: benchmark, 2017)
Mavenisation possible	Not applicable	Yes	Yes	Yes
Dynamic Reconfiguration Possible	Yes, but only using JMX or re-reading the configuration	Yes, can be done programmatically.	Yes, can be done programmatically.	Yes, can be done programmatically.
Mapped Diagnostic Context	No	Yes	Yes	Yes
Exception Handling (recovery from I/O failures)	No	No	Yes	No
Configuration file type (XML/properties)	Properties	Both	Both. Logback offers groovy format too.	Properties

REFERENCES

1. Gulcu, C. (2003). The complete Log4j manual: The reliable, fast and flexible logging framework for Java. *QOS. ch, Lausanne, Switzerland.*

2. Lars Vogel (c) (2007, 2016). vogella GmbH. (n.d.). Java Logging API - Tutorial. Retrieved from http://www.vogella.com/tutorials/Logging/article.html.

3. Jenkov, J. (2017). *Java Logging: Overview.* Retrieved from http://tutorials.jenkov.com/java-logging/overview.html

4. Java Logging Overview. (n.d.). Retrieved from https://docs.oracle.com/javase/8/docs/technotes/guides/logging/overview.html.

5. Gülcü, C. (2003). *The complete log4j manual.* QOS. Ch.

6. Goers, R. (n.d.). Log4j – Overview – Apache Log4j 2. Retrieved from https://logging.apache.org/log4j/2.x/manual/index.html.

7. Logback Home. (2017). Retrieved from https://logback.qos.ch/

8. Gülcü, C., & Pennec, S. (2011). *Logback Manual.*

9. SLF4J Manual. (2017). Retrieved from https://www.slf4j.org/manual.html

10. SLF4J Binary files. (2017). Retrieved from https://www.slf4j.org/download.html

11. tinylog: Lightweight Logging Framework for Java. (2017). Retrieved from http://www.tinylog.org/

12. Benchmarking Java logging frameworks | Log Analysis | Log

Monitoring by Loggly. (2017, October 25). Retrieved from https://www.loggly.com/blog/benchmarking-java-logging-frameworks/

13. Which Java Logging Framework Has the Best Performance?— SitePoint. (2017, April 10). Retrieved from https://www.sitepoint.com/which-java-logging-framework-has-the-best-performance/

14. tinylog: Benchmark. (n.d.). Retrieved from http://www.tinylog.org/benchmark.

15. SLF4J 1.8.0-beta0 API. (2017). Retrieved from https://www.slf4j.org/api/

16. Apache Log4j API 2.9.1 API. (2017). Retrieved from https://logging.apache.org/log4j/2.x/log4j-api/apidocs/index.html.

17. Logback-Parent 1.2.3 API. (2017). Retrieved from https://logback.qos.ch/apidocs/index.html

18. Java logging framework. (2016, December 31). Retrieved from https://en.wikipedia.org/wiki/Java_logging_framework.

19. Tutorialspoint.com. (2017, August 15). log4j Architecture. Retrieved from https://www.tutorialspoint.com/log4j/log4j_architecture.htm.

20. FileHandler (Java Platform SE 7). (2017, October 9). Retrieved from https://docs.oracle.com/javase/7/docs/api/java/util/logging/FileHandler.html.

21. Level (Java Platform SE 7). (2017, October 9). Retrieved from https://docs.oracle.com/javase/7/docs/api/java/util/logging/Level.html.

22. Handler (Java Platform SE 7). (2017, October 9). Retrieved from https://docs.oracle.com/javase/7/docs/api/java/util/logging/Handler.html.

23. Logger (Java Platform SE 7). (2017, October 9). Retrieved from https://docs.oracle.com/javase/7/docs/api/java/util/logging/Logger.html.

24. java.util.logging (Java Platform SE 7). (2017, October 9). Retrieved from https://docs.oracle.com/javase/7/docs/api/java/util/logging/package-summary.html.

25. Welcome to Log4Delphi. (n.d.). Retrieved November 01, 2017, from http://log4delphi.sourceforge.net/.

26. tinylog 1.2 API. (2017). Retrieved from http://www.tinylog.org/javadoc/

INDEX